I0890028

Praise for JOHNNY LEWIS: THE BIOGRAPHY

'This is a rollicking read and a fascinating behind-the-scenes look at boxing. Johnny Lewis took Jeff Fenech and Kostya Tszyu to world titles but that's only the public story of the man regarded as Australia's best boxing trainer. Kent chronicles what happens behind closed doors: the broken promises, the struggles to strip weight off for fights and the underappreciated tactical battles that go with the "sweet science".' *Adelaide Advertiser*

'Johnny Lewis is unquestionably Australia's most successful boxing trainer. Over the past thirty years he has trained six world champions, among them some of the greatest names in the sport … this book is not only for the boxing fans, but for anyone interested in how to get the best out of those around them.' *Western Star*

'[Kent] writes this biography of Australia's most famous and successful boxing trainer … with a clever combination of empathy and sensitivity, which results in a gripping account of a street-smart kid from Erskineville who became a gifted trainer and an inspirational role model ... a wonderful picture of Sydney's colourful boxing and criminal underworld in the 1970s and '80s.' *Sydney Morning Herald*

'Journey the cobbled back streets of inner Sydney, where violence, mischief, generosity and old school values fashioned the psyche of legendary Australian boxing trainer Johnny Lewis. Face the underworld; run with scamps; absorb each punch with Kostya Tszyu, Jeff Fenech and others … and prepare for million-dollar betrayal. Greed, deceit, friendship, love and loyalty prove engrossing bedfellows. Paul Kent … finally gets the trainer of six world champions to drop his guard.' *Illawarra Mercury*

'Blood, sweat and cauliflower ears—Johnny Lewis knew all about them ... This intriguing bio shows how the former Erskineville signwriter inspires his fighters to greatness with a mixture of intuition, kindness and cunning.' *Men's Health*

'Finally, the story of Australian boxing's most beloved character can be told in Paul Kent's unputdownable new book ... Find out what makes Oz's most successful trainer tick both in and out of the ring.' *People Magazine*

'Perhaps the most surprising aspect of the book is Lewis' familiarity, given where he grew up, with notorious Sydney figures such as Neddy Smith and Kevin Gore, boss of the infamous Toe-Cutter Gang. The book travels from the tough streets of inner-Sydney to the corner of champions.' *Daily Telegraph*

'Johnny Lewis is the high priest of Australian boxing. In a sport too often sullied by thugs, conmen, drama queens and palookas, the legendary trainer is the last bastion of credibility. In the past 30 years, he has trained six world champions, among them two modern day greats. And along the way he has saved countless other lost souls from themselves with the type of discipline and compassion that belong in a Rocky movie.' *Newcastle Herald*

JOHNNY LEWIS
THE BIOGRAPHY

PAUL KENT

ALLEN&UNWIN

This edition published in 2012

First published in 2010

Allen & Unwin
Sydney, Melbourne, Auckland, London

83 Alexander Street
Crows Nest NSW 2065
Australia
Phone: (61 2) 8425 0100
Email: info@allenandunwin.com
Web: www.allenandunwin.com

Cataloguing-in-Publication details are available
from the National Library of Australia
www.trove.nla.gov.au

ISBN 978 1 74331 086 1

Set in Janson by Midland Typesetters, Australia

10 9 8 7 6 5 4 3 2 1

To my parents, Alf and Marge, and my brother Robert, and everybody who ever lived in Erskineville that, in some way, made me the person I am. You all did in some way. To the Indigenous fighters who, for many years, were used up or under-appreciated and who, I believe, are members of the greatest sporting race on earth. There is great opportunity out there—all you have to do is believe.

—Johnny Lewis

To my wife Fiona, with love and admiration, who comes along only twice in a lifetime. And to Evie, who has no better example than her mum.

—Paul Kent

CHAPTER 1

THE FIRST TIME, he was taping Kevin Kelly's hands.

It was at The Octagon in Sydney in July 2001, and Kelly was to fight Josh Clenshaw. That was the first time I ever saw it.

He pulled a length of white Elastoplast tape about four inches off its roll and tore it clean off. He then took the torn piece and ripped it lengthways and secured one skinny half to the end of a table for later. Then he pressed the other strip down the back of Kelly's fist, gently smoothing its wrinkles. He took the second piece from the table, ripped it in half crossways, and laid one of the short pieces across the first to make a small white cross.

He is Johnny Lewis, the fight trainer, and he tapes a small white cross on the back of each fist before he wraps his fighter's hands before a fight. He does this every time, for every fighter he ever handles, and I ask him why.

'Just a sign of the cross,' he says. 'One for Kevin and,' on the other fist, 'one for his opponent.'

There was a small pause.

'We all want 'em to go down. But we want 'em to get up after the count of ten, don't we, mate.'

Kelly smiled.

Perhaps that, more than anything else that can ever be said or written, is why they go to him.

In a sport too often callous and mean and uninterested in the losers, here was a small act of unprompted kindness towards an opponent in the moments before a fight, and it was beautiful.

Friendships are made in such moments. You get to know such men.

That is why my business here is Johnny Lewis. His act of blessing his fighter and his opponent, so foreign to the sport, is everything we believe we know about Johnny. It is the small kiss on the cheek he gave Jeff Fenech after stepping through the ropes to leave Fenech in the ring before the first bell. It is the way he led Kostya Tszyu to the ring with his gloves resting high on Johnny's shoulders and his head buried deep in Johnny's back, shutting out the world, with only Johnny to guide him. It is the time he grabbed Jeff Harding at the end of the eleventh in Atlantic City, when Harding was behind on all three judges' cards and cut and bleeding over both eyes and under one as well, and Johnny found the words that saw Harding bounce from his stool and go back and dig like few men can, and knock his man out to win the title.

It is all of that.

Yet it is still more.

Bob Fulton, the Australian rugby league coach, watches his work, and decides a man like Johnny Lewis is what he needs on his coaching staff. So Johnny tours with the Kangaroos and the players are drawn to him. The Sydney Swans, the Australian football team, hires him for cross-training sessions, and soon it's not about that at all. Basketballers and netballers and footballers and jockeys come to train with him because he has the reputation as the best, but more than that. When they talk about what he does for them, they don't talk about fitness, or their form. They talk about the man.

The answers are right in front of them, in the small white crosses on the back of Kevin Kelly's fists.

The question is ... why?

It all really got going one afternoon in 1981. It was late October. Johnny was working one of those good young boys he'd promised another man he'd help—Mark Cribb was his name—through the pads in the gym.

They were upstairs at Newtown Police Boys Club, in Sydney's inner-west, working three minutes at a time. Around them were the rhythms of the gym. A couple of fighters worked the heavy bags. One was working the speedball next to the mirrors. More fighters were skipping, their leather ropes clicking lightly across the hardwood floor in a tempo to send a baby to sleep. Along the bench across from the windows, the windows Johnny had painted shut, the locals used to sit. They used to come in and watch the fighters, talking fights, but those days were gone, the fight game fading.

The fighters who'd finished working the bag and the speedball, finished working the pads with Johnny, they shadow-boxed in front of mirrors that had misted over.

It was the same as every day, only this day was different.

The door opened and two young men, or perhaps they were still boys, walked in.

A few heads turned, not all. Only to make sure the door didn't stay open too long. The boys took a seat on the bench that ran alongside the ring.

'Time,' Johnny yelled and, like that, the music stopped. The fighters walked around, getting their wind back, because that's what they always did. Nobody sat. Nobody bent over, hands on knees. You don't show weakness in front of other fighters.

The shadow-boxers took their towels and, in the minute they had to rest, wiped the condensation from the mirrors. Some used the palm of their hand. The boxing room inside the Newtown gym was often ten, fifteen degrees hotter than outside. Johnny liked it like that. Helped the boys sweat. Helped them pull weight in the weeks before weigh-in. That's why anybody who walked through the door got a stare. They were letting the heat escape.

So they wiped down their mirrors, knowing that by the time they finished their next three-minute round the glass would steam over again to the point where they again couldn't see themselves. Rivulets of sweat ran down the mirrors to the floor.

'Time,' Johnny said, and they started again. Everybody at once. Bags and skipping ropes, and fighters snorting in front of mirrors.

By now he had been training twenty years, so he was used to working his fighters with one eye somewhere else. On the clock. On a boy hitting the bag down the end of the gym. As Cribb worked the pads, he peeked over at the two young men—or were they boys?—sitting on the bench. He figured one to be Turkish. The other, he wasn't sure. Maybe Aboriginal, maybe Italian. They were both very slight. Still teenagers, he decided.

'Halfway,' he said, at a minute-thirty.

Cribb kept working the pads. A sharp, steady rhythm, his punches even and nicely weighted.

'Minute to go.'

The boys watched.

'Thirty seconds … ten seconds,' and then Johnny leaned into Cribb's ear, 'bring it home, mate …'

Five … four … three …

'Time!'

He slapped his pads. Cribb had done his rounds.

The mirrors had steamed up again.

The boys sitting on the bench would hardly have noticed. They wouldn't know that fighters shadow-box in front of mirrors to spot faults in their technique. That they might drop their left hand after jabbing then bring it back in a small arc that is completely harmless except that for one small moment it leaves their chin open for a straight right-hand counter. It can end their night right there.

Other fighters might draw their right hand back just slightly before throwing it. Cocking it, or telegraphing. It's a sign as tell-tale as if the fighter has announced out loud what he is about to throw. That's why they shadow-box in front of the mirrors, sweat flicking off their fists and elbows as the glass slowly steams up. Shortening their punches, keeping their defence tight. There is more in those perspiring mirrors than sweat. The mist over the mirrors is commitment. The residue of sacrifice. But the two boys on the bench wouldn't know that.

How could they?

'Mate,' Johnny said to Cribb, 'we're gonna have to get you some good sparring.'

'I'll spar him.'

It came from nowhere. A small voice, hardly one to make you think it will change your life.

Johnny turned around. It was one of the boys on the bench. The Aboriginal kid, or was he Italian?

'That's not the way we do things here,' Johnny said.

The kid didn't say anything else. But even in that, Johnny saw something. Maybe it was the way he came to his feet. 'You ever done any boxing before?'

'Nuh. But I'll be all right.'

No, Johnny said again, not today. 'If you're so keen to be a fighter, how about coming up here tomorrow and doing some training?'

'If I come tomorrow, can I spar him, then?'

'Yeah, but be here by four o'clock.'

He could easily have let the kid spar, he knew. What did it matter to him if some kid off the street took a few licks? At least his boy would have got some needed rounds. But there were ways to do things in the gym, and the trick was to have the discipline to stick to them.

At two-thirty the next afternoon, Johnny washed his brushes and cleaned up at work; he was a signwriter with Sydney County Council. He left for the gym and turned into Angel Street a little before 3 p.m.

He saw him as he pulled in. There already, waiting for the doors to open, was the young kid.

Johnny got out of his car and walked towards the door. The kid didn't say anything. Nothing when Johnny unlocked it, either. He began wondering. Is this kid shy? Or is he too arrogant to say hello? Normally, Johnny considered himself a good judge with his first read.

Yet he couldn't figure this one out.

Still, what did it matter? A few minutes later Cribb arrived. He began warming up. Johnny gloved up the young kid. Made sure his headgear was on tight. The kid bounced around, shaking out nervous energy. Johnny turned and talked softly to Cribb.

'Just go easy.'

Not because he especially wanted him protecting the kid—he might never see him again after today—but because he didn't want Cribb knocking the confidence out of him before he could get any decent work out of him. He looked at the clock on the wall, waiting for the second hand to roll around to the twelve.

'Time.'

The fighters moved toward each other; the kid attacked. In this way he was no different from any kid that ever stepped into a boxing ring. First time in is like a barroom brawl: all offence.

The kid went after Cribb. Cribb had too much for him. He used his experience to stay on his jab and stay away, remaining in control. He flicked his jab. Picked off the wild attacks coming at him. He countered or laid off when he began to overwhelm, taking what he could from the spar.

But still, for three minutes, the kid went after Cribb.

'Time!'

Johnny checked that the kid was OK.

'Yep,' he said. It was all he'd said.

'That's good, Mark,' Johnny said. He gave him a drink.

Time …

The second round started slower than the first. Again Cribb got the better of it. Yet while the kid slowed, Johnny watched him. He was defiant.

When it was over, Johnny told the kid he ought to think about coming along more regularly. 'You might be able to have a fight yourself in twelve months or so.'

Encourage him, he thought.

'You shouldn't really be sparring someone like this fella anyway,' Johnny said. 'He's a bit too experienced for you.'

'I'm right,' the kid said. 'I'll spar him again tomorrow.'

Johnny looked at him. He had to think again. By now he had been training fighters long enough to see all kinds, but this one … there was something uncommon about this one.

The next day they were back in the ring. When the first round was over, Johnny gave them both a drink and he pulled Cribb aside. 'Just give him a couple underneath.'

Cribb nodded.

The round began like the others. Soon enough, Cribb went to work. He ripped one underneath, right in the belly. The kid still moved in, throwing punches. Then came another. Then another. Johnny watched the kid start to slow down. That's what body shots do. You can recover from head shots, but body shots take a little from you each time, and whatever they take you cannot get back.

Still, he kept fighting on. While his body slowed, his spirit remained, and inside Johnny was thinking, What else? Johnny was thinking, This is wonderful.

The next day, the kid started training regularly with him. Before long, Jeff Fenech was ready for his first bout.

And Johnny Lewis was about to unleash one hell of a fighter.

He knew early. Normally, he kept them in the gym for as long as twelve months before putting them in the ring. The good ones could do it in six months, from scratch to being ready to win. Some might go a little earlier, but not if they were only ready to fight.

They had to be ready to win.

Fenech had started talking a little now, and Johnny learned he was trialling for Newtown's Jersey Flegg side, the local rugby league junior representative team. He was seventeen. He wanted to get fit. He thought boxing could help.

One of the police officers running the Police Boys Club pulled Johnny aside. Fenech was reasonably well known to them, he said. He didn't say any more. Johnny knew. Johnny watched him train.

This kid Fenech, he lived with a wonderful simplicity. He wanted for nothing he couldn't steal before the day was over.

He hated school, so he left and became a brickie's labourer, which he didn't particularly like, but it kept him fit. He had no desire to be world champion, no great ambition to be anything other than the best thief in Marrickville. Or maybe a footballer. It was too close to call.

But Johnny saw something more, something that perhaps no one had ever noticed in Jeff Fenech before. He wanted to win. He wanted to train harder than the bloke next to him. He wanted to hit the bag harder, to do more sit ups, to spar one more round. If somebody did something that impressed him in the gym, Jeff Fenech wanted to do it too, only better.

And perhaps for the first time in his life, somebody got it. Somebody saw that he had desire.

He wanted to win, like no fighter Johnny had had before. What he lacked was focus.

Early, they worked in baby steps. Johnny taught him the jab. Snap it out. The most basic boxing tool. The most important punch a boxer can have, and the most unnatural. It is the only punch you do not see in a street fight, which is fought all on instinct. But it's often the first punch a fighter will throw in any combination in the ring, as everything works off it.

The following day, it was still there. There was no need to go over what they'd done yesterday. They could just build on what they had.

Soon Fenech started dictating the spar with his jab.

Cribb, a national amateur champion, still handled him all right. But Fenech was learning quickly. Sparring with Cribb, watching how the other fighters worked, there was example everywhere.

Across the gym floor was Jeff Malcolm, the former Australian light-welterweight champion. Johnny was hoping that Malcolm would fight the American Saoul Mamby the following year for his World Boxing Council (WBC) belt. In late August, Mamby had earned a tough fifteen-round majority decision against the Indonesian Thomas Americo. Johnny planned to have Malcolm fight Americo early in 1982, the sooner the better, and he wanted to roll that into a shot at Mamby. The promoters told Malcolm's manager, the rugby league great Tom Raudonikis, they must beat Americo and then regain the Australian title. Then they could have Mamby.

Johnny was pleased enough. With a fighter of Malcolm's quality, both fights were easily winnable. Raudonikis, just a month past leading Newtown to an almost unlikely Grand Final win against Parramatta, listened to Johnny. Two fights, and then Mamby would be ripe to be taken.

But there was a rule in the gym. The next fighter to go in the ring was always the most important fighter. So while Malcolm prepared, Fenech was ready.

His first fight was a November night at Blacktown Police Boys Club. Johnny found a kid from Fairfield Police Boys Club, a kid named Craig Easey, as Fenech's first opponent. Fenech weighed 109 lb, just under 49.5 kg. So did Easey. At that weight they could be riding in the first at Canterbury, but on this night they were two light-flyweights.

Until now, Johnny's best fighter was probably a kid named Phil McElwaine. McElwaine was a beautiful boxer. A true boxer, the kind that accumulates punches. In 1978 he went to the Commonwealth Games in Edmonton, Canada, and came home with a gold medal in the middleweight division. Johnny thought McElwaine was going to be anything as a fighter right up to a motorcycle accident in 1983. It left him in a coma for three weeks and gave him severe head injuries that stayed with him forever. It ended his career.

Whenever he was asked, Johnny rated McElwaine alongside Tony Madigan as perhaps the best amateur Australia had produced. Madigan lost in the quarter finals at the Melbourne Olympics in 1956. He won the bronze medal at the 1960 Olympics in Rome after being eliminated in the semi-finals by a young American, Cassius Clay. It was an improvement on Melbourne.

Craig Easey was not quite a Madigan. But this night he stepped in against a young, unpolished Jeff Fenech and felt right away what the world was about to see. Fenech did not box so much as fight. It was a performance straight from the street, and it overwhelmed Easey. Fenech won the fight relatively easily, and everybody who saw it was impressed.

Except for Johnny.

Fenech showed him nothing he wanted to see. His one concern about Fenech had been there since about the kid's third day of training.

'The one question with Jeff is if he can become disciplined,' Johnny said to the copper running the gym, Brian 'Chicka' Moore. Chicka had been Johnny's friend since they were young boys. He is also a former rugby league centre with Newtown, and a Kangaroo in 1967.

'Like when a referee says break, or gives a reprimand or whatever. The thing with Jeff is, he gives so much so quickly. This kid could be something very, very special. He just has to stay focused and disciplined.'

Johnny didn't see focus or discipline against Easey. He saw a kid in a street fight with gloves.

When the card was over they packed their bags and, as a team, headed home. As they walked out of the Police Boys Club a mini-bus drove past with a drunk hanging out the window. He yelled a drunken comment at Fenech's girlfriend, Tania.

'Come here and say it,' Fenech yelled.

Johnny saw the bus's brake lights glow red. The bus stopped, and a man no bigger than a small building dropped out the bus door, only he moved quicker.

As quick as that, the big bloke was on Fenech, and Johnny watched it end almost as quickly as it had begun.

The big bloke charged Fenech, who went in low and drove his shoulder into his midriff. Then he drove the big bloke's legs until he took enough weight out from him to lift his feet off the ground. From there it was all a formality, really. With the big bloke's centre of balance gone, Fenech flipped him upside-down and drove him head first into the concrete gutter. Then he finished the job with his fists.

By now Johnny was on him, pulling Fenech off.

'Stop it!'—he gave him a shake—'Stop it.'

Almost immediately, Fenech climbed off.

'Mate, what was that?' Johnny said.

'He called Tania a slut.'

'I don't care. There's no reason for you to do that.'

'But, Johnny …'

'Bugger this,' Johnny said, and walked off.

That night, Johnny lay in bed thinking. It was nothing about the fight in the ring. He kept replaying the incident outside. The bus going past. The brake lights. Most of all he kept thinking of Fenech lifting this big man up and spearing him into the gutter. He kept thinking about Jeff, skinny little Jeff, and the hard rope of muscles he felt when he tried to pull Fenech away.

'The strength this kid's got,' he thought.

Still, gyms are full of the prodigious, and Johnny had been at this for twenty years. Jeff needed to show more than strength. Fighters do not win without discipline.

He went to sleep thinking disappointment. Part of him thinking about what might have been had this kid been disciplined. Then he reminded himself that you can't win anything without discipline. But gee, what the kid could do if ... And he drifted off to sleep.

When he woke the next morning, he was straight back on last night. The strength of the kid ...

He heard a knock on the front door. It was still early. He found Fenech on the front step.

'I'm sorry about last night,' he said.

They were the first words out of his mouth, and, Oh, mate, Johnny thought. What a godsend.

He invited him in.

He did not say it, but he thought Fenech was one hundred per cent correct to defend his girlfriend's reputation. Where he came from, where they both came from, you protected your own.

But because of his uncertainty about Fenech's discipline, Johnny didn't tell him that. Instead, this morning Johnny saw something else.

Fenech was a tough kid off the streets. His father, Paul, was often laid up in hospital with a bad heart, and his mum, Mary, was either visiting him or working three jobs to pay for it all. She was the only wage earner. So Jeff, with no direction and no responsibility, was a street-fighter, a petty thief, a young kid heading one way.

It was easy when no one believed in Jeff Fenech.

And even if he was first to the gym every day, he wasn't in the whole way. Until now.

Sitting there at his kitchen table, Johnny saw that Fenech did not want to lose this chance. Sitting there, Johnny saw that he had reached him.

It was then he knew he could do something with this kid.

CHAPTER 2

He had him.

Years later, you talk to Fenech and he will say he could have walked into any gym and, right away, the trainer there would have had a potential world champion. He is probably right. But Johnny, he says—Johnny wasn't just a trainer. Johnny didn't work on the fighter, but the man.

Fenech has no doubt that is why he became a world champion.

Johnny gave Fenech love. The only condition was that Fenech try to be the best he could be. With that simple offering it showed that Fenech, the hard young fighter, needed something after all.

In those days, Fenech was absolutely ripe for Johnny. What is less considered is that Johnny was absolutely ripe for Fenech.

Still only thirty-seven at the time, he had been training fighters for twenty years when Fenech walked into his gym that day in 1981. Besides Phil McElwaine, he'd had any number of Australian champions. Now he handled Jeff Malcolm, and a world title was looming.

But his great joy still remained in the sport at its purest. A young boy with no confidence and less ability would come to the gym saying he wanted to learn self-defence. Johnny would work with him slowly and patiently, building him. Soon he would suggest that the kid get into the ring. Have a novice bout.

'No,' the boy would say. 'I just want to learn self-defence.'

By now Johnny knew it wasn't about fear or courage, it had nothing to do with that. It was confidence.

'Trust yourself, son,' he would say. And Johnny would go back to gently building his confidence, until one day the kid would suggest a fight himself. 'Do you think I can?'

It was the look on the kid's face afterward, after the fight, when he was back in the dressing room and he looked at his trophy and began to understand what he had done. That's what stayed with Johnny.

And that's why he had never harboured any great ambition for world titles or personal glory. Certainly not in the professional side of the sport. Indeed, it was in the charter of the New South Wales Police Boys Clubs that its gyms were not-for-profit charities, for amateur athletes only. Professional athletes were not supposed to train at them, although the rule was rarely, if ever, applied.

Jeff Malcolm, for instance, was only a couple of fights away from a professional world title. By the end of 1982 Johnny was confident they would have the belt.

But Fenech, he was something different again. He opened possibilities. For the first time, Johnny began to wonder.

As for how Fenech would deal with success, he didn't know.

After all, he had really begun training by accident. All of this was unplanned.

HE WAS thirteen. He began fighting under Snowy McFadyen and Jack Blom at the Police Boys Club at Newtown in 1957. Snowy was a straight-down-the-line bloke, family oriented. For him, fighting and training were simply your duty. You're in there, you do it. Jack was the other way. Jack was a scallywag. He would tell you what you needed to hear to get you ready for a fight, no matter how far from the truth he had to go. Jack said what he needed to say, but he got you where you needed to be.

Training alongside him in those days were Freddy Casey and Jacky Bruce and Billy Males, and Billy's brother Danny. They went all over the state together. To places like Cowra, Griffith and Singleton and Orange, places an inner-city kid like Johnny had never seen before. He stayed in pubs or was billeted by local families, and they shared wonderful times on those long, endless bus rides.

After several years, Snowy McFadyen and Jack Blom left the gym. A new trainer took over, Dick O'Connor.

He brought a new set of rules.

He was to be called Mr O'Connor. You never spoke to him unless spoken to. If you spoke first, you were sent home and banned till the following day. Johnny, quiet and respectful always, had no problems with Mr O'Connor.

For all the stiff formalities, he immediately felt something different. It was in the way Mr O'Connor spoke to him. Not just at training, but in the dressing room before fights, in the corner between rounds.

He did not understand at first, but he soon worked it out. Mr O'Connor took the fear out of him. He was always a small boy that struggled to put on weight. He always felt at a physical disadvantage.

'If I turn sideways in class they mark me absent,' Johnny said. Mr O'Connor understood.

His struggle with weight meant he struggled to put on muscle. So he was never a strong boy. When you can get so far in junior boxing simply by being the stronger fighter, it was a tremendous handicap. Under Mr O'Connor, though, Johnny finally understood what boxing was about. The art of it. With that, and with Mr O'Connor's perfect words in his ear, he no longer fought scared, and he fought differently.

He never lost a fight while Dick O'Connor was in the corner. It is something he remembers still, and for it he will forever love the man.

Others understood it, too.

Over time Johnny saw fighters from other gyms, fighters with other trainers, sneak into Newtown for private lessons with Mr O'Connor. He would close the doors so there was only him and the fighter and Johnny inside, and he would teach technique and vision better than any trainer Johnny had seen then or since.

'Don't tell anyone about him coming up here,' he said to Johnny about one fighter. Why would he? He was getting the best private lessons himself, just watching.

It stayed like that until he was seventeen. He wished it had stayed that way forever. But one day Mr O'Connor pulled him aside. 'I'm going to be missing for a little while.'

His voice was no different than if he'd said he was stepping out for a loaf of bread.

Johnny believes it might have been family matters, but he isn't sure. All he knows is that Mr O'Connor left that afternoon and did not come back. As far as he knows, he never trained again. Certainly he never saw him again.

After months of no fights and no trainer, Ken Shorter, the policeman running the gym, walked into the boxing room.

'We're going to Parramatta for a tournament,' he said.

'Oh yeah?' Johnny said. 'Who's going to train us?'

'You are.'

'I can't do that,' Johnny said, shaking his head.

'Well, you're gonna … you and me.'

'No, no,' Johnny said. 'I'm not going to do this. I don't even know what I'm going to say.'

'Well, we're going,' Shorter said, and they went.

Who knows what he saw in Johnny? Whatever it was, six fought that night and six won, and it was some trip back in the bus.

He trained them like he thought Dick O'Connor would train him. He trained them all that way for all the years after he took over the gym, at seventeen years old.

'Modelled myself on Dick O'Connor, grabbed a bit from Jack Blom.'

That's how it began, and even then he had something, a sensitivity uncommon in fight trainers.

Months later, he was working a corner at South Sydney Juniors. He was there primarily as a second, helping another trainer who needed an extra pair of hands for the bucket and sponge. He was now eighteen years old. Maybe it was a sense, this way he had with his fighters. Maybe it came from the gentle nurturing he'd got from his mother, a woman of immeasurable kindness. After a fairly brutal round, their fighter headed back to his stool and, as he turned to sit on it, Johnny saw something.

A look in his eyes, who knows?

There was a nick over the fighter's eye, and his trainer worked on closing it. Johnny kept looking at this young man, though, seeing what his trainer couldn't. The referee was Jimmy Carruthers, Australia's first professional world champion, now retired, and he headed towards their corner.

'Are you all right?' Johnny said before Carruthers arrived in the corner.

The fighter said nothing. He just looked at him with dish-plate eyes. Carruthers came up. 'How you going, mate?'

The trainer didn't bother looking up. 'He's all right, mate, he's all right.'

Carruthers ignored the bravery of the trainer and asked the fighter again, 'How are you, mate?'

The fighter said nothing.

'He's got a cut there,' Johnny said, stepping in. 'It's no good.'

Carruthers looked at Johnny and back at the fighter. 'Yeah, yeah,' he said. Then he turned and walked across the ring and put his hand on the other fighter's head to crown him the winner.

The fight was over.

Back in the dressing room, trainer Ernie McQuillan, who was the promoter this night, was filthy. Ernie was from the 'He can't hurt us' school of training. Nobody ever hit one of Ernie's fighters with a punch Ernie couldn't take. Ernie did not make money as a promoter by having fights stopped before the crowd got its spill of blood.

'Jesus Christ. Why'd you stop that?' Ernie said.

The trainer, who wanted to work again, pleaded ignorance. 'It wasn't us, it was the referee.'

'Jesus Christ,' Ernie said again. 'You've only done two rounds. Jesus.'

Johnny wasn't listening to Ernie, though. He was looking at the fighter's face, washed with relief.

Later, the night over, Johnny was walking through the club, heading out past the poker machines. An arm reached out to stop him. It was Carruthers. Johnny had never spoken to him in his life.

'Son, how old are you?' Carruthers said.

'Eighteen.'

'Well, son, let me say what you done there tonight was a fine act. That kid didn't want to be in there. For someone so young to show such maturity, good on you, son.'

Working a corner, Johnny had already figured out that all a trainer can do is react to what he sees. That is the only tool he has. By telling him he was spot-on, Jimmy Carruthers was telling him he could trust his instincts. He was doing the job right.

And for that to come from Carruthers, well ... that made it so much better. Jimmy Carruthers had been an idol since Johnny was eight years old and his father took him to Snowy Robbins's gym, above the dry-cleaner's along Erskineville Road, to farewell Carruthers as he left for South Africa to fight Vic Toweel for the bantamweight championship of the world. This was in the days when there was only one world champion in each division, and only eight divisions. Only eight men at any one time could call themselves world champion.

Carruthers was having his final sparring session at Snowy's gym, and on this last day the press came to interview him. As a farewell gift, they presented him with a travel bag.

Johnny stood in the background with his elder brother Robert and his father Alf, standing there star-eyed and saying nothing, and watched Carruthers accept the bag with slight embarrassment. He was a humble man, and he said, 'I hope I can bring the belt back in this bag.'

The fight lasted 139 seconds.

In that time, Jimmy Carruthers threw 147 punches to knock out Vic Toweel. And became Australia's first recognised world champion.

That afternoon at Snowy's gym had started Johnny's love for boxing.

Now, after talking to Carruthers, he walked out of Souths Juniors this night believing he might really know what he was doing in the corner.

Over the next few months he fought less himself and trained others more, slowly giving up his own career to continue coaching other fighters in the gym. He took on more and more boys, and he needed to keep up with the success they were having. He began travelling a lot.

Some years later he found himself in Thailand with the amateurs, and it was time for great change.

He did not invent the form, stealing it directly from a Thai trainer he saw on the trip. But he figured nobody holds a copyright on good ideas and, with that, he took this idea and would soon change forever the way they trained in Australia.

Traditionally, trainers stood in boxing rings and caught punches with big, eighteen-ounce gloves as they moved around with their fighter. Occasionally they parried back. It was always done that way, move and counter, throw the punch when the trainer finally got the glove up there to catch it. Johnny found it stilted and slow. With the big gloves, you just couldn't catch the punches fast enough. This Thai trainer, though, did not use gloves. He used target pads instead. Johnny watched the speed at which the Thai fighters worked their punches and thought, This is for me.

He brought the pads back to Newtown. Today, target pads are in every boxing gym in Australia.

Back then, though, not everyone liked them.

In his newspaper column, Bernie Hall, a former lightweight contender and one of the country's leading trainers, wrote that there was a trainer around town downgrading P platers to L platers with his unusual training methods. He didn't name Johnny, but it was cheap and spiteful and Johnny knew who he meant.

But by now Johnny trusted himself. To hell with Bernie.

If Johnny's methods caused one problem it was indirectly, through the publicity that Fenech's emergence got. That publicity probably ruined a hundred young fighters over the next twenty years. Trainers, catching a glimpse of Johnny on the evening news working Fenech through the pads, would start working their fighters through round after round of one-twos, over and under. They were mimicking the style, without realising the fundamentals behind it.

Most of all, they couldn't replicate Johnny.

Schooled by Dick O'Connor and Snowy McFadyen and Jack Blom, he understood the fundamentals, and how to teach them. Some things don't change, and boxing resists change more than any sport. Old-timers would moan long and hard about Fenech's mauling style, for instance. They couldn't see past his ferocity to recognise the subtlety of skill. Fighters recognised it, though. In the coming years, seeing how quickly Johnny was progressing Fenech, Jeff Harding would move to Sydney from Grafton as an amateur to train under him. The Russian world amateur champion Kostya Tszyu would turn professional and knock back an offer from Korea to migrate to Australia and fight under Johnny, all because of the speed with which Johnny secured Fenech a world title. American Virgil Hill, having just lost his world light-heavyweight title, would move to Australia to train at Newtown and regain the crown with Johnny in his corner. Joe Bugner would come out of retirement for one last campaign and hopefully a shot at heavyweight champion Mike Tyson. Justin Rowsell would begin his professional career under Johnny and be another headed for a certain world title until, well ... to this day Justin remains Johnny's greatest disappointment. Gairy St Clair would put together the most courageous performance Johnny ever saw, bracketed next to Harding, to win a world title in South Africa. Billy Dib would win his first and, so far, only world title after switching trainers to have Johnny in his corner.

But while other fighters would come, and there were other fighters before, it started with Fenech.

His style was not the classic amateur style. Johnny didn't care, or dare change it. Every day in the gym, he trained Fenech like a pro. It is important to understand here that in the early 1980s there was no great difference between the amateur and professional styles. The chief difference was that amateurs fought three rounds and pros anywhere between four and fifteen. Both disciplines were scored basically the same way, with a judge awarding the round to the better fighter based on his control and effectiveness, and the fighter with the most accumulated rounds won the fight. Today the pros and amateurs are almost two different sports. Amateur boxing is scored by computer, with judges required to register a point for each clean punch they see. The fighter who scores the most points, regardless of how hard or effective his punches are, wins the fight. It has become a sport for sharpshooters.

So when Johnny began steering Fenech towards the Olympics, which were for amateurs, he didn't change anything to make his style more amateur friendly. Fenech's natural instincts were enough to make him very good even if Fenech himself believed his true calling would be the pros.

Several weeks passed after that first fight at Blacktown. Fenech was in the gym every day. Johnny found him another fight.

They arrived at the venue to find Fenech's opponent almost seven pounds over the weight.

'Nope,' Johnny said, 'we're out.'

Boxing is divided by weight, and not by height or age or any other classification, for very good reasons. Boxing is all about the weight of the punch. Almost always, if I hit you harder, I win. It simply stands to reason that a bigger man can throw a harder punch. Not always considered, but equally as important, is that a bigger man can also absorb a bigger punch. The lower the weight division, the greater the advantage of extra weight. Seven pounds was too much.

'Nope, we're out,' said Johnny.

'Come on, Johnny,' Fenech said, adrenaline running. 'I still wanna take the fight. Who cares?'

'I said no,' Johnny said, and did not turn back.

Later, when the disappointment passed, Fenech looked deeper into what had happened. He realised that Johnny hadn't called it off out of fear or a lack of belief that he could win. It was something Fenech was not conditioned to look for, which is probably why he didn't recognise it immediately: Johnny had Fenech's interest at heart.

By showing Fenech respect, Johnny earned his loyalty. From that day on, Fenech never questioned Johnny's judgement once a decision was made.

Johnny, for his part, needed Fenech the street fighter to know he was the boss. When a decision was made it was made, and that was the end of it.

Fenech got back in the ring soon after. One Friday night, he and Johnny turned up at a club ready for another bout. Johnny walked into the dressing rooms to register.

'Your opponent's fallen through,' the official told him. No fight.

Not again, Johnny thought. He looked around and spotted another fighter.

'Look,' he said. 'There's a bloke the same weight.'

'He's had forty fights.'

'That'll be all right,' said Johnny.

Even in amateur boxing, which is at least half as ruthless as its professional cousin, it is not hard to find trainers who are braver than their fighters. Figuring Johnny for one of those, the official barely paused before writing Fenech's name into the slot. Officially Fenech was still a novice. In Australian amateur boxing, forty fights was well experienced. These two shouldn't be fighting. Yet Johnny saw something in Fenech's new opponent that gave him confidence. This bloke might have had forty fights, but he still had the body of a boy. Fenech was small, but he was mature through the chest and shoulders. He already had that strength.

Right there, Johnny knew Fenech had this kid beat. He also knew something the other guy didn't: he knew the engine in his fighter.

Later, after the match was made, the trainer of Fenech's opponent came over to Johnny for a quiet word.

'Look, mate, I want to be honest with you,' he said. 'My bloke can fight.'

'Thanks, mate,' Johnny said. 'But my bloke's a tough little rooster. It'll be all right.'

'It's up to you,' the trainer said. 'But I'm telling you—remember I told you, my bloke's a very good fighter.'

Fenech jumped on his opponent from the bell and didn't allow him to get off. The other kid backed off to create room to throw his punches and Fenech was on him again before he got set. He knocked him out in the second round. Already the style was there: swarming his opponent, throwing flurries the other fighter could not stand up to.

After the fight, the rival trainer found Johnny in the dressing room. He spoke with the bitter tone of a man who felt he had been set up.

'Your bloke can't fight,' he said.

'You're right, mate, he can't,' Johnny said. 'But your bloke can and we just stopped him in two, so take out of that what you want.'

All the way home, Johnny allowed himself to dream.

For many years in Australia, decades really, the two most important people in boxing had been Harry Miller and Ern McQuillan. Miller ran boxing at the Sydney Stadium, the old tin shed, and McQuillan trained most of the fighters.

Every Monday night Miller would sit in his office at the Stadium and not even watch the fights in the arena, just sit there talking to promoters and newspapermen like the *Daily Mirror*'s new young boxing writer, Bill Mordey. After each fight an employee would walk in and tell him the result of the fight just finished.

'He went all right?' Miller would ask.

'Yeah, he went all right.'

'Put him on again. What about the loser, he worth putting on again?'

Fighters weren't worth bringing back if they could not sell a ticket. They needed to be entertaining, and even more so in defeat.

As the country's leading trainer, McQuillan was tight with Miller, so tight that many fighters could not get on the Stadium card unless they became McQuillan fighters first. That was the way it worked.

By the time Fenech began fighting, the Stadium had been closed for more than a decade, levelled to make way for the Bondi Junction train line. Harry Miller too was long gone, and all Ern McQuillan's best fighters were retired or breaking not much better than even. Sydney people hardly cared about boxing anymore. The old *TV Ringside*, a weekly staple on Channel Seven, was no longer televised. The game struggled for coverage in the mainstream press.

Fenech had all this to overcome when he started. Yet Johnny believed.

CHAPTER 3

In January 1982, shortly after Fenech's fight with the kid who could fight, but evidently not as well as his trainer thought, Johnny headed to Newcastle with Jeff Malcolm.

It was about to begin.

Malcolm had been pro for about eleven years by then, and was suffering the usual fate of the Australian fighter. He couldn't get a crack at a world title.

Even when they had the talent, local promoters often did not have the money to lure the world champion to Australia. They often lacked the smarts and the connections to manoeuvre their man through the rankings until he was No. 1, which would force the champ to a mandatory defence. They lacked exposure on the American market, where the belt—which was just the residue of the true game, which was money and control—lay. And without money and smarts and connections and exposure, they could change nothing.

It surprised exactly nobody, then, that Australia's first world champion, Jimmy Carruthers, had beaten a South African to win his world title while the second, Lionel Rose, had beaten a Japanese fighter. They had been able to bypass the American stronghold.

Frustrated at his lack of progress, Malcolm had turned to Tom Raudonikis to manage him. Raudonikis had no experience managing fighters, but maybe that's what Malcolm needed, somebody from outside the fight game.

'On one condition,' Raudonikis said when Malcolm approached him.

'What's that?'

'Johnny Lewis trains you.'

Johnny had been on the Newtown Rugby League Club committee since 1973, the year Jack Gibson was coach. He was still there when Raudonikis joined the club in 1980, and Raudonikis soon began heading to the Newtown Police Boys Club gym for extra training sessions, where of course he trained with Johnny.

Tommy, the great Australian football champion, saw one thing early about Johnny the trainer. He has no idea what it is, he says. But 'Whatever it was, it's what makes men great.'

The admiration was mutual.

Johnny continued knocking off from work as a council signwriter at about 2.30 each afternoon to head to the gym. Raudonikis would often be there before him, and Johnny always found him in the same place, downstairs on the basketball court. He would walk in and find neighbourhood kids spread around the court. The kids weren't gym members. They'd just heard Tommy Raudonikis was at the gym, or that there was a cricket game going on inside.

Tommy organised the cricket games. He turned a garbage bin upside down and found a bat from somewhere, and if a bat couldn't be found he'd grab a plank of wood and, when they put a tennis ball with it, they had themselves a game. Kids everywhere, and Tom Raudonikis—the Australian halfback and one of the biggest names in Australian sport—up to his elbows in it. That's the quality of Tom Raudonikis, Johnny thought to himself.

Driving to Newcastle now with Jeff Malcolm, they were about to tick the first box in the two-fight deal that had been put to them. Tonight they were fighting for the Australian title. Next stop, a shot at Saoul Mamby's World Boxing Council light-welterweight title. The Australian champion was Peter Berrigan.

They hadn't been in Newcastle five minutes before Johnny suffered great pain between his eyes. The referee, it turned out, was a fighter out of the promoter's gym. And the promoter was the trainer of the champion, Berrigan.

On top of that, so was one of the judges.

It was the curse of the small promotion. Where the big promotions can afford to bring in impartial officials, often flying them in, small promotions require local help. Local officials are often connected to the local promoter, who is often the local trainer too. It is not unusual. Berrigan's training partner just happened to have a referee's ticket. He was an affordable choice.

Johnny's headache began to ease when the fight started. Malcolm, a southpaw and one of the loveliest boxers Johnny ever saw, dominated the fight. It was all there, the beautiful footwork, the ability to move in and out behind a wonderful balance. He would hit Berrigan and be gone by the time Berrigan responded. Between rounds, Johnny did nothing but keep him calm.

'Keep doing what you're doing, mate.'

He did not need to say any more. Why should he? Alongside Johnny in the corner were Tommy Raudonikis and another Newtown footballer, also a childhood friend of Johnny's, Col Murphy. For round after round Malcolm built his lead, until the bell rang to end the tenth and final round. Billy Males, Johnny's old teammate and now a leading referee and judge, scored every round to Malcolm. The other two judges scored every round to Berrigan. There is no reason to believe Berrigan had anything to do with this or even any knowledge of it.

But Johnny did not see it coming. As soon as the decision was announced, the crowd roared up in appreciation of a well-worked rort. On the ring apron, Col Murphy knew they were rubbing it in.

Forget diplomacy, he said to himself. He threw his bucket of water over those near him.

'Youse can all get fucked,' he said.

Then he stood there, the crowd wet and quickly silent, waiting for just one of them to step up and take issue with it. Not one rose from his chair.

What do you say to a fighter after this? Johnny never spoke to the promoter again.

It was only later, on the way home, that he came up with a plan to still get to Mamby. So they'd lost the Australian title. But what if they fought Thomas Americo next, and beat him even more convincingly than Mamby had? It might convince the Americans to take the fight anyway.

It was a small hope in a dark evening.

A month later, the New South Wales Rugby League season kicked off. Tommy Raudonikis was five months past leading his club to what was nearly its greatest moment. Now, in his final season at the club, he was starting in reserve grade.

He was on the outs with the coach, Warren Ryan. But there was one small positive. The early start for reserve grade allowed him an early exit.

February 27, 1982. Saturday afternoon. Behind the grandstand in a chauffeured hire car with the engine running is Johnny. Tommy walks off Henson Park muddied and spent and goes straight into the dressing room. He grabs his kit-bag, goes straight back out again, gets in the car and pulls the door shut behind him. And he sits there, still in the mud he's just played eighty minutes of football in. He hasn't even had time to put his teeth back in.

'I'll have a shower when we get there,' he says.

Alongside Johnny in the hire car is Jeff Malcolm. Tommy has made the match for Malcolm to fight Thomas Americo at a promotion he is bankrolling at the Sydney Opera House. The co-promoter is millionaire

Sydney ad-man and Newtown benefactor John Singleton, Raudonikis's great friend.

They met more than two years ago when Singleton invited Raudonikis into his office and told him he wanted him to play for Newtown. Tommy couldn't do that, he said. He had just been awarded life membership at his own club, Western Suburbs.

Singleton explained the virtues of playing for the Jets, who had just run last but had great plans, and Tommy sat there completely unconvinced. Then Singo pulled out the greatest sight a semi-professional footballer can see, for rugby league was still semi-professional in those days: a paper bag filled with money. Tommy didn't need to count it, just weigh it. Suddenly the Jets had their biggest signing in years, the current Australian Test halfback.

Now Singo and Tommy are promoting fights together, and the publicity run for the Opera House card is about to begin.

Malcolm will spar at a four-round exhibition at Griffith, in south-western New South Wales. He comes from near there, so it is billed in town as something of a homecoming for the local boy.

First, though, they need to get to the airport.

The driver starts towards Bankstown Airport, and Tommy leans forward and peels the electrical tape from his football boots, sprinkling mud across the floor. He pulls off his boots and, finally, his socks. Naked white feet contrast with his muddy legs. Then Tommy leans back and finally begins to relax. All of a sudden, he sits up and tells the driver to divert. It sounds urgent.

When Tommy finally tells the driver to stop, they are in front of a bottle shop. Tommy walks into the bottle-o still dressed to play football and comes out with a carton of Toohey's cans. He plants the carton at his feet and sits back and cracks his first ring-pull. Now he is right.

It is no more than a two-can trip to Bankstown Airport. They drive right up alongside a small four-seater plane on the tarmac, and

Johnny looks at the pilot, thinking, He looks much younger than I thought he'd be. Next to him is Paul Ferreri, the Commonwealth bantamweight champion, who is also coming to Griffith. Ferreri's job is nothing more than to wave to the crowd. He is smartly dressed, politely spoken. He comes from Melbourne, where they don't play rugby league. So Ferreri has no clue who this character might be in a rugby jumper, caked in mud, getting out of the car with a kit-bag under one arm and a carton of cans under the other. All he knows is they are late.

They all get on the plane. Johnny is sitting on one side of the plane, facing Ferreri, with Tommy and Malcolm facing each other on the other side.

Now, Johnny flies as well as most, which is not very well at all, and certainly not any better than Ferreri and Malcolm. When they finally get in the air, the pilot turns and tells them that he's actually a trainee and has only enough hours to get them to Bathurst, but not to worry—once they land, someone else will be waiting to fly them to Griffith.

Johnny sits back in his seat. How many different ways can you say Jesus Christ?

The only one unconcerned is Tommy. He is about four cans in, sitting back carefree and painless. He doesn't care about the rookie pilot or the impromptu stopover. And he doesn't notice Ferreri, who is staring hard right at him.

No, Tommy drinks.

Somewhere about now, nobody is sure exactly where but it must have been somewhere over the Blue Mountains, Tommy realises there is no toilet on this little four-seater. Never mind. He picks an empty can, awkwardly manoeuvres to the edge of his seat, and pulls the leg of his shorts to the side. He positions himself as best he can over the empty can and lets go. Ferreri, who has never heard of this man, and so has had no chance to fall in love with him like the rest of us, can only watch.

This worries Johnny. He can see Ferreri is real unimpressed.

Tommy shuffles and starts his business and it is here, well, it is here it gets awkward. One aim is good, and one aim is missing.

A mischievous side stream shoots off from the main one, and, as you would have it, all over a startled Ferreri.

He reacts like a boxing champion might.

He lunges towards Tommy. As he does, Johnny leaps between them. Ferreri is angry. Angry and wet, which for a proud man like him is the worst kind of angry.

Eventually Johnny talks him down, and he sits back in his seat, unhappy, but no longer with murder on his mind.

Eventually the rookie pilot touches down in Bathurst and everyone gives a small prayer. If nothing else, a full-grown pilot is waiting to take them the rest of the trip to Griffith. Or so they think.

The new pilot takes one look at them and walks away.

'Mate, I can't take four,' he says. 'They told me there was only three.'

Apparently, Ferreri originally planned to make his own way to Griffith, so he had not been counted. Johnny protests.

'No way mate, I can't do it,' the replacement pilot says, and walks off.

The trainee pilot is still standing there.

'Come on, mate, we gotta get there,' Tommy says. Nobody is happy, least of all the kid, who has used up his hours. But he agrees to fly them to Griffith.

They take off again.

Things have calmed considerably. Malcolm and Johnny start to relax and even Ferreri leans back in his seat. Not that Ferreri has forgiven Tommy, though.

Nice and comfortable, now eight or nine cans in, Tommy lights up a smoke.

The calm lasts no more than a minute.

It starts up front. The kid pilot starts checking the instruments in small panic, trying to determine what's wrong. His eyes scope the engine through the windscreen.

'Something's on fire!' he yells.

He turns.

'Anyone back there smoking?'

'Nah,' says Tommy. He folds his arms across his chest to tuck his cigarette under his armpit. Right up against the cabin wall.

The pilot keeps checking the instrument panel.

'There's something burning,' he says. 'There's something burning.'

Now, nobody else is all that worried, because they know it's only Tommy smoking and, not that they are happy about it, but they know that the engine isn't on fire, either. They aren't going down.

But in 1982 the décor can scare a dog off a bone, and small four-seater planes are no exception. Running high up the inside wall of the plane is a brilliant shagpile carpet.

The smell in the air changes. Tommy leaps up. Flames are coming out of the wall. Johnny does what any sensible man would do. He grabs one of Tommy's cans, gives it a shake and cracks the ring-pull.

'Don't do that!' Tommy yells, reaching out. His solution is to pat the fire frantically, trying to smother the flames. Johnny pushes past him and douses the cigarette and the flaming carpet with Tommy's beer.

While it certainly succeeds in putting out the fire, the mood after this is less than cosy.

Tommy is filthy because Johnny has wasted a perfectly good can of beer. Johnny is filthy because Tommy nearly set their plane on fire eleven thousand feet in the air and cared more about wasting a can of beer.

Ferreri is worse than filthy. He doesn't say a word, just sits and looks at Tommy with full-blown evil in his eyes.

He sees past Tommy to a black scorch mark the size of a garbage-can lid that Tommy, somewhat embarrassed now, thinks he can hide if he turns his shoulder and sort of leans in front of it.

At the venue in Griffith, the promoters too are filthy because they're late. If only they knew, thinks Johnny.

The main event has been held up waiting for Malcolm to arrive and spar his exhibition. By now the crowd has had a gut full. All the goodwill has left the room. Worse, Malcolm's opponent for the exhibition has dropped out.

Nothing has less patience than a fight crowd waiting for the next bout, unless it is the promoter worrying about a walkout from this very same crowd. Tommy, always brave, volunteers to step in. Now, here in the auditorium Tommy is swaying and beginning to slow, the soreness from his earlier football game setting in. He puts his arm around Johnny and wonders ahead about this exhibition.

'This is just going to be an easy spar, isn't it?' he says to Johnny.

'It was gonna be,' Johnny says.

Doing a quick count, Johnny figures Tommy has downed about eighteen cans.

While Tommy showers, Johnny begins wrapping Malcolm's hands. Both of them have had enough of Tommy, but they also know they have no choice.

'What'll I do?' Malcolm says.

'I'll tell you what you're gonna do,' Johnny says. 'Don't hit him hard in the head. But rip him up the guts. Fuck him. He's made this trip a misery for us. Rip him up the guts.'

For three rounds they move around, Malcolm working with Tommy, giving a show for the crowd who, truth be told, are as pleased to see Tommy as they are him. Then Malcolm hits the go button.

He rips a punch underneath, right into the middle of Tommy's belly. He moves around a little more and rips another right. Each time, Tommy swoons and his cheeks puff like a goldfish.

Malcolm goes underneath a third time, Tommy steps back, raises his chin, and lets go a fountain of white foam. Almost before it hits the canvas, the promoter is in the ring, screaming.

'Get them out,' he yells. 'That's fucking *it*!'

Much later, after the main event, Johnny finds Tommy in a bar at the club, drinking with the locals.

'Tom,' he says, 'I'm going back to the motel, mate.'

'I'll stay for a little while,' Tommy says. 'There's some good blokes here.'

'That's all right mate.'

'What room are we in again?'

Johnny pulls the key from his pocket. They are sharing a room at one of those roadside motels where you can drive straight up to the door of your room. The tag says Room 8.

'Sixteen,' he says.

'Righto, mate, 16. Righto Johnny, I'll see you back there mate, I won't be long.'

Johnny closes the door and, after a day like this, climbs into bed for eight hours of uninterrupted sleep. After the flight and the fire and the fights, it is glorious.

Next morning, he wakes and pokes his head out the door. There, along the walkway, is Tommy, curled up on the concrete in front of Room 16.

'Tom!' he yells.

Tommy wakes immediately. 'Mate, I've been knocking all night. You couldn't hear me?'

'No, mate, we're down here,' Johnny says.

'I thought you said 16?'

'No mate, we're Room 8.'

'I'm fucking freezing,' Tommy says.

Later that morning, Johnny and Tommy go back to Sydney. They go by bus.

■ ■ ■

THE DAY after they got back, Tommy was cited by the New South Wales Rugby League for breaking the jaw of an opposition player called Earnie Garland. He was suspended for thirteen weeks.

Banned from playing, Tommy stayed away from training for a month. When the Jets committee next met, a proposal was formally put forward to sack Tommy. He hadn't trained for four weeks, said Frank Farrington, the Secretary. That was grounds for sacking right there.

Johnny spoke up. 'No, Frank. He trains every day with me.'

'Does he?' said Farrington.

'Every day, mate.'

It was only a small lie.

Johnny called Tommy as soon as he got home.

'Tom, you get up to the gym tomorrow and bring your wet-weather gear,' he said. 'Don't you ignore me, mate, because they'll check up. Don't let me down.'

'I won't let you down, Johnny.'

The next afternoon Tommy walked in. He put on a raincoat and Johnny grabbed his pads and walked to the middle of the ring. For three-minute rounds, thirty seconds' rest between them, they worked.

There was nothing fancy in it. It was about effort. Johnny had put his fighters through this same routine thousands of times and, knowing its toll, came prepared for Tommy. He filled a bucket with sand and put it in the ring next to him.

Soon Tommy started dry-heaving.

'Come on, mate,' Johnny said. 'Keep going.'

Of course he kept going. Tommy kept punching, and dry-heaving, and after every dry heave he turned and spewed into the bucket and turned straight back into the pads.

'Come on, Tom.'

Tommy Raudonikis worked that day like Johnny had seen no man work before. He just kept on giving. He hit the pads and grew so tired he couldn't even turn and find the bucket and spewed down the front of his raincoat. But he kept punching. That afternoon, Johnny Lewis saw why Tommy Raudonikis was a champion footballer, why he was a winner. He did not have the skill of the other top halfbacks, but nobody ever finished over the top of Tommy. If he had to, Tommy would drag them down to his level and then finish over the top of them.

It was that toughness that Johnny admired most about Tom Raudonikis.

'He gave,' Johnny said.

Here was an exertion he had not seen in the gym before. But he would not have to wait long to see it again. Jeff Fenech was just starting to come into his own, and Johnny honestly believed Fenech was learning something about hard work by watching Tommy train alongside him.

CHAPTER 4

STILL, THINGS WEREN'T going well for Tommy Raudonikis.

Having recovered from the spar with Jeff Malcolm, he was still in the midst of his thirteen-week suspension when big time boxing finally took place at the Sydney Opera House. At which, remember, he was co-promoter.

Johnny helped Tommy organise much of the card while training several fighters involved. The date was April 2, 1982, and should never be forgotten. The Opera House people certainly cannot.

It began as a slow boil.

The steep tiering of the auditorium might have been perfect for Vivaldi but it soon became a problem for the boxing crowd, where drinking was at least half the night's entertainment.

Jeff Malcolm fought Thomas Americo in the second fight on the card. He won on points over ten, with Johnny, Tommy and Fenech in his corner. No one disputed the decision.

It started for real in the ninth round of the main support, though. Australian light-middleweight champion Alex Temelkov fought challenger Ken Salisbury. In a clinch, Salisbury bent too far forward and Temelkov rabbit-punched the back of his head. As the referee separated them to warn Temelkov, Salisbury's trainer Bernie Hall, last seen taking pot shots at Johnny in his column, climbed to the ring apron and took two great handfuls of Temelkov's hair to wrench him backwards.

As Temelkov pulled away, his trainer, who was also his brother, flashed across the ring to launch a flying karate kick at Hall, who avoided the kick by simply dropping off the ring apron. An old welterweight, Bernie always had good footwork.

Apparently frustrated at missing Hall, Temelkov's brother then turned and started throwing punches at Salisbury.

As it turned out this was particularly bad news for Temelkov's brother. The referee who'd just separated Temelkov and Salisbury was Charkey Ramon, a former Commonwealth light-middleweight champion and a fighter Johnny thought should have won a world title in fairer circumstances. In other words, he could handle himself.

Ramon also just happened to have trained under Bernie Hall. As Temelkov's brother rebounded from his Bruce Lee lunge at Hall and started laying into Salisbury, Ramon grabbed him and, after a short spot of in-fighting, stepped back and threw a lovely long right hand that landed flush. By this time, of course, others had joined in around the ring.

As the brawl went on, Tommy stood outside the ring holding a big bag of money and watching his whole promotion disintegrate in front of him.

The money was the bets Temelkov's supporters had made against Salisbury's supporters. Tommy was the only one they trusted to hold it, but now he had a problem. He had this bag of money, which was considerable, but as the promoter he believed he was supposed to be the one stopping this brawl. He stashed the bag of money under a chair and climbed into the ring. He thumped across to Temelkov's corner, palms raised, pleading for a truce. It was a lone finger in the wall of a crumbling dam. Fights started to erupt throughout the crowd and soon supporters began tumbling down the steep tiering.

Johnny could only watch from ringside as the brawl ran on. Then he saw one of them in the ring turn on Tommy. Others joined in. Johnny watched Tommy going boom ... boom ... boom, knocking them down as quick as they got to him.

The brawl lasted the best part of thirty minutes. Oh, it wasn't constant fighting. But each time the peacemakers thought they had it calmed down in one area, it flared again in another. Good behaviour was restored, after a fashion. The judges gave the decision to Salisbury by disqualification on account of the original foul.

When the main event, starring Paul Ferreri, began, scuffling continued throughout the Ferreri fight. Even more toppled down the steep tiering. Only now most were being tossed down. Johnny could do nothing but sit in the crowd and watch, and in some cases admire. Some showed good arm strength.

Tommy's troubles were nowhere near over, either. He retrieved the bag of money and handed it to the Salisbury camp. They won the decision, they got the money. But not everyone agreed. Temelkov's supporters thought their man's rabbit punches didn't warrant disqualification. They thought Salisbury should have been disqualified on account of Bernie Hall's attack. They had done their money, and they were angry. They started threatening Tommy. As the Ferreri fight ended, one of Tommy's supporters slipped him a pistol.

'Use it if you need it,' he said.

Tommy pushed the pistol into his belt and made for the door.

'BRAWL!' screamed the *Sun* on Monday morning. 'Boxing at Opera House Is Banned After Drunken Fans Slug It Out'. The following day it carried an exclusive with Tommy. 'Raudonikis Tells: Fight Bet Death Threats'.

The death threats lasted days, the promotion such a brilliant failure that boxing was never held at the Opera House again. Tommy still had eight weeks left of his suspension.

Jeff Malcolm after beating Americo, now felt he was back in line for a title shot. It would not happen. In late June Saoul Mamby lost his title to Leroy Haley and the opportunity was gone. This is the cost of larceny. For the price of their small victory in Newcastle another man's dream was taken. Jeff Malcolm fought for sixteen more years, but he never fought for a world title or was even in a position to do so.

Eventually he left Johnny to pursue opportunities in America. Johnny understood. A fighter must do what he believes is best for himself. This is the fight game.

A month after the Opera House brawl, on a night in May, Johnny's phone rang. It was Mick Fernandez, and he sounded upset. Mick Fernandez trained across town.

'Mate, you're not gonna believe it,' he said. 'You know how Kenny was working with that bloke doing the floors? A bloke's walked past and flicked a cigarette on the floor and blown him up.'

Johnny could hardly believe it. Ken Carmody was dead. He was lacquering a floor when he went up in flames. Ken Carmody was Mick Fernandez's fighter, and now he was dead.

Right away, Johnny thinks of a night in Canberra in 1969, and of Ken Carmody and the fun he made for them.

A year after Johnny's mentor Dick O'Connor left the Newtown gym, about 1962, Snowy McFadyen had walked right back in. He and Johnny trained side by side for nearly three years until Snowy had a blue with the policeman running the gym and told him to shove it.

'Stay solid with me,' he said to Johnny on the way out.

'Not a problem.'

Johnny didn't want to leave. The fight was nothing to do with him, and he loved Newtown, but you pick and you stick. He left Newtown.

Then Snowy disappeared and Johnny was left gymless. For months, Frank Keane and the brothers, Martin and Kevin Ross, wandered gymless with him. For a while, he worked out of other trainers' gyms. Then one Friday night in 1966 he ran into Kevin Gore at the fights. Gore was a former bouncer at the illegal casinos, a trotting driver, a safecracker and standover man. He liked Johnny.

He backed Johnny's fighters whenever they fought and made a lot of money because they so often won against better credentialled opponents. He got the price and so, his pockets filling with money, he naturally had a very solid reason to like Johnny. But he liked Johnny beyond the money.

Johnny knew enough about Gore never to ask. Gore was a Toecutter. During the 1960s and '70s, the Toecutter Gang terrified Sydney's under world. Nobody knew where they were doing the business of toe cutting. Nobody knew for certain who they were. All anybody knew was that big jobs were happening in Sydney, hundreds of thousands of dollars being knocked off from payrolls and banks all over the city, and later those who were whispered to have done the robberies were also going missing. The Toecutters were grabbing them right off the streets.

It turned out the Toecutters were doing their business in the basement of the Iron Duke Hotel, in Botany Road, Alexandria. They would tie up the thieves and ask them where the money was hidden. For every question not satisfactorily answered, a toe, with great care, was removed with bolt cutters. They were effective and deadly and nobody ever walked away from the Toecutters, not even with a limp. Along with their toes, the thieves also disappeared.

Kevin Gore ran the Toecutters.

Anyhow, this night in 1966, Johnny was at the fights at South Sydney Leagues Club when he ran into Gore and mentioned that he'd left Newtown.

'I've got the gym in Botany Street,' Gore said. 'Why don't you bring the boys over there?'

It sounded solid enough. Johnny spoke to his fighters and they decided to try it.

It turned out better than they expected.

Mick Fernandez ran the gym. Mick had fought and trained out of the old boxing tents. The tents travelled from town to town with the shows and called on locals to step into the ring with the house fighters. 'A pound or two for a round or two,' they called. Last two rounds with the house fighters, and you'd win two quid.

In the tents, Fernandez learned all the tricks. Boiled milk was rubbed into cauliflower ears. It eased pain and reduced swelling. In his corner he carried a two-shilling piece and a handkerchief in an ice bucket. Between rounds he pulled the handkerchief tight around the cold coin and pressed it against his fighters' eyes to bring down swelling. These days, purpose-built End-Swells do the same. Mick was ahead of his time, and soon he was sharing his secrets with Johnny.

He was very important to Johnny, for those reasons. In between they laughed every day as Mick recalled his days on the show circuit.

One of the attractions on the show route was a dancing duck, Mick told him. People paid their money and the bloke running it would turn on the 78 rpm record and suddenly the duck would start picking its feet up, trained to dance to the music. Kids loved it. The dancing duck.

Nobody knew the minute the music started, the burners started underneath. The dance floor was a hotplate.

When fights were taking place inside the tents, the other fighters used to stand around the edges of the tent, leaning into the canvas. It all added to the show, see. Mick was standing there one day when—*whack!*—somebody from outside king-hit a fighter through the canvas. Three more went down throughout the afternoon. The fighters were filthy. Every time they shot outside after one went down, the culprit was long gone. Mick, though, was cunning. He took the small lid from the incinerator inside the tent. It was not very big and not very round, but it was all cast iron and when he pressed it against the canvas it must have looked, at least from the outside, just like another dumb head leaning back into the canvas.

The next *whack!* was more a metallic, ringing sound, and it was immediately followed by the long groan of agony. When the fighters got outside, the bloke was still on the ground, holding his hand, which was probably broken. In case it wasn't, they gave him a hiding anyway. Then they threw him in the river.

Mick trained strictly pros when Johnny arrived, Johnny only amateurs. Johnny's fighters liked the gym, so they stayed. At times a big, raw-boned bloke would come in to punch the bag. He stood a good six-four, six-five, but he was not overly interested in fighting competitively. Johnny thought that was a pity. Neddy Smith, as it happened, was making money elsewhere, on his way to becoming Australia's biggest heroin dealer.

Mick started taking Johnny with him when he travelled to a fight. He taught Johnny how to wrap hands. How to clean a cut in the forty or so seconds you actually get to work on a fighter between rounds and, more importantly, how to stop it bleeding. Johnny used a secret solution with a Friar's Balsam base to stop cuts, and he carried peppermint oil for his fighters to sniff before and during a fight. Homespun remedies that do nothing but work. Boxing is full of them.

Mick also taught Johnny how to gauge the health of his fighters leading up to a fight. 'Look at their hair and eyes,' he said. 'If their hair's really looking good and their eyes are clear and sparkling, it's a good sign. Always look at someone's hair.'

Before long, Mick Fernandez had Johnny wrap his fighters' hands before the fight. During the fight Johnny looked after the cuts.

Mick taught him all these things. He introduced him to Melbourne trainers Leo Berry and Jack Rennie, two of the most influential people in Johnny's career as a trainer. Rennie was most famous as Lionel Rose's trainer, and when Rose started training at Botany Street whenever Ronnie had a fight in Sydney Johnny found he liked his company, and they would often have lunch together, or dinner, sitting there talking fights.

In Berry he saw a lot of qualities he had seen in Dick O'Connor. Over the years there came many phone calls, Johnny calling up to say he was putting his fighter in against this fighter, and what did he think?

'That's a good fight for you at this stage,' Berry would say.

Johnny was still a young trainer then, and Berry taught him many things, while reassuring him what he was doing was right. He offered guidance and friendship.

And now hearing Ken Carmody was dead, all those days flashed through Johnny's mind. And so did Ken. Mick's fighter Ken.

Sometimes he fought under the name Ken Carmichael. He was adaptable that way. When he fought at South Sydney Rugby League Club he was introduced to the crowd as 'South Sydney's very own …' and, as he stood there in his red and green trunks (the colours of the South Sydney rugby league team), the crowd cheered. A month later he would fight at North Sydney Rugby League Club, where he'd be introduced as 'North Sydney's very own …' And the crowd would cheer him in his black and red trunks (the colours of the North Sydney rugby league team). Kenny knew how to win a crowd.

After a particularly good fight one night at Souths, Carmody lost and was interviewed in the ring afterward. He told the crowd he was disappointed to lose because this was going to be his last fight, and he wanted to go out a winner.

Well, the crowd responded and then some. Coins started showering into the ring. More than $300 when they counted it later.

Back in the dressing room, Johnny said, 'I didn't know you were retiring mate.'

'Oh, that,' Carmody said, turning up his mouth and shaking his head, 'Tell 'em anything.'

Then he turned to Mick. 'Go and get me an orange juice, would ya.'

'Go and get it your fucking self,' Mick said. 'They just gave you a fortune.'

In 1969 Kenny fought Ken Bradley in Canberra for the New South Wales featherweight title. Johnny was in the dressing room with Kenny before the fight. Mick walked in. Evidently, the promoter thought Bradley was going places. Although not too far, you might argue.

'Listen, Ken,' Mick said. 'I was just talking to the promoter, and they've got bit of a rap on this bloke. They wouldn't mind seeing him win this one.'

Carmody knew what every syllable of that meant. He sagged.

'You want me to take a dive?'

'I'm just saying they've offered to throw in a few hundred extra if you go down. I'm not saying to take it. It's your choice.'

Carmody sat back making small noises to himself.

'I can't believe you'd ask me that.'

'I'm just passing on the offer,' Mick said. 'I didn't say we'd take it.'

Carmody shook his head and muttered to himself a little. He looked at Mick.

'How much?'

Kenny groaned. It was just a few hundred dollars, and he said he couldn't believe it.

Kenny groaned again. 'What do you think, Johnny?'

'It's nothing to do with me, mate.'

'No,' Kenny said, 'I'm interested in what you think. You think I can win tonight?'

'Oh, I don't know anything, mate.'

'No,' Kenny said, 'I respect your opinion. Do you think I can win?'

'Mate, to be honest I think this bloke might have a little too much for you.'

Carmody digested that for a small moment.

'Fuck it,' he said, looking at Mick. 'Tell 'em I'll take it.'

Kenny Carmody fought with uncommon courage that night. He took the fight to Ken Bradley, but by the middle rounds he was losing, though not by much. Mick told him to start looking for a way out.

'The first solid shot you take,' he told him, 'go down.'

Kenny fought on through the seventh and eighth rounds, brave but outclassed, and as the fight reached the ninth Mick started worrying. 'Go down this round,' he said. Kenny fought on, refusing to fall.

Coming into the last round, the tenth, Mick was worried.

'Listen,' he said, 'go out and give it your best for thirty seconds, and the first solid shot you take, you go down. I'm throwing in the towel, and when I do, come over and have a go at me.'

Carmody went out and let everything go. Bradley was just as game, and landed several heavy shots. The crowd was up and roaring. Here was this little bloke from Sydney doing his best to score a last round knockout and steal the fight against the local.

Then the referee stopped the fight. Kenny looked up in surprise.

'Your corner's thrown in the towel,' the referee said.

'Whuh?'

Kenny turned and saw the towel on the canvas. The fight was over.

He shook his head, walked back to the corner and whacked Mick square in the mouth. Mick, surprised, and with his lip split, grabbed him by the throat. Kenny, in his boxing gloves, couldn't get Mick off. Johnny had to jump to the apron and pull them apart. As a convincer that the stoppage was on the level, it served its purpose, though Mick had the shits real good.

The ring announcer stepped in and declared Ken Bradley the new featherweight champion of New South Wales. Interviewed in the ring, Ken Carmody complimented him on a gutsy fight.

'I'm a little disappointed, though,' Kenny went on. 'Last week I asked my little boy what he wanted when we went to Canberra and he said, "Dad, all I want you to bring back is the title. I don't want nothing else." I'm just disappointed I couldn't win the belt for him.'

Well, you can guess what happened. The coin shower started.

In the dressing room, Kenny was still counting his money when the venue's secretary walked in, saying that was one of the most heart-wrenching things he'd ever witnessed. In fact, he said, he was going to call the club's bistro and organise it so Kenny and his wife and son could go down there after the fight and eat whatever they wanted, on the house. Kenny thanked him sincerely. What a wonderful gesture.

As soon as the door shut behind the secretary, Kenny handed Johnny a $20 note. 'Go and find me a good sort with a young kid and tell her I'll buy her dinner,' he said.

And now Kenny Carmody was dead. Burned to death.

In 1971, two years after Kenny's night out in Canberra, a Mayne Nickless armoured van was robbed in Guildford, a western Sydney suburb. Three thieves took about $500,000. Toecutter Kevin Gore enjoyed a particularly close relationship with Detective Sergeant Fred Krahe, Sydney's most notorious policeman. Shortly after the robbery, three Melbourne crooks suspected to have been involved disappeared. Rumour had it that they'd been taken by the Toecutters, tipped off by police in a bid to get at least some of the money back. Then midway through 1972, Kevin Gore went missing. Payback from Melbourne. It was said that he'd been bound, tortured and dropped over the side of a boat off Sydney Heads, most likely with a handsome weight attached. That was also where many of the Toecutters' victims were said to have ended up.

Johnny heard it another way: that Kevin Gore was buried under the reinforced concrete runway at Sydney airport. While it has a certain Jimmy Hoffa touch to it, much of Sydney's underworld, in their quiet moments, will tell you the same. Try digging that up.

With Gore gone, Johnny left the Botany Street gym and moved with Mick Fernandez to Snowy Robbins's old gym in Erskineville, the gym he had farewelled Jimmy Carruthers in all those years before. It was the gym where Johnny's father Alf had pencilled for Sydney's illegal SP bookmakers on weekends. Johnny had begun working there too when he was twelve, on account of his neat handwriting.

It was a nice gym, and Johnny stayed there through most of the 1970s, but it was Newtown he longed for. That was the gym he loved.

It took tragedy for him to go back home.

Steve Donkin was the trainer at Newtown Police Boys Club, and he did everything with his fighters. He ran with them, trained with them, boxed with them. One of those fighters was Michael Jerban. And one day, the day after he won a fight and went home with great dreams in his head, he got out of bed and fell down dead with a brain haemorrhage.

Steve Donkin sat in a fog for days. Then he rang the amateur boxing authority and told them he was quitting. He no longer wanted to train fighters.

But what about his boys? He needed someone to train them.

He got into his car and drove to a little prewar flat in Swanson Street, Erskineville, and he knocked on the door and Johnny Lewis answered.

'I'm quitting,' Donkin told him. 'I want you to take over the gym.'

Johnny knew what had happened to Michael Jerban.

'That's not your fault, mate,' he said.

'Johnny, we ran together, we did sit-ups together, did our chin-ups together, did everything.'

'It's not your fault.'

Donkin shook his head. He had a gym full of good kids, kids like Mark Cribb. National champions. Johnny paused. He tried another way.

'You've probably got the best club in Australia,' he said. 'You can't walk away.'

'My heart's not in it any more, Johnny. There's some good kids up there. I want you to look after them.'

Johnny saw his pain. He understood it and remains glad he does not know it.

So Johnny promised Steve Donkin that he would look after them.

That was the day he returned to Newtown.

CHAPTER 5

EVERY SUNDAY NIGHT the men would come back to their house. The door would open and Johnny's father Alf and several mates would walk through to the kitchen and dump sheets of paper and wads of cash on the table. Barely as tall as the table, Johnny would watch them tally up accounts, figuring out who was owed what so they would have it ready for settling time tomorrow.

Every Friday night the trots were on at Harold Park. Saturday was the races and Saturday night the dogs. On Sunday the gym was turned over to two-up. Johnny's father worked as a penciller for an SP bookmaker, and Sunday nights were when they settled for the weekend.

Every pub had an SP back then, and almost every corner shop was one. SP dens were housed in small rooms above shops or behind them, wherever they could run a phone line. Johnny's nan used to send him out with a shilling in his hand and instructions to back whatever George Moore was riding. Every Christmas the bookie would send a hamper her way, as well as to all his other clients, then put on a Christmas party for the kids.

Men wore hats, and did long hard hours in jobs where they didn't know phrases like job satisfaction or career path. They worked because they needed the money, and when they knocked off they headed to the pub for the six o'clock swill, filling themselves with as much beer as they could before the pub shut.

Fights at the pub were always out the back, one on one. If one man got knocked down, the other waited for him to get up. The winner bought the drinks afterward.

As a boy Johnny saw quite a few good fights behind the pubs.

His family lived in Erskineville, in Sydney's inner west. Nearby were Newtown and Redfern and Marrickville, Glebe and Balmain.

Alf Lewis knew the people of his neighbourhood and worked comfortably beside them, getting by with a quick wit and unbreakable honesty. Johnny's mum, Marge Lewis, had one of those big, soft hearts that go on forever. She always told her boys Johnny and Robert to look for the best in people.

Johnny remembers a neighbour around the corner doing it a little tough. Ill health. The local mums took turns cooking soup, keeping it warm in the oven for supper that night. Johnny's mum called him in to go and deliver it. Other times someone might come home with a particularly big catch of fish. The spare would be offered to a neighbour, or someone down the road. Early on, one woman named Maureen Oliver, a mum looking for nothing more than something for her boys to do, started up the local rugby league club. She gave so much, for so long, a plaque in a little park along Erskineville Road now bears her name.

'There was a lot of that stuff going on,' Johnny remembers. 'It made the place as good as it was.'

People were honest with each other. They looked out for each other. They were up front. They stuck by each other. Nowadays, somebody finds an angle, a way to make a dollar, and before the money is in their pocket someone else has made the call to Crimestoppers. And less out of honesty than small jealousy. If I can't have it, you can't have it.

Johnny was walking down Erskineville Road one day when he ran into Slim Rolls, standing outside the train station.

Slim's brother Cec trained horses for Perc Galea, one of Sydney's biggest illegal-casino operators. When the Cec-trained Eskimo Prince won the 1964 Golden Slipper, Galea celebrated by throwing handfuls of money into the crowd. Men like Slim Rolls were everywhere in Johnny's youth. He accepted them simply because his parents did.

Slim was wearing a long coat designed to carry sunglasses and 45 r.p.m. records in pockets sewn into the lining. The crude term for this is selling hot gear. In Johnny's neighbourhood it was looked upon more as a public service.

'How you going, mate?' Johnny said.

'I've got the shits, Johnny,' Slim said.

'Oh, what's up?'

'Look, I'll show you this,' Slim said, and opened the newspaper he was holding. 'Read that.'

Kamahl, the singer, had been awarded a gold record for selling ten thousand copies of an album. Johnny read it. 'Oh, yeah. So … What's wrong with that?'

'I've sold more records than him and they never give me a gold one.'

The thing about people like Slim, Johnny soon learned—and the SP bookies and the guys selling stolen suits—was that they were the first people in if someone needed a hand. Take a record, they'd say. Have a pair of sunglasses. You doing it a bit tough? Here's a couple of dollars. Today, Johnny says, the TAB is open seven days a week, all day Sundays, pumping punters to stay on and back the horses in Hong Kong or maybe the next in Macau and Johnny asks, What's more immoral? That, or the local SP in the old days giving out Christmas hampers and putting on parties for the kids.

No, they weren't bad people. They looked after their own. Every few months a benefit seemed to be held to help someone. They'd be put on at the town hall or a local pub to raise money to pay off the coppers when someone got in trouble with the law. Food and alcohol would be provided and throughout the day money would be collected and later handed over to the arresting cop, or his superior, or sometimes the prosecutor, and before the court appearance the case would be 'no-billed'. Evidence had suddenly gone missing. A witness could not be found.

JOHNNY saw Erko and its people through the eyes of his mum and dad. They had been married four years by the time he came along, late in the night of March 18, 1944. Johnny was born in Bankstown Hospital, but his family were living in Wallangarra at the time, on the New South Wales–Queensland border. In 1947 they moved to Sydney to a housing commission flat in Erskineville. It was 34/5 Swanson Street, a block of twelve flats that for Johnny remains the one great place on this earth.

'We had nothing,' he says. 'But we had everything.'

As a boy, it was simple and innocent. Later he learned how people looked down on housing commission residents, but the Lewis home, filled with love, was—well 'we thought it was Buckingham Palace'.

His nan lived around the corner, in Malcolm Street. Her habit of misplacing her front door key was easily overcome: she just left it permanently in her front door. That's how much of a community it was.

It gave Johnny the two things every child needs: safety, and room to dream.

The Newtown Bluebags played just down the road, at Erskineville Oval until 1954, when they moved back to Henson Park. There was no television, and the wireless was big enough to jump start a car. As a kid, Johnny spent his days racing sticks down the stormwater drains, or playing cricket before school in his pyjamas in the middle of Binning Lane, behind St Mary's Catholic Church, with an old fruit box as the wicket. A car came along every so often and, as one, young boys would explode in small fury. 'What are you doing?' the kids would say. 'Use another road. We're playing here.'

Johnny had a paper run at the newsagency that ran alongside the railway tracks. McLean, the owner, let Johnny and his mate Geoff Sewell build a pigeon coop behind it. They must have had a hundred birds over time.

Every afternoon one neighbourhood boy, Warren Allen, walked down to Erskineville Oval, cut out a perfect square of turf and carried it back to the unused tennis court across from the Lewises' block of flats. There he planted it. Square by square, watering it as he went, he filled the hard earth tennis court with the lush grass from Erskineville Oval. It became the best backyard footy pitch in the city.

Come Saturday during the rugby league season, Johnny and his mates would jump on the old red-and-cream Lowes bus and head to the Sydney Cricket Ground for the match of the day. They would run home after the game, too excited to wait for the bus.

Sundays growing up were spent working the scoreboard at senior Aussie Rules football games at Erskineville Oval. Between quarters, Johnny would jump down from the scoreboard and run on to listen to the coach's pep talks. Between games he would carry a big tray secured around his shoulders by a leather strap. 'Chips, chocs, sweets, peanuts.'

When the footy was over, Johnny and his mate Geoff Sewell would go back to their paper run. Sewell told him that after the footy was the best time to sell newspapers. Most spectators had a belly full of beer, and tipped more heavily. They would also jump on the trams and walk through the carriages. The trick to selling papers here was the timing. People on trams were nearly always in a hurry, even when sitting down. 'Watch,' Sewell said. He would sell a paper and the bloke would give him sixpence, then he would fumble in his moneybag for the tuppence change. He'd take an awfully long time. 'Oh, just keep it,' the bloke would say.

'That's how we make our tips,' said Sewell.

They had a thousand ways.

Selling papers at the footy, Johnny would fumble for the tuppence in change while deliberately standing in front of people, blocking their view. The trick was to find the right person to stand in front of.

'Sit down!' It always came.

'Go on, mate,' the buyer would say, waving him off.

Other times Johnny would yell, 'Get your final!' This was always a Saturday, race day, and the punters would want to get the results from Randwick or Rosehill or wherever they were racing. They always wanted the final edition, containing the full dividends and racing strips.

'Last race?' they'd say.

'Yeah, mate,' Johnny would answer, taking their money and skipping away quick.

'Hey!' he'd hear in the distance. 'This is the early edition.'

They organised a daily raffle with their paper run. The tickets declared it was raising funds for the Eastern Suburbs Baseball Association. Whose two shareholders turned out to be Johnny Lewis and Geoffrey Sewell. They sold two hundred tickets for a shilling each, which came to £10. First prize was five pounds, the rest profit.

The winning ticket was the one that matched the last two digits of the day's wining lottery ticket. Sewell showed Johnny how to approach the winner's front door with the £5 ready, curled up in his hand ready to hand over but out of sight just in case ... 'If they don't say nothing,' Sewell told him, 'say nothing.'

If the winning ticket holder said nothing, hadn't remembered ...

Beautiful. Profit, £10.

One Saturday night, when Johnny was twelve years old, he and some mates were playing in the streets. The SP bookie on the corner had one of those new transistor radios. Nobody could believe how small they were making them. This one was no bigger than a house brick. It sat on the fence. Between races, the bookie's bagman, out by the fence, switched stations and listened to the rugby league Test, Australia playing Great

Britain at Bradford in England. Johnny and his mates heard the commentary from the radio as they walked past. Further on down the road, another neighbour was sitting at his front window, listening to his big old wireless.

'No. 1 just won that race,' the neighbour said. Then, nodding towards the bagman, 'He don't know.'

The boys turned to see the bagman still caught up listening to the footy. He had forgotten about the race. Johnny and his mates trotted down to him and backed the No. 1 dog.

They waited a bit.

'Geez,' one of them said, 'you better put that race on.'

'... and dividends on the fourth at Wentworth Park,' the announcer said, 'No. 1 the winner, paying ...'

They collected on the next race as well. At this, the bookie walked out to the fence and smashed the transistor radio.

Johnny was making friends for a lifetime, boys like Brian Moore, known all his life as Chicka, and Bobby Lanigan. Both would go on to play league for Newtown. Johnny played Aussie Rules through his teens, reaching first grade in the local comp when he was seventeen. (He was also an A-grade tennis player back when Australians could play tennis, but it was all cut short when, at nineteen, he fell off a ladder at work and broke his ankle. The injury, which numbed most of his foot, still gives him trouble today.) Every second week in the juniors there was an away game, and one of the fathers, Les Markham, would take all the kids to it on the back of his flatbed truck. You'd go to jail for that today. Some years later, somebody stabbed Markham. That and diabetes meant his legs had to be amputated. When he needed a few hundred dollars for a wheelchair, they organised a benefit at Newtown Police Boys Club to raise the money. People came from everywhere. They raised thirteen thousand dollars that afternoon, looking out for one of their own. Johnny Lewis can't remember meeting anyone in his youth who was a bad person. Everyone he knew was always ready to help a mate. If someone was down there was always someone to bring them back up again.

Erskineville is a different place now, a suburb of soy lattes and conversations about real estate and new dance beats. All Johnny's friends have moved on. But Johnny remains. He lives not more than five minutes' drive from the street where he grew up.

ONE Monday when he was about twelve, Johnny was walking along Erskineville Road when Reg Marbuck pulled up beside him in a car.

'What are you doing?'

'Nothing,' Johnny said.

'You want to come to the fights?'

Johnny had spent many Monday nights sitting with his father listening on the radio to Freddie Dawson and others fighting at the Sydney Stadium, then reliving it all in the morning papers, where there'd always be a photo of the main event shot from above the ring.

Johnny went to the fights and Marbuck, one of those good blokes you run into in life, paid his entry. Watching it live, putting pictures to the sounds he heard over the radio, something came alive inside him. This was boxing. And this was him.

CHAPTER 6

As Jeff Malcolm's career flailed, the improvement in Fenech was rapid. He won the New South Wales State amateur light-flyweight title in his fourth fight. Soon nobody wanted to fight him, in fear of his reputation. At one point he went six months without a fight, matchmakers unable to find anyone prepared to step in against him.

Then Johnny had to go to Hawaii. Jeff Malcolm was trying to fight his way back after his robbery in Newcastle, trying to chase down Leroy Haley. He had a fight in Honolulu against American Francisco Roche, a journeyman who was nothing more than a night's pay for Malcolm. This is the way it was to become for Malcolm. Chasing ghosts.

He would never get Haley.

Finally in 1982, they got Fenech a fight against Joey Glover at Cronulla Leagues Club. It was his first fight without Johnny in his corner. Johnny was in Hawaii with Jeff Malcolm, so Tommy Raudonikis and Phil McElwaine stood in for him. Glover, predicted to be Australia's first Olympic gold medallist, was slick and clever and moved well. He was the great hope in Australian boxing. He danced away from Fenech and, for the first time, Fenech's professional-style preparation counted against him. He was cautioned four times for ducking too low, unacceptable in the amateurs but OK in the pros, and he lost the fight.

Fenech believed he had won despite the warnings, but he knew Joey Glover had a big reputation. It was a reputation he planned on taking for himself. But that bout started a pattern: Fenech would lose only when Johnny was not in his corner.

Next, Fenech headed to Tasmania to fight Greg Vanson. Representing New South Wales as amateur champ, he was obliged to have a designated coach with him, not his own trainer. Johnny was forced to stay home.

Knowing that in Fenech they had a good one, the amateur coaches wanted to do what they always do when they get a good one, which is put their own stamp on him. They wanted to give him a more 'amateur' style, so their game plan for the Vanson fight was to have him retreat and jab. In the history of great ideas, this misses the cut. It cost Fenech the chance to fight at the Commonwealth Games in Brisbane in October 1982.

Johnny, back in Sydney, hands tied, knew now that Fenech was different. If he kept improving the way he was, he could even win a medal at the Olympics in a couple of years. But these amateur coaches, they had to be kept away from him.

The losses without Johnny in his corner only drew Fenech closer to him. When they were away for a fight they walked every day, and throughout their walks they talked. They laughed and joked, and Fenech told stories about his neighbourhood, and Johnny quietly counselled him, laying out the future that could be his.

Fenech was immature at times, and he was still very much the tough street kid, but he impressed Johnny with his loyalty. Fenech had character. When he made a mistake, which he did often, he was quick to apologise. More, he worked to make up for it.

After losing to Vanson in Tasmania, Fenech beat Glover in the return, then knocked out Warren Luland in three rounds in Dubbo. The Luland bout gave Fenech a scare, though. For the first time in a fight, he was nearly knocked out.

And then again after it.

As they walked out of the hall—Johnny, Fenech, Fenech's best mate Peter Mitrevski and Brian Wilmot—a drunk approached. He was holding a broken bottle, and he announced he had come to defend Warren Luland's reputation. Through slurred words, threats were made. Fenech remembered the drunk insulting his girlfriend outside Blacktown Police Boys Club. He held his temper.

Just as it became clear that the drunk was not going to be talked down, Johnny said, 'Run.'

As one, they turned and fled. The drunk gave chase. Now, the success of an evacuation plan such as this is firstly to be able to outrun the pursuer. If that fails, then it is absolutely vital that you can outrun at least one of your offsiders. Only one is necessary for it to be a success.

The drunk began to close on Johnny. Fenech, well ahead with the other two, looked over his shoulder and saw what was about to happen. He turned in a step and headed straight for the drunk.

He planted his foot and drove his shoulder through him. As rugby league tackles go, it was copybook. Then, in a move not unlike the one he'd performed at Blacktown that night, he picked up the drunk and speared him into the ground.

Only this time the drunk held him, dragging Fenech down with him in a headlock. Fenech's head crashed into the ground as well. The drunk slashed at him with the bottle and tore a large gash in his scalp before Fenech landed several more punches than was probably necessary.

Fearing that the drunk might have mates, they ran all the way back to their hotel, owned by a mate of Johnny's, Joe Lang. They banged on the door for Joe to let them in. In their room, Johnny took out his medical kit and began cleaning Fenech's cut, stitching it closed.

Then the lights went out.

They grabbed what they could from the medical kit, anything sharp or pointed, and stood ready at the door.

And they waited.

For ten, fifteen minutes they waited for whoever had killed the lights to burst through the door.

Nobody came.

After a while one of them sat down. Then they all began to relax.

Next morning they learned that it had just been a blackout.

Fenech went on to win another state title in 1983, then catapulted it into his first national title with a points win over Michael Fry. Again Johnny was not allowed in Fenech's corner, although it's fair to say he was within shouting distance of it.

The national title put Fenech in place to contest the Oceania title, which he also won. After just twelve amateur fights he had qualified for the World Cup in Rome.

Johnny went to Fiji with Jeff Malcolm. While he was there, he wrote Fenech a letter.

'Dear Jeff …'

It was a letter of dreams and hope. Johnny wouldn't be able to go to Rome, because only designated coaches could, but Fenech should 'enjoy the experience,' he wrote, 'and learn from it. It will all come to fruition in 1985, you'll see,' he said. Be good. Fenech read the letter over and over again. He folded it and unfolded it and read it again.

He tried to see what Johnny saw. He read it with more hope than expectation.

It's not that he disbelieved Johnny. But could he really do what Johnny was saying he could? He thought about the faith Johnny was showing in him and wondered, if he believed it would come true, did that mean it would?

'This old guy,' thought Fenech, 'who I love …'

■■■

A DAY after he returned from Fiji, Johnny got a call at home from Frank Farrington, the secretary of the Newtown Rugby League Club. He was crying.

'Johnny, we're gone,' he said.

'What do you mean?'

'We're out.'

'What are you talking about Frank?'

'They've kicked us out.'

A lifetime of memories disappeared right there. The New South Wales Rugby League had kicked Newtown and Western Suburbs out of the competition. Facing financial trouble, they had hoped to relocate to Campbelltown in outer Sydney to take advantage of its thriving population, but the League had decided it was all too late and kicked them out.

Johnny took it hard. His one ambition all his life had been to pull on the royal blue jersey of Newtown. Failing that—he had everything but the talent—he'd followed them every weekend, and when the club had been struggling in 1973, Farrington had convinced him to put his hand up for the committee. He had been on it ten years now, and now the club was dead. Tommy Raudonikis was no longer there. He'd retired at the end of 1982 to go to Brisbane and play one final season for Brothers.

As silly as it might sound to some, Johnny isn't sure he ever really got over the demise of Newtown.

But it's funny how things happen. Newtown was dead and Tommy had been gone for almost a year and the next person through the door was Steve Mortimer, the Canterbury and New South Wales halfback. Mortimer was looking for extra training and Tim Pickup, the Bulldog that trained at Newtown most afternoons, had convinced him that Johnny might be his man.

When Johnny put him through the pads, Mortimer had one thought the whole time. 'This is the hardest training I've ever done.' He was dying. He'd never encountered anything like it.

Fenech, young and cheeky and anonymous, couldn't resist taking a shot at one of the great Australian rugby league players.

'You're soft,' he taunted. 'You'll never make a boxer.'

Then Mortimer joined all of them—Johnny and Fenech and all the other fighters—for a road run. Mortimer was so far gone by this time he felt numb. He was just gliding along. When they got back, almost flattened by exhaustion, he thought the others must be taking bets on him never coming back again.

FENECH won a bronze medal in Rome after going down to South Korea's Heo Yong-Mo in the semi-finals. From there the Australian team went to Belfast for the inaugural Commonwealth titles, where Fenech lost his only fight, but got the bronze anyway through a quirk in the draw.

He was emerging as a leader in the Australian team. Soon he was the outstanding fighter in the amateurs, and was made captain of Australia's Olympic team about to head to the 1984 Games in Los Angeles.

He had only one problem.

Once again, nobody wanted to fight him.

CHAPTER 7

Nobody ever got more out of a training session than Jeff Fenech. His capacity for work was unrivalled.

Australia's best amateur by now, he was fighting in the sport's lightest division, flyweight. For all that work, making weight was a struggle. He needed to train every day to keep his weight down, and he needed to fight regularly to prevent himself from going crazy with the frustration of training.

He began consuming daily doses of Nulax, the fruit laxative to help in the battle with his weight.

They were on the pads one day, Fenech again squeezing what he could into the three-minute round, when suddenly he looked up at Johnny.

'Oh, Johnny, I just shit myself,' he said.

'Shut up and keep punching,' said Johnny.

There was a reason Johnny had told him to keep punching. Every round builds endurance, like bricks in a wall. For Fenech to stop would have been to throw away the work he'd already done. A marathon is much easier to run, for instance, if broken into stages. To stop would mean having to start the whole session again.

Fenech understood. As dirty as he felt, he kept training. He never complained again.

At nineteen, and with just twenty fights, Fenech was picked for the Olympic team. At the Olympic trials he brought a tall middleweight over to meet Johnny.

'This is my trainer, Johnny Lewis,' he said to the tall kid. 'Johnny, this is Jeff Harding.'

Jeff Harding was the direct type.

'I want to train in Sydney,' he said.

'Well, come along to the gym any time you want,' Johnny replied. As far as invitations go, that was it.

From the trials on, everything that happened in the gym at Newtown for Fenech was geared towards the Olympics. Johnny's great dream as a trainer was to train an Olympic gold medallist. He thought Fenech was a long way from that, but he also knew Fenech was improving so fast he would be an altogether different fighter in six months' time. Given that, he thought he was an outside hope at a gold medal.

Slowly it looked to be coming together.

The Eastern-bloc countries looked like they would boycott the Games, meaning the favourite in the flyweight division, Cuba's Pan American champion Pedro Reyes, would probably not be there. Johnny went through the field and figured that with the Eastern-bloc countries gone, Fenech had one true threat between him and Australia's first Olympic boxing gold medal: South Korea's Heo Yong-Mo, who had beaten him in Rome.

First they had an international tournament at Sydney's Town Hall. Johnny wanted to use this to help lead Fenech into the Olympics, six months off. Tournament fighting was different from the club circuit, which goes down a fight at a time. Boxers fight every second day in tournaments, and as well as being fit to fight they must weigh in before each bout, which means stabilising their weight for as long as two weeks.

Several weeks before the tournament, Johnny called Arthur Tunstall, the head of Australian amateur boxing, to clear up a few details.

'That's off, pal,' Tunstall said.

'Oh, geez, no one told me,' Johnny said.

This really upset Johnny's plans. Fenech had no one around to fight, and he needed the rounds.

Back at the gym, Johnny ran into Grantlee Kieza, a young journalist from the *Daily Telegraph* and one of the promoters of the upcoming Australian middleweight title bout between Ritchie Roberts and Billy Johnstone, who also played league for Canterbury. Kieza was cosying up to Fenech. When he heard the Town Hall fight was off, he told Johnny that while setting up Johnstone's title shot he'd met a bloke from Fiji who might be able to help. Not much later, Fenech and Johnny were heading to Fiji, invited to a tournament there. It kept Fenech's preparation on track.

Johnny took Fenech's mate Mitrevski along with them, also to fight. They both won. They considered the tournament a success until they got back to Australia and Johnny was called in to see the boxing authority. They wanted to know, these men that wouldn't know, why he had taken Fenech away without permission.

Why? Because he was Fenech's trainer and Fenech needed the fight. The authority was its own law, however, and in one of the great examples of stubborn idiocy, it suspended Johnny for twelve months for leaving the country without permission.

Johnny was shattered. Not allowed in Fenech's corner, he lost a great deal of faith in the amateurs after that.

He appealed, and the suspension was cut from twelve months to six. There was no explanation for this, just as there had been no real explanation for the original suspension. And they wonder why Australia hadn't won a gold medal in eighty years.

■■■

Meanwhile, Billy Johnstone lost to Ritchie Roberts, disqualified in the twelfth and final round for head-butting. Hard as a coffin nail, Johnstone was leading the fight and about to comfortably crown his career with a national title when, as he would say later, he had a moment of madness. The head-butt was too blatant for referee Billy Males to ignore. When the judges' scores were revealed, Johnstone led on all three cards and needed only to survive the last to win. He retired, never to fight again.

Fenech left for the Olympics. The Games began, and what Johnny had feared would happen started to happen.

In fight after fight, Fenech began rolling over his opponents. For all his trouble making weight, his advantage became obvious the second he stepped into the ring. Few flyweights were as big as he was. Given his strength, the advantage was considerable.

Johnny tried to keep up via TV. Early on, Fenech's fights were televised, but often on delay and never advertised. So Johnny watched as much coverage as he could in the hope of catching a Fenech bout.

He stopped Bolivian Rene Centellas in the third, then beat Tanzanian David Mwaba 5–0. Under a new Olympic ruling system, five judges scored the fight, and if it was 4–1 or 5–0 the decision was final. If it went 3–2, the decision was passed on to a five-man jury, who could overturn the result only if they then voted 5–0 or 4–1 the other way. Judges are chosen because they are deemed well qualified to judge. So why the need for a jury? There is no other way to describe this system than as absolutely ridiculous—which made it absolutely perfect for amateur boxing.

In the early rounds Fenech was flying. Mwaba of Tanzania was a tough opponent, and the win over him left, really, only the South Korean Heo Yong-Mo between Fenech and gold. At least that's what Johnny believed. The Olympic favourite was American Steve McCrory, but

Johnny knew Fenech would be too strong for him.

The Americans didn't seem to rate Fenech. When an Australian reporter asked McCrory about him, he answered: 'Jeff who?'

Then came the quarter-finals.

It was a Wednesday, and before the fight Fenech called Johnny in Australia. He sounded edgy. He was fighting Yugoslavian Redzep Redzepovski. A win would guarantee him a bronze medal and put him a win away from the gold medal fight. Johnny encouraged Fenech and then went to bed.

He got up at 5 a.m. to watch the fight. Press attention meant it was being broadcast live in Australia. Right from the opening bell Johnny got concerned. Fenech was showing Redzepovski too much respect. Johnny got angry watching. Once again, he knew, the coaches had underestimated what they had in Fenech. By the second round Redzepovski was on empty. But Fenech was boxing carefully, frozen with caution. Johnny urged Fenech to step it up, to roll over him … Fenech wasn't experienced enough to recognise Redzepovski was gone, and the coaches clearly weren't aware that all Fenech needed was to be told to finish the job. After the fight Johnny felt sick. He knew that if he'd been there in Fenech's corner, there would have been no need for the judges.

Then the score was announced. Fenech 3–2.

For a brief moment, for an eye-blink, Johnny felt relief.

Then he remembered that under the new Olympics rules this meant the decision now went to the jury. The minutes ticked by, and the delay began to tell the story. Fenech appeared to already be sensing the outcome. Waiting in the ring, he got fidgety, kicking his legs, turning his head from side to side. Then came the announcement.

The five-man jury overturned the decision 4–1. Fenech clapped lightly when Redzepovski's hand was raised, then held it up in recognition of the decision. Around the arena, the largely American audience booed.

Four years later in Seoul, the judging system at the Olympics would be investigated when Roy Jones Jr was decreed to have lost a fight he had won easily against South Korean Park Si-hun. It was the gold medal fight and Jones had dominated all three rounds. The widely respected Compubox, which counts punches thrown and landed, found Jones landed 86 punches to Park's 32, which in any language is a hiding. Yet the judges gave it to Park 3–2. One judge, the Moroccan Hiouad Larbi, who qualifies only as an idiot, explained his decision for Park this way: 'The American won easily, so easily, in fact, that I was positive my four fellow judges would score the fight for the American by a wide margin. So I voted for the Korean to make the score only 4–1 for the American and not embarrass the host country.'

An investigation found not only that South Korean officials had entertained the judges beforehand, but that widespread corruption existed throughout the judging. The judging system was thrown out and a new system introduced at the world titles the following year.

Perhaps in spite, perhaps not, it was alleged that the judging in Seoul was rigged in retaliation for the heavily pro-American judging in Los Angeles four years earlier. Fenech's loss to Redzepovski certainly took him out of McCrory's way. But why his decision was overturned can only be guessed at. Anything is not only possible, but also quite likely. Far too late for Jeff Fenech, who had lost his one chance at Olympic gold.

Not long after his loss, McCrory came over to Fenech. Fenech later related it to an Australian journalist: 'You been robbed man, but I'm glad. We thought you was the dark horse.'

The American later beat the Yugoslav 4–1 to win the gold medal.

The day after Fenech's loss, a newspaper journalist found Johnny for his verdict. He had taped the fight and watched it three times, back to back, Johnny told the reporter. 'And each time he wins it easier. He's a loser in one way, but he'll be a winner in others. Boxing has helped him become a better person. He won't let anyone down.'

Far away in Los Angeles, Fenech battled his emotions at a press conference.

'I've worked so hard for the chance to win Australia's first boxing gold medal at the Olympics, only to have the chance taken away by a bunch of senile old men,' he said. He then thanked everybody that had ever helped him, and as he went through his list his voice broke. He couldn't get Johnny's name out.

CHAPTER 8

A FORTNIGHT after Fenech returned home, on a Sunday afternoon, Father's Day, news began breaking about a shootout in Milperra, an outer western suburb of Sydney. There were fatalities.

As the afternoon went on, more details came through. Rival bikie gangs had taken to each other in the car park of a pub, the Viking Tavern, and there were seven dead, including a young girl.

An uneasy feeling came over Johnny when he heard that. Phil McElwaine was a bikie. So were his older brothers Mark, who also trained at Newtown, and Greg.

A little while later, Johnny's phone rang. The McElwaines had been at the Viking Tavern.

Phil was nicknamed 'Knuckles', Mark was 'Gloves', and Greg was more formally known as 'Dukes'. All three were Comanchero bikies until the gang split in late 1983. Not always a democratic process when it involves bikies.

This split was particularly acrimonious, and happened after the club president, Jock Ross, was found to be sleeping with another member's wife. The McElwaines, along with another group of brothers called the Campbells, split to form the first Australian chapter of the Bandidos. The Bandidos and Comancheros remained enemies until August 1984 when their feud turned into a war over the attempted murder of Ross.

On this Father's Day, the two gangs had come armed to a swap meet for bike parts. When the violence stopped, four Comancheros and two Bandidos were dead. One innocent, a fifteen-year-old girl, had been killed in crossfire. It became known as the Milperra Massacre. Thirty-two bikies were arrested, including all three McElwaines. Each was charged with a collective seven counts of murder.

The trial would last thirteen months, and until it ended, in June 1987, Phil McElwaine and his brothers stayed in jail.

IT WAS the second great blow to come Johnny's way.

Three years earlier, Paul Hayward had been sentenced to twenty years in a Bangkok prison for trying to import 8.4 kilograms of heroin into Australia.

Little Pauly.

Johnny's heart broke a thousand times at the news.

Paul Hayward must have been eight years old when Johnny first met him. Johnny had a young boy, Desmond Locksley, fighting at South Sydney Juniors. Desmond had asthma and had taken up boxing to help his lungs. This night, in the last fight of the night, he went in against a little ginger-haired boy. Paul.

It was one of those fights that could have gone either way. What was not in dispute was that, even at eight years old, these kids showed the bigger boys how to fight. Paul won it in a close one.

Johnny remembered the ginger hair and started seeing it often around the streets. Hellos soon became chats and, unlikely as it was given their ten-year age difference, they became friends.

'Why don't you come and watch me play footy?' Paul said to Johnny one day. He was now ten.

Johnny was in his early years as a trainer. He went along and saw Paul play football at a level above the rest. He was an obvious talent, cutting through the defence so easily, scoring almost at will.

Yet what clinched it for Johnny was not Paul's talent but his generosity. Paul could have scored all the tries. Yet Johnny watched him making breaks, doing all the hard work to create the try, and then at the last moment passing to a teammate so he could score instead.

Most twenty-year-olds would not have noticed this. Johnny not only noticed, he understood. There's something special about this kid, he thought. There was a depth to him. That he was built like George Barnes, one of Johnny's all-time favourite fighters, didn't hurt either.

And this is how it goes with Johnny. If we are to understand him, the clues are in Paul Hayward.

One day when Paul was in his early teens, he turned up at Newtown and told Johnny he wanted to train there now. Johnny trained him for several fights, and when Paul got a bit older he got him a trial with the Newtown Jets rugby league club in 1972.

Paul got graded and looked set for a good football career, but he still had the odd fight under Johnny. In 1976, he made the Sydney representative team and toured New Zealand with it. Tommy Raudonikis was the captain.

At the end of the 1978 season, the Jets were off to holiday in Hawaii. Paul, around at Johnny's place to pick up his son, who Johnny was babysitting, was thinking about not going.

'You should go, Paul,' Johnny said.

Paul paused briefly.

'No, I don't think I'll go.'

A couple of days later, early in the morning, Johnny was getting in his car when his neighbour called out to him.

'Did you hear what happened to Paul Hayward?'

It was the way he said it. Johnny didn't want to answer, as if that might hold off whatever was coming. 'No,' he said.

'He got arrested for drugs in Bangkok.'

Johnny felt sick. It didn't make sense. Paul had never touched drugs as long as Johnny had known him. And what was he doing in Bangkok?

He got in his car and turned on the radio, waiting for the news. It was the first story of the bulletin, the Newtown rugby league star arrested in Bangkok on drug smuggling charges.

Paul Hayward's trial lasted more than two years, the longest narcotics trial in Bangkok history. He got twenty years, while the two men arrested with him, Warren Fellows and Bill Sinclair, got thirty-three years each. Sinclair was later freed on appeal.

The judge said a photo taken in Australia and presented as evidence, showing Paul with Neddy Smith, was evidence that he was part of a drug-smuggling syndicate. Neddy Smith, still in Australia, was named in court as the head of the syndicate.

Whatever reputation Paul Hayward had in Australia was shot. But despite that Johnny still says of Paul Hayward, 'He is the finest man I know.'

It wasn't until 1998, when Warren Fellows published his memoir, *The Damage Done*, that the quality of Paul Hayward emerged.

Though the court was never told this, Paul's sister-in-law happened to be Neddy Smith's de facto wife, which explained why he and Neddy were often together.

Fellows wrote in his book that after he became a drug smuggler he met Neddy Smith in a bar in Bangkok. He soon began working for Neddy. One day, he was in Sydney with Neddy planning another pick-up in Bangkok.

At the same time Neddy had asked Paul Hayward to take money up to a business associate of his in Bangkok, the man that had introduced him to Fellows. Fellows wrote that during his meeting with Neddy,

Neddy casually suggested that since he and Paul were both going the same way they might want to travel together for company. It sounded good to Fellows, who then made his great mistake. He booked his and Paul's plane tickets on Neddy's home phone, which was bugged. Suddenly, Fellows and Hayward were both on the police radar, and were under surveillance from the moment they left Australia. A similar story is told in Neddy Smith's book, *Neddy*.

Shortly after Paul delivered the money in Bangkok, Fellows took possession of the drugs. By now Paul knew why Fellows was there. Believing he was helping, he offered to stash the drugs in his room in case the cops went kicking in Fellows's door. That was Paul.

He thought hiding the heroin in his room would help if Fellows was being watched. He didn't know he was being watched as well. This is Fellows's version, not Paul's excuse. Paul never made an excuse. Fellows told it as a man with nothing left but the guilt for the catastrophe he pulled Paul into, and admiration for the man Paul was throughout. Soon after his arrest Johnny received a letter from Paul. It was full of the trivialities of his day, and of strength. In not one paragraph did Johnny sense weakness. Johnny finished the letter hopeful that if anybody could get through this, Paul could.

He sat down and wrote him a letter back.

Twenty years. There is not a day goes by that he will not think of Paul Hayward.

CHAPTER 9

HERE is Bill Mordey, the newspaper's finest.

He was tall and thin, with a long face that looked somewhat fuller when there was a cigarette hanging out of his mouth. He was a journo from an era when journos wore hats and drank at the same bars as the bookies and the crims and coppers. He wore suits without socks, wouldn't walk into a racetrack if he saw the colour green, which is considered bad luck on a track, and once pawned his typewriter so he could get on the last at Gosford.

Bill Mordey wrote for one of the two afternoon papers then published in Sydney, the *Daily Mirror*, and spent his Monday nights in Harry Miller's office at the Sydney Stadium when Miller still had his office there.

Mordey came into Johnny Lewis's life when Jeff Fenech was about to fight Wayne Mulholland at Dapto, near Wollongong on the NSW south coast. It was early 1985.

By then Fenech had turned professional. He left the Los Angeles

Games early after his disappointment. The whole flight home, he considered his future. Part of him wanted to stay amateur four more years. Go back again, next time the Olympics would be in Seoul, and win Australia's first boxing gold medal. But what guarantee was there that it wouldn't happen again? These senile old men …

Johnny met him at the airport.

'I'm turning pro,' Fenech said.

Johnny knew the emotion of the moment. 'Let's think about it', he said. Australia's first Olympic gold medallist was something that would stay Fenech's forever. If they turned pro, there was no going back.

Fenech watched McCrory win the gold medal in Los Angeles on television at home. Within days the Australian Amateur Boxing Union approached him, asking him not to turn professional. It would approach Redzepovski and fly him to Australia for a rematch.

But Fenech had made up his mind. He was turning pro. The time was right.

By this time Bill Mordey had left the newspaper business, resigning in 1980 to become publisher of *Big League*, the New South Wales Rugby League's official publication. Colin Love, Johnny's friend but also the League's lawyer, managed Fenech from his first pro fight. He thought Mordey might help promote this young kid who'd been robbed of gold.

It is important to understand the sense of injustice Fenech's Olympics loss sparked around Australia. He returned from the Games a household name, which is very different from when he left, where only friends, family, and a few select law enforcement officers knew of Jeffrey Fenech. His hurt was obvious from his comments about the judges, but the way he tried to live with the verdict won a lot of people's support.

Johnny knew it was important to get him in the ring as soon as possible. Less than two months after his Olympics loss, Fenech fought Bobby Williams at Marrickville RSL Club, right around the corner from where he lived. He put Williams down three times before the referee called enough in the second round. Williams was no world-beater, but neither was he a bum. Less than two years earlier he'd been good enough to fight Frank Cedeno, who would win the World Boxing Council (WBC) flyweight belt six months later.

Wins came quickly after that. Fenech stopped Percy Israel in seven, then won the Australian super-flyweight title in his third fight, knocking out Junior Thompson in four.

He was just twenty, still growing. The struggle to boil down to the 115-pound junior bantamweight weight limit got to be too much. Johnny pushed him up to bantamweight. They flew to Fiji, where Fenech stopped Iliesa Manila in two, then headed home and challenged Mulholland for the New South Wales and South Pacific bantamweight titles. That's when Mordey was asked to come aboard.

'You know that kid that got beat at the Olympics? That got robbed?' Love said to Mordey. 'Well, Johnny, my mate, is training him and he's approached me to ask if you'd promote him.'

Mordey's credentials as a fight promoter amounted to having known Harry Miller. He was a link to the long-gone golden era of Australian boxing, and to Johnny that seemed good enough.

'Yeah, we'll give it a go,' Mordey said. He called his offsider, Michael Dann, at the *Big League* office in Albion Street, Surry Hills. 'We're going into boxing promoting,' he said.

One Sunday morning, Johnny and Fenech went to Colin Love's home at South Coogee to meet Mordey. Mordey would come on board after Fenech fought Mulholland in Dapto.

Johnny told him what he believed Fenech was capable of.

Already the benefits of Johnny's experience were evident. Nothing had been random about Fenech's pro fights. There was no guesswork. From the start Johnny had deliberately put Fenech in against different opponents with different styles, although largely one-dimensional. This allowed Fenech to concentrate on one aspect at a time without having to focus much on anything else. Williams was heavily experienced, for instance, having fought sixty-nine times by the time he stepped in against

Fenech. Johnny believed Fenech would be too strong for him, but he wanted him to experience the ringcraft of a seasoned professional. Yet at the same time Johnny was clever. Williams did not have the punching power to seriously hurt Fenech, so Fenech would be kept safe.

In the next fight, Percy Israel had a considerable height and reach advantage over Fenech, giving Fenech a look at a different type of fighter again. Try to solve this problem, Johnny was saying. After him came Junior Thompson, small, muscular, undefeated, and determined to stay that way.

Iliesa Manila had one of those chins that, once hit, stays hit. Fenech dropped him after Thompson and he did not move for a full five minutes.

Stylists and brawlers, toilers and sharpshooters. The only type Johnny avoided was the big puncher. The big puncher can be hopelessly outclassed for every second of a fight but turn it all around with one pool-hall shot. It can bring your fighter's whole campaign undone.

The first thing Mordey did for the Mulholland fight was hire a bus. He stocked it with beer and filled whatever space was left with every sports journalist he could squeeze aboard for the trip down the old Pacific Highway to Dapto. He even bought them dinner.

Fenech did his part by knocking Mulholland out in the fifth.

On the way home, Mordey organised for a hotel to stay open for a victory celebration. The bus pulled in and the journos poured out and into the pub, even happier when Fenech and Johnny turned up. They drove the pair of them batty all night with their questions.

The following day Mordey sat in his office with Dann.

For a novice promoter, Mordey had some advantages. He knew everybody and, most of all, everybody liked him. During his days as a rugby league roundsman Mordey had spent every Saturday afternoon in the bar at the Sydney Cricket Ground, where they played the match of the day. The bar was filled with SP bookmakers, illegal casino operators, thieves, hustlers, racing identities, journos, footballers, doormen, glovemen and gamblers. There were even respectable types, although few of those would admit to it. They were terrific days. If something was going on in Sydney, somebody in the room knew about it. On top of that, few journos knew how to manufacture column inches like Mordey. And this young kid Fenech already had a story behind him. All that was needed was to work the angles.

'You know how we're going to get this off the ground?' he said to Dann one afternoon in their office. 'We've got to get people there. We're going to get people who've got money to come to the fights. Like they used to in the old Stadium days.'

Mordey thought the best way to do that was to form a golden ringside club and fill it with Australia's best-known people. Politicians, sportsmen, celebrities. If those sorts of people watched this kid Fenech, the punters would follow. The press would take care of itself.

Dann called the racing writer John Holloway. Shortly afterwards, he had the full mailing list of the Australian Jockey Club calendar. Jockeys, bookies, trainers, owners and socialites. Dann and Mordey's son, Craig 'The Clone', started working the phones.

Dann rang Tom Powell, ageing now but once one of Australia's biggest bookmakers. Powell wore a diamond tie-pin that ran nearly the width of his tie. He had cash just ripe for spending.

'Mr Powell, Michael Dann is my name,' Dann said.

'Yes, what do you want?'

'I don't know if you are aware, but Bill Mordey is kicking off boxing, and I know you were a regular at the Stadium—'

'I was.'

'And I'd like to offer you the opportunity of joining the golden ringside club whereby—'

'What's this involve?'

'Your tickets would be available, the same seats at each fight coming up. Obviously we would like to put you in the front row.'

'Well, that would be decent.'

'We're looking at this first fight with Jeff Fenech, and it will be $150 a seat—'

'I beg your pardon? You mean to say you'll be charging me $150?' The pause was only small. 'I'm not interested.'

They had better success with others.

The Mulholland fight was Fenech's fifth as a professional, and at bantamweight. Again, the step in weight was done carefully. Here was a fighter who did not have the punch to seriously hurt Fenech but who was also big enough and talented enough to keep Fenech at his very best. Shortly afterwards, Mordey called Johnny.

'I can get him a world title fight,' he said.

'What?' Johnny said. He thought Mordey was mad. 'Bill,' he said. 'The kid's had five fights.'

There had already been talk in the papers about Fenech getting a world title fight. Melbourne promoter Cos Sita had hoped to match Fenech against Japan's International Boxing Federation (IBF) champion, Satoshi Shingaki, on the undercard of Lester Ellis's shot at the IBF super-featherweight title in Melbourne. Johnny had knocked it on the head, saying he wasn't ready. Nothing had changed since.

Now Mordey was saying he could make the same fight. Sita had put him in contact with the American matchmaker Don Majeski.

If Lewis-Fenech-Mordey became the holy trinity in the resurrection of Australian boxing—and they did—then Majeski was the silent hero. He worked out of a small apartment in New York where he pressed his clothes by placing them under his mattress before he went to sleep. So good was he at his job that for years after this Johnny and Mordey did not take a step without speaking to Majeski first. On Shingaki, Majeski told Mordey, 'He's a world champion just for the taking.'

Johnny couldn't help but remember Jeff Malcolm and his frustration. Now, after five fights, Fenech was getting his opportunity. If they knocked it back, would he get another?

Aside from Majeski, Mordey's advantage was the formation in 1983 of the IBF, established by Robert W. Lee as an international arm of the United States Boxing Association. Lee was a former World Boxing Association (WBA) official who lost his bid to become its president. He said he feared the WBA was being lost to the unsafe hands of South and Central American nations, which he claimed were making life difficult in the lower divisions, particularly for fighters from outside the Americas. So Lee started his breakaway. It could not have been better scripted for Fenech.

While the IBF drew considerable criticism, Lee, who answered his own phone in a small office in New York, knew he had a ready-made market in Asia, which was home to the majority of smaller fighters but lacked heft in boxing politics.

'We were forced to the Orient,' Lee told the Australian *National Times* newspaper in 1985. 'Latin Americans are fearful to fight for us because they could be ostracised by the WBA or WBC.'

Lee's coup came when he convinced Marvelous Marvin Hagler, the undisputed middleweight champion, to fight for the IBF belt against Wilford Scypion in May 1983. Both the WBA and WBC threatened to strip their belts from Hagler if he took the fight. Hagler, stubborn as a rental mule, called their bluff. He knew he held the power.

The WBA and WBC withdrew their threats, and the IBF was on the road to legitimacy.

So Mordey, who might have made a phone call to Cos Sita in Melbourne, told Johnny he could get Fenech a title shot with the IBF's champion, Shingaki.

Johnny said no. He was still living in the 1950s and '60s, when world title fights actually determined the best fighter in the world. Fenech was good, Johnny knew, and he was always improving, but he wasn't yet the world's best.

Some time later, Fenech heard that Mordey could get him a world title fight if Johnny was prepared to take it.

'Johnny, please let me fight,' he said. 'I'll win it now. I'll win it for you.'

He said it so often that Johnny finally agreed to take a look at Shingaki.

'Get me his last three fights,' he told Mordey. Soon afterwards, tapes arrived. After watching the tapes, Johnny rang Mordey. There was a sing-song lilt to his voice. 'Mate, bring him tomorrow,' he said.

He was convinced Fenech would win. He would be just too strong for this kid. *Daily Mirror* columnist Ron Casey was to say that Shingaki was so small he'd fallen off a charm bracelet. Still, Johnny said to Mordey, 'It's a hard job for Jeff.' For one, the fight was fifteen rounds, and so far Fenech had not fought any longer than seven. But given Fenech's rate of improvement, Johnny was optimistic. He told Mordey to get Fenech another fight before Shingaki, though. Shingaki was a southpaw, meaning he led with his right hand instead of the left, like most fighters. One type of fighter Fenech had yet to face in his five professional fights was a southpaw.

Mordey booked the Hordern Pavilion and signed Filipino southpaw Rolly Navarro. Since the old Sydney Stadium had shut down in 1971, Sydney's big fights had been held at the Hordern. Once again, Mordey filled the joint with his mates from the press, who did their part in the lead-up by carrying the hype. More than 3500 tickets were sold. Just as the fight was about to go off, the news came in that American fighter Jerome Coffee was seeking an injunction to stop the upcoming Shingaki fight. He claimed he, not Fenech, was the rightful challenger to Shingaki's title.

As Mordey was learning all too quickly, everybody has a price. Eventually a deal was made for Coffee to step aside and drop the injunction, so long as the winner made his first defence against him.

Still, for all the hiccups and backroom dealing, such was the job Mordey did in his first promotion that people dared to talk about the return of big-time boxing to Sydney.

On the big night, the golden ringside section held the Federal Minister for Sport, John Brown; former champions Jimmy Carruthers,

Johnny Famechon and Joe Bugner; and other former high-profile fighters such as Tony Mundine, Rocky Gattellari, Vic Patrick and Tommy Burns. Champion jockey Malcolm Johnston was there, along with former NSW Rugby League boss Kevin Humphreys, league stars Jack Gibson and John Raper, as well as Kevin Ryan, Ian Walsh, Tim Pickup, Chicka Moore and other current and former footballers. Cricketers and rugby union players took their seats, and so did George Freeman, the illegal-casino owner and biggest SP bookmaker in the country. The *Daily Telegraph*'s sportswriter Ray Chesterton created a small commotion by wearing a red sports jacket that at least one suffering eyewitness described as 'vivid'.

A low buzz went around the waiting crowd.

Fenech walked into the Hordern wearing a screen-printed T-shirt designed by Johnny: 'Jeff Fenech, proudly sponsored by Marrickville Hotel.' Marrickville Alderman George Savvas, who owned the hotel, was funding Fenech's career. He met all costs, right down to his $65 a week rent. Five years later Savvas would start a stint of twenty-five years' jail for conspiring to import eighty kilograms of heroin into Sydney.

Fenech kept his end of the bargain by flogging Navarro throughout the first round.

Johnny, worried that Fenech was bombing him out too quickly, told him to hold Navarro up.

'We need the rounds,' he said.

Fenech then started boxing Navarro. One of Fenech's quirks was that for all his street-fighting ability and his thirst for the fight when it got rough, he had a lovely jab.

The jab came naturally for Fenech. At least early in his career, he dictated fights by jabbing and jabbing until he finally backed his opponent onto the ropes, when he could then swarm with the roughhouse brawling.

He jabbed Navarro solid for two more rounds, then finally tired of the charade and finished him in the fourth. The win left

Australia's boxing establishment nonplussed about Fenech's chances against Shingaki.

Tommy Burns claimed he'd had tougher spars in the gym.

'Fenech still has a lot to learn,' said Tony Mundine.

'A very good fighter, but, after all, he had nothing to beat,' said Johnny Famechon.

Rocky Gattellari said Fenech was still three years away from a world title. He called it madness to take the Shingaki fight.

Vic Patrick said that if Fenech was really ready for a world title he should have stopped Navarro in the first minute.

Johnny dismissed the lot. Here was the start of what became almost a crazy trend with Fenech, one that dogged his career. His knockers talked down his chances before every fight. Yet when Fenech punched holes through them they then dismissed the challenger, saying Fenech had nothing to beat. Johnny even had a bloke at work always telling him that Fenech couldn't fight. Before every fight, here he came, telling Johnny his boy Fenech was about to get beat.

Only three experts picked Fenech to beat Shingaki. The first two were Leo Berry and Jack Rennie. The third one was Jimmy Carruthers. Grand old Jimmy, who said it on TV, with absolute conviction: 'It's a good move at this stage of Fenech's career. I think Fenech can win.' Theirs was quite a friendship. At home today Johnny keeps a big framed photo of Jimmy Carruthers in his prime, shaping up. Just the way he'd looked that day long ago when Johnny and his dad and brother farewelled him at the gym.

Carruthers' belief was born of many nights at South Sydney Juniors, when he had been referee and the young Johnny had read the fights absolutely perfectly. He had no reason to believe Johnny had got it wrong this time.

Between them, the three that picked Fenech shared one common trait. They were the three that knew Johnny best.

CHAPTER 10

At home, Johnny's family was growing. He had two children now, Brent and Leisa. And he has another family in the gym.

Fenech was the star, the eldest son in a way, and he treated all the others, especially the young kids, like his little brothers. When he signed a sponsorship deal with Reebok, he kitted them all out in brand-new Reebok gear. There is a generosity of spirit with Fenech. And he treated Johnny like a father. More than a father. 'Johnny was my mother, my father, my whole family,' he said.

He trailed Johnny to the ring with his gloves perched on his shoulders, his head buried in Johnny's back to block out all that is around him, knowing nothing but that Johnny was leading him to where he needed to be. Before he turned to hear the bell; every time, he kissed Johnny on the cheek.

'It is beautiful stuff,' Johnny tells a reporter. It goes beyond fighter and trainer. 'So much of it is done on a lot of trust and hard work together.'

Trust is the most important quality a trainer can share with his fighter. Without it, you go only as far as talent, and talent only ever goes so far. With trust, you reach for greatness.

Steve Mortimer, still training with Johnny and on the verge of leading New South Wales to its first State of Origin win against Queensland, watched the family relationships develop. He was working in the gym one day when out of nowhere, Johnny called a halt. 'Have a look and appreciate what's around you now,' Johnny said to everyone. 'When success comes it'll be different.'

'I saw the wildness in Jeff Fenech, and in other kids in the gym, and I saw how gracefully and softly Johnny Lewis would change their attitudes for the better,' Mortimer said.

The benefit of this was not lost on Mortimer. Always regarded a brilliant talent, his commitment to Newtown and to Johnny's methods brought a steel to his game that answered the one big question left of him. He could dig.

'He just responded,' Johnny said. 'He complemented that great skill with a newfound confidence that no one was going to stand over him.'

The Shingaki fight approached. Mordey negotiated a purse of $20,000 for Fenech. Shingaki, the champion, would get $US60,000.

Once again, Johnny took Fenech and Peter Mitrevski to Fiji for their final preparations. The small steamy islands were their unofficial training camp, perfect to help Fenech boil down to weight. After Fenech finished his roadwork and before they headed to the gym, they would walk together and talk.

This was 1985, remember, and just as Johnny had promised in his letter two years before, it was all about to change. All those hopes and promises ... Now they were about to fight for a world title. The dreams were about to come true.

Years later, Fenech and Mike Tyson sat in Las Vegas reminiscing about the men who came into each of their lives, and the difference they made because they allowed themselves to trust.

For Tyson it was trainer Cus D'Amato. A guard in the juvenile detention centre Tyson was in had seen in the twelve-year-old street thug a prodigious talent for boxing.

D'Amato had taken one look at young Mike and immediately picked him as a future heavyweight champion. He moved him into his home and later legally adopted him.

Fenech too had spent two months in a juvenile delinquents' home at twelve, sent away on assault charges after a fight on a train.

Whereas Tyson's father had been absent and his mother mostly absent, Fenech's father Paul had been ill and his mother Mary had worked three jobs to support the family. 'The only person I ever listened to,' he said, 'was Johnny.'

There is a vulnerability to Fenech that few people ever spot. He can be callous and cruel, and cocky to the point of extreme arrogance. But he can also be deeply sensitive. Talking with Tyson about his family life, he opened a window into his private hurt. 'My family was dysfunctional,' he said. 'But Johnny, he gave me everything. He gave me something I never had. With Johnny ... I felt safe.'

D'Amato trained both Floyd Patterson and Jose Torres to world titles, and when he began telling Tyson he could follow them, young Mike listened but did not really believe. D'Amato kept telling him until he died, one year and seventeen days before Tyson became, at twenty, the youngest heavyweight champion in history.

'Cus used to tell Mike things like Johnny did me,' Fenech says. 'Like how he was going to be the youngest heavyweight champion ever when he was twenty. He'd tell him all these things and they came true. That's what Johnny did with me. It just happened. There's not a chance in the world I would have been the person I am today without Johnny Lewis. Johnny didn't just develop me as a fighter. He developed more important things in me as a person.'

Tyson told Fenech he remembered sparring Larry Holmes as a rising heavyweight, and D'Amato taking him aside afterward. 'You could knock him out now,' D'Amato told him. Mike struggled to believe it.

Fenech didn't. 'That was the difference between me and him. I used to spar them all, all the ex-champions and the big names, all the pros, and Johnny used to say to me "Jeff, you're going to be better than all of them. You can beat them all." I believed I'd smash them. I was sparring guys from other gyms, all the big names, and Johnny wouldn't say nothing, but after it I'd know. Quietly, I knew how proud he was of me.'

Soon after, they arrived in Fiji to prepare for the Shingaki fight, staying in a little motel and training every afternoon at the church next door. Fenech sparred Mitrevski and Fijian featherweight Vereniki Raiwaula.

Back home in Sydney, Mordey was busy selling the fight. He didn't send out press releases. Instead, he picked his reporters and selectively placed stories with a phone call. It was so simple, and nobody ever did it better.

The celebrity journalist Jana Wendt flew to Suva to do a *60 Minutes* interview. The reality of it, a world title challenge, was hitting Fenech. His skin began breaking out from the stress, and he picked at his face relentlessly. But he trained hard, and when they returned to Sydney he was on track.

They went into camp at the Travelodge Motel, in Rushcutters Bay.

Johnny relaxed the way he liked to relax. He went to the footy to watch Souths play at Redfern Oval. In the toilets he bumped into Jack Gibson. While Gibson had coached Newtown in 1973, Johnny's first year on the club committee, that was a long time ago now. Johnny wasn't sure if he remembered him.

'Hello, mate, how are you?' Gibson said.

'Good thanks, Jack,' Johnny said, walking out. Gibson, he thought, was just being polite.

Johnny went back into the grandstand and sat down.

Gibson walked up.

'I liked the interview the other night, son. I loved every bit of it. Keep the good work up.'

'Thanks,' Johnny said.

'You still watching Newtown?'

The Jets were now playing in a secondary competition.

'Oh, they're gone,' Johnny said.

'Yeah. You watching Souths now?'

'No one will take Newtown's place.'

'Mate,' Gibson said, 'I'm very impressed with you.'

He walked away with those words bouncing around in his head. He admired Jack as a coach. He had learned so much from him in the year he spent at Newtown. Talk little, say a lot, that sort of thing. Jack got clever with his simplicity, and so his words resonated, and Johnny never mastered that. What he could do, though, was get to the heart of what mattered. It stirred a wonderful confidence in his fighters.

Five days before the fight, Shingaki arrived with full entourage. Now the sportsmanlike thing to do in boxing is to at least play the part, so the Japanese fighter arrived with his promoter, cornerman and advisor, Hisashi Ikeda, his manager Henry O, his sparring partner Shinobu Kawashima, and even his masseur, Kiyoshi Kazama.

Half the thrill of boxing is the larceny involved. A promoter that does not try it on every once in a while is not really trying at all, so as Shingaki stepped off the plane with his entourage, so did the vice-chairman of the IBF championships committee, a Mr Hisashi Ikeda. Shingaki's advisor and promoter.

Mordey could only look. Ikeda, who was massively wealthy, believed he had done a pretty good job as vice-chairman. He had managed to sign Fenech to fight his boy, and avoid—for a year now—a fight with the undefeated American Jerome Coffee, which meant certain defeat. He was rumoured to own the McDonald's franchise for all of Japan and to be linked to more colourful enterprises. He certainly looked the part. When he and Shingaki showed up to a Manly–Balmain rugby league match at a boggy Brookvale Oval, Ikeda was in a white suit and white shoes.

Johnny had more important things on his mind. Several nights before the fight he sat down with Fenech after dinner to see where his head was at.

'Jeff,' he said, 'if you lose this fight these blokes are gonna slaughter me because I put you in.'

'Johnny, no one will be slaughtering you,' Fenech said. 'I'm gonna knock him out. Don't worry, Johnny, don't worry. No one's gonna beat me. I won't let you down.'

Anything less from Fenech would have been a concern. He was perfect.

What Johnny didn't know was that Fenech, more than likely, had a broken hand. He'd hurt it sparring several days earlier, then refused to get it X-rayed. All an X-ray would do was confirm the break, he figured, which would put the fight at risk. Not now, Fenech said. Not days before a world title.

THE HYPE about the Fenech–Shingaki bout reinvigorated the fight game in Sydney.

Channel 9 bought the rights to air the fight live on TV around Australia. The fight would be up against the Logies, the Australian TV awards night that was usually the year's ratings winner. In Melbourne, Lester Ellis was making the first defence of the IBF super-featherweight title he had won two months earlier, and Channel Seven was televising it live in Victoria. Boxing had not been on television for going on six years, and now the broadcasters were transmitting it live on two channels.

The last televised bout had involved Tommy Raudonikis's old sparring partner, Paul Ferreri, at his absolute peak against a long-retired Rocky Gattellari, who was coming back after six years. It ended in controversy when Gattellari withdrew in the third, claiming an injured hand.

Now, as the reigning Australian and Commonwealth bantamweight champion, Ferreri was moaning that Fenech shouldn't have got the world title shot first. It was only Fenech's seventh fight as a pro, he said, while he had been fighting professionally since 1968. The fight should be his. Despite his public protests, he agreed to work as one of Fenech's sparring partners in the lead-up to the fight.

Still, Ferreri was not alone. Many people were wondering whether Fenech had been brought along too quickly. Shingaki was by no means a great fighter—he had had only eleven professional fights himself—but Fenech was still so … raw was the word.

Aware what people were thinking, and with Johnny's words from several days earlier still in his head, Fenech spoke up the day before the fight. 'Blokes in the street are saying Lewie has put me in over my head,' he said. 'But I'd fight this bloke for nothing for the opportunity.'

'Johnny has me so strong that I'll walk right through Shingaki,' Fenech went on. 'Why should I have to wait any longer? The people who arranged this, who agreed to the fight, obviously think I'm ready. I know I am, so let's get on with it.'

The fight was a sell-out. It eclipsed the biggest gate ever taken at the Hordern, $120,000, set some twelve years earlier when another champion bantamweight, Frank Sinatra, took the stage. But Mordey never revealed the exact gate. Before the fight he had figured the whole production would cost in the vicinity of $250,000, and when new federal laws prevented him from taking up a $100,000 sponsorship from the Benson & Hedges tobacco company, he groaned and felt his head hurt. Fenech had drawn 3500 people at the same venue to fight Navarro, when Mordey claimed he had finished only slightly ahead. Given the rise in purses, plus sanctioning fees, Mordey needed at least a full house to break square. He got that.

Before the fight he put on a dinner at a hall alongside the Hordern for all the golden ringside ticket holders. Alongside the likes of Federal Sports Minister John Brown and his state counterpart, Mike Cleary, were renowned Sydney hit man Stan 'The Man' Smith, underworld boss George Freeman and Gerry Reilly, Sydney's biggest ticket scalper.

There was also a Parramatta Road used-car salesman named Vlad Warton, and a woman who ran a nail salon. She'd been one of the first to join the golden ringside. Telling Dann she wanted four tickets, front row, she was going to bring along some of her girls.

Unfortunately, Dann didn't have a front row seat left.

'I'll give you row five,' he told her. 'You don't want front row, you'll get a sore neck looking up all night. I'll give you row five, right in the middle.'

After they filed into the Hordern, MC Johnny Tapp, the race caller, introduced all the past champions to respectful applause. Except Rocky Gattellari, who got booed. Long memories.

Looking around at the officials, Mordey thought the Japanese judge looked awfully familiar.

The referee for the main event was New Zealand's Bruce McTavish. The IBF had appointed three judges, Australian Paul Moore, American Ric Bays, and this Japanese guy.

Mordey pointed him out to Dann.

'He look familiar?'

The judge, Kiyoshi Kazama, was Shingaki's masseur.

With the crowd building inside, Mordey confronted Ikeda.

'What's he doing?' he asked, pointing to Kazama.

'Oh, that,' Ikeda said. 'He is a trainer, but tonight we have got him as a judge. Same difference.'

It was beautiful in its brazenness.

A Pommy kept walking the aisles calling, 'Back the Jap,' and taking whatever money came his way. Shingaki was the betting favourite, commanding 10–9 on with the bookmakers. One big punter, an illegal-casino operator known as Hungarian Tony, entered Fenech's dressing room to wish him all the best. He claimed complete confidence in him, then walked out and put $30,000 on Shingaki.

But if Ikeda was doing his best to swing the advantage his way, he found a willing adversary in Mordey. Mordey had booked the fight for a Friday night, 26 April. It was the day after Anzac Day, memorial day for fallen Australian and New Zealand soldiers. During World War II, Japan, Shingaki's homeland, had bombed Darwin, Broome and Townsville and sent mini submarines to raid Sydney Harbour.

Throughout the lead-up to the fight much of the press had centred on Fenech's unfair treatment at the Los Angeles Olympics and how, now, redemption was near. It all worked to stir up the crowd.

In the dressing room, Johnny remained calm, as always.

He is always nervous, but believes fighters pick up on their trainer's vibe, and so he works hard to project nothing but confidence. With Fenech, that was easier than with most. Johnny talked softly but firmly. Every action in the dressing room was deliberate.

Somebody knocked on the door to tell them they would be calling for Fenech soon. They went to Shingaki's dressing room to say the same.

As challenger, Fenech walked first to the ring. The crowd crackled. He appeared in a green and gold robe with a boxing koala on the back, his gloves perched on Johnny's shoulders. The image of the fighter lost in his thoughts, leaning on his trainer brought drama to the moment. The crowd charged up.

Fenech climbed into the ring and began bouncing around. He looked straight ahead, acknowledging no one around him. He threw light punches, he felt out the ring. He focused.

The crowd waited for Shingaki.

Johnny stood in the corner, his arms resting calmly on the ropes. Fenech continued moving. The crowd continued waiting. Fenech threw more light punches, stretched his neck and looked up at the green and gold balloons above the ring and waited. He looked towards Shingaki's dressing room.

Where was he?

The mood of the crowd began to shift.

Shingaki was in his dressing room, it seemed, quietly waiting for the call to come out. Mordey had held back the knock on his door, deliberately stalling his entry.

As Shingaki waited, and the impatience mounted, Mordey called over ring announcer Ray Connelly. He spoke to him briefly, then Connelly made a short announcement to the crowd.

'Ladies and gentleman, sorry for the delay, but the champion Shingaki is exercising his right to enter the ring when he is good and ready.'

Immediately boos rained down.

'Send him home,' somebody yelled.

The anti-Shingaki feeling escalated. Over the next several minutes the crowd grew more and more boisterous. Finally Mordey gave word to bring out the champion. When Shingaki walked into the arena, there was only one reaction.

What's Japanese for, Oh shit?

The fighters walked to centre ring for the referee's instructions, Johnny massaging Fenech's shoulders. Just before the bell, Fenech turned and kissed Johnny on the cheek.

'I love you,' he said, and then turned for the bell.

He boxed carefully the first round, taking a look at Shingaki while sitting behind his jab. The crowd was quiet. It often is in the early rounds, when two fighters are feeling each other out and the fight has yet to take shape. From the second round on, though, Fenech began to dominate Shingaki. Everything the champion had planned was failing. He did not have the strength to back Fenech up, so Fenech kept pushing through him, wrestling him onto the ropes, banging to the body when he got him there. More, Fenech was beating him to the punch from the outside too.

Ringside, Johnny's confidence picked up. 'He's gonna win this,' he said to Mitrevski.

It was clear from the early rounds that Fenech was winning the fight and needed only to stay safe until the final bell to win. In the ninth, though, he stepped it up and battered Shingaki on the ropes. Shingaki was taking punches without answering back. Worse, he was not avoiding them. Referee McTavish stopped it with seventeen seconds left in the round.

Fenech, the new world champion, leapt in the air and collapsed on his back. Johnny was first through the ropes, leaning over and picking him up in a hug. Above them, the green and gold balloons began to fall.

How BIG a moment was it? To grasp that, Johnny says, you had to consider the era. Nowadays, boxing has so many governing bodies that any world champion is just one of an alphabet soup of world champions. Alongside the recognised and respected World Boxing Association (WBA), World Boxing Council (WBC), International Boxing Federation (IBF) and World Boxing Organisation (WBO), there are many other bodies all claiming to decide world champions—the IBO, WBF, WBU, IBC, IBA and the rest. Most of those belts aren't worth the bus fare home unless there's a $5 note pinned to the side. But back then, even in the relatively new IBF, a world title meant something.

In the ring, Fenech grabbed the microphone and thanked seemingly everybody who'd ever been involved with him. But the audience remembered only four words. Those words said everything about where he was from and what he felt and, with that, a nation opened its heart.

'I love youse all.'

Later, Mordey got the judges' scorecards, even though they were now redundant. It was just as he'd figured. After eight rounds Moore, the Australian, had it scored to Fenech 80–72. He had given him every round. Bays, the American, had an identical scorecard. He just hoped Kazama, the masseur-cum-judge, massaged better than he scored fights. Kazama scored the fight 80–80. In other words, he had scored all eight completed rounds even.

Afterwards, they went back to the Marrickville Hotel. Five years earlier Fenech had earned his spending money by picking up glasses in these same bars. This time, George Savvas already had the champagne on ice. They poured champagne and sprayed each other with it and Fenech's right hand swelled as big as a glove. The following day the papers would claim it had been broken during the fight. They had photos of Fenech spraying his handicapped mate Con Spiropolous with champagne.

They were all there, except Johnny.

Before the fight Chicka Moore had asked him what he was doing afterwards. Johnny didn't know about Savvas's celebration plans.

'Nothing,' he said.

'Why don't you meet me at the Kurrajong Hotel for a beer?' Chicka said.

'Righto,' Johnny said.

Johnny kept his promise. They sat and had a beer. After a while, Chicka said, 'Let's get to the turnout in Marrickville.'

'No, mate, I'm not gonna go.'

'Come on, mate, let's go and have one beer.'

Johnny was reluctant. He does not like crowds. His favourite times after a fight are when he and the fighter and those close to him, those that contributed, get together for a quiet celebration among themselves. But eventually he agreed to go.

The party lasted most of the night. At one point Fenech looked around. 'Gee,' he said. 'I wish the pub was like this all the time.'

CHAPTER 11

Two DAYS LATER, Johnny was back in the gym. There were kids to train.

'Do up those glove laces,' he told one boy.

Another two were sparring in the ring.

'Peter, keep your hands up. Have you two gone three rounds yet? Two? One more, then.'

Around the gym were some twenty kids, skipping and working the heavy bags, two sparring in the ring and more lined up. There was always a fight coming up somewhere.

In all the time Johnny trained at Newtown not once would he nail a photo of one of his fighters to the wall. His reluctance was well-meant. He was not in the business of shrines. One fighter might begin to dominate other fighters in the gym. The only photo he would ever raise to the wall did not belong to a fighter. It was of Julian Stewart, the son of an old Johnny fighter, Bobby Stewart. That would be years later, though.

Julian had been going to the gym for two years by the time Fenech won his title, ever since the day his dad brought him in and spoke to

Johnny. Bobby Stewart explained how Julian had cerebral palsy and watched some children kicking a ball around at the park, and got upset because he realised, for the first time in his life, he couldn't do it with them, and would never do it with them.

Johnny called the fighters to a halt.

'This is Julian,' he told them. 'Julian's part of our team.'

Fighters would come and go, titles and careers and all that, eventually the council would even shut the gym down, the miserable bums. But Julian will never leave. Johnny will keep him close all his life, in the corner for nearly all his fights.

The photo he keeps is of Julian crossing the finish line in the fourteen-kilometre City to Surf race. Julian goes the whole distance on crutches.

There, says Johnny whenever the photo is noticed, went courage.

On the night of his title fight, in the dressing room at the Hordern Pavilion, Fenech had wrapped little Julian, now seven, in his arms, sealing their friendship.

Within a week of beating Shingaki, Fenech was back in the gym nursing his broken hand. Easter was approaching and Fenech asked Julian what he wanted. Julian asked Fenech if he would go to his school so the other kids could meet him.

So Johnny and Fenech and Peter Mitrevski and Fenech's disabled mate Con piled into the van and headed for the Spastic Centre at Allambie Heights. They were driving along when Fenech yelled, 'Stop the car!'

They hit the brakes and pulled in to the kerb. Johnny looked around. 'What's going on?'

The moment the car stopped, Fenech slid the side door open and disappeared. They sat for several minutes, wondering where he'd gone.

Then Fenech got back in, carrying three large bags of toys.

He'd noticed a toy shop as they were driving past and wanted to take presents to the kids.

When the champion of the world showed up with all these gifts, the children were ecstatic. It was a glorious day.

'It was a very special time for a lot of kids,' Julian recalls. 'Jeff was just a kid himself at the time, but he was on top of the world, and it just gave those kids a very special time. A bit of inspiration was what we needed.'

Nobody outside the school ever heard about it.

Johnny always kept that one to himself. He saw Fenech maturing into the man he wanted him to be.

WHILE Fenech rested his broken hand, Mordey started looking for his first defence. In Tennessee, Jerome Coffee was training in the firm belief that, after being bypassed for Shingaki to fight Fenech, he would now get his shot. He had some waiting to do.

Mordey considered finding someone else as a warm-up before Fenech fought Coffee, with even Mark Cribb considered as an opponent. That was the paper talk, anyway.

Then he got a shock. Shingaki's promoter Hisashi Ikeda and manager Henry O protested to the IBF. They claimed referee McTavish had jumped in too early to stop the fight, given that Shingaki was still on his feet.

Mordey was angry. 'The Jap was gone,' he said.

But Shingaki's complaints found enough sympathetic listeners. There was a belief in fight circles that champions were entitled to exit the game in their own way—on their shield and all that.

IBF championship chairman Bill Brennan also believed so, and launched a round of negotiations.

During those talks, it emerged just what a superb job Mordey had done to secure Fenech the world title shot in the first place. Taking advantage of how little the IBF knew about Fenech, he had somehow leapfrogged him over the far better qualified Coffee.

IBF President Robert Lee said at the time that the Australian Boxing

Commission has asked that Fenech be rated based on his amateur record. This was extraordinary. Fenech had fought only twenty-eight times as an amateur, *including* his Olympic campaign. He was in many ways still a novice. The IBF's Brennan told the *National Times*, 'We had no problem rating Fenech on his amateur career and few pro bouts. All his pro fights were ten rounds.'

Before meeting Shingaki, Fenech had not fought beyond six rounds as a pro.

Unhappy at the way Mordey had manipulated them, the IBF sought redress. It ordered a rematch.

Shingaki was never going to win a rematch as long as he wore left and right gloves. Johnny was more worried about Jerome Coffee. He was no world beater. *Ring* magazine ranked him only thirteenth among its sixteen best bantamweights worldwide. (The division was ruled by American Richie Sandoval.) Yet Coffee was vastly more experienced than Fenech, whom *Ring* didn't rate at all. He had been the gold-medal favourite at the Moscow Olympic Games but lost the chance to fight following America's boycott. He'd turned professional later that year and was undefeated.

Coffee did have a claim on Fenech's first title defence, since he'd agreed to step aside for Fenech to fight Shingaki.

Then Johnny said, 'Hey, Bill, we can use this.'

Mordey was unsure what he meant.

'We can get Jeff another fight. These people are demanding another fight [with Shingaki]. Let's give it to them, and we can stall Coffee.'

It was certain that at some point Fenech would have to fight Coffee. As champion, he couldn't avoid it. The trick, Johnny knew, was in the timing. He told Mordey there was something nobody else was considering.

'The way Jeff's going, at the end of every month we've got a new fighter,' he said. 'He's just taking to it like a duck to water.'

Mordey loved it. The way Fenech was going, if they got Shingaki again, he would roll over him. And then he'd roll right over Coffee after that.

It didn't look good to accept too quickly, though. So in public they disputed the Shingaki protest.

'I just think it's scandalous,' Colin Love told the *Daily Telegraph*. 'Anyone who watched the fight could see the referee acted properly. But in any event we are quite prepared to defend the title and give Shingaki another chance.'

The IBF ordered the rematch to a purse bid. Mordey, meanwhile, battled away, frowning and sighing and publicly wondering how he was going to win a purse bid against a Japanese millionaire. He'd evidently forgotten all about the four-fight *Fight of the Month* deal he had signed with Channel Nine after the Shingaki fight, and about the big sponsors Fenech was attracting.

Then Mordey learned that Shingaki's promoter Ikeda had announced the rematch for July 18 in Japan. Mordey had wanted it to be at the Hordern Pavilion on August 9. Mordey cabled the IBF President, Robert Lee, in New York to protest. He was about as angry as anyone can recall seeing him.

MEANWHILE, Johnny, figuring there was nothing he could do, went to Melbourne to see a friend.

At Victoria Park, Collingwood was playing Hawthorn.

'Hello, Russell,' he said, walking up on his mate. 'How are you, son?'

'Hello, John,' Russell said, putting out his hand.

Russell Cox had called him John ever since they'd met thirteen, fourteen years before, at a benefit at Leo Berry's gym in Richmond in Melbourne. Russell Cox was Australia's most wanted man. A former armed robber sentenced to life over a failed escape attempt, he'd been on the run for eight years on the day he met with Johnny, which, if it is not a record then is certainly in the photo finish, after breaking out of what was considered Australia's only escape-proof prison, Katingal, in 1977.

As police in three states looked for him, Johnny sat next to him at the footy.

Johnny met Cox as often as he could, which wasn't often, circumstances being what they were. The last time they'd met was shortly after Cox's escape, when he was hiding out at Saratoga on the Central Coast.

Mostly, when they met, Cox wanted to know what was going on in Johnny's life. He'd ask about various blokes they both knew. Johnny would have a rough idea what Cox had been up to from reported sightings in the news. This day at Victoria Park it was different.

Instead of Johnny reading about Cox in the papers, Cox had been reading about Johnny. He picked up the paper one morning to read about Jeff Fenech, Australia's new world champion, and, wouldn't you know it, his trainer was one Johnny Lewis out of Newtown. Russell Cox had smiled to himself. Good to see something like that happen to such a good bloke, he'd thought.

Now he could congratulate him in person.

As NEGOTIATIONS dragged on over the purse bid, Johnny saw an opportunity to sneak in another fight before the Shingaki rematch. This was just getting better. With Fenech's improvement from fight to fight, even Shingaki was going to face a different fighter by the time they got back into the ring. Fenech knocked out Filipino John Matienza in six. It was a strange day. At 4 a.m. the day of the fight Mordey was awoken by the phone beside his bed. Ikeda was threatening to withdraw Shingaki from the rematch.

The fight was finally scheduled for August 23 in Sydney.

The Japanese had outsmarted themselves, though. All the stalling had already allowed Fenech at least one rematch, and now time to squeeze in one more. He went to Brisbane and knocked out John Farrell in nine. 'Oh, hit him with a beauty!' commentator Mike Gibson told the audience. Fenech was ready for Shingaki.

But Johnny had other worries. A couple of days after he returned from Melbourne, there was a knock at his door. It was 12.30 a.m. He had to be up for work in five hours.

Standing at the door was Jeff Harding, crying.

Harding was leaving soon with the Australian amateur team for a ten-day tour of the British Isles: London, Cardiff and Belfast. It happened when he was applying for his passport. Harding's mother admitted that his father was not the man who had raised him, as he believed. His real father was a Dutch sailor, a man he did not know.

Johnny looked into Harding's tears with no idea how he should handle it. What do you say to a kid at a time like this? Johnny thought. Not surprisingly, he went back to his football days, and to Tom Raudonikis. As far as tough men went, Johnny put Harding right alongside Tommy. He knew you could talk to Tommy differently than you could to other men. You could tell Tommy straight.

'Jeff,' Johnny said to him, 'it's half past twelve. What do you want me to do about it?'

'What?' Harding said, confused.

'Who gives a shit about how we got here? It's about where we're going, mate.'

Harding looked at Johnny, more confused than ever. Johnny wanted to hug him.

'What am I supposed to do now?' Harding said.

'Know what I'd do?' said Johnny. He was talking quieter, softer.

'That's what I've come here for.'

'I'd go home, and you know that bloke that you think has been your father for twenty years? I'd wake him up and kiss him and tell him what a wonderful person he is, because that's what he is.'

For a long time after Harding left Johnny was uneasy. He didn't believe he'd handled it well.

It was something that will never stray far from Jeff Harding for the rest of his life. Difficult most of the time, anyway, he becomes a little more difficult. More prickly.

A month or so later, Harding fought with the NSW Amateur Boxing team in a tournament against Yugoslavia, and flattened Damir Skaro, a former Olympic bronze medallist, with a left hook. Harding was giving Johnny everything in training, and the win made Johnny only more certain he had a very good fighter in his gym.

SHINGAKI arrived back in Australia saying all the right words. He knew the mistakes he'd made, he said. He'd trained harder this time. He knew Fenech's style much better now.

What he didn't know was that he was fighting a different fighter. Fenech was improving not only with each fight but with each week in the gym. And the wins over Matienza and Farrell had only given him more confidence.

Johnny and Mordey had pulled it off. They had stalled Jerome Coffee (until November 9, IBF's orders) and got Fenech another payday against a man they were certain he would beat.

Mordey was starting to get comfortable as a promoter. He had admitted to making between $10,000 and $20,000 profit from the first Fenech promotion, against Rolly Navarro; at first he'd claimed he broke even. Certainly the $60,000 it had cost to promote that fight was money he mostly didn't have. For this fight he told the press Fenech was being paid $100,000, while Shingaki's end came to about $A60,000. Hire of the State Sports Centre at Homebush Bay, tickets, staff wages and insurance came to another $20,000 or so. Then there were sanctioning fees, expenses for American referee Jay Edson, whom Mordey had to fly in, and American judge Lou Tabat. If Bill couldn't sell just about all the

5800 seats available, he was going to have trouble making a profit at all. In any event, he would tell the press he broke even.

'We have been struggling along paying our bills …' he said.

But Mordey had nothing to worry about.

Watched by 5000 people, Fenech broke Shingaki's nose in the first round, cut him over the right eye in the second, and stopped him coming out altogether after the third. The Japanese fighter quit on his stool.

'Fenech is going to be great very soon,' referee Edson said later. 'I have seen the best bantamweights in the world—the WBA and WBC champs—and he is up there with them. His rate of progress is phenomenal.'

'We had nothing, but we had everything.' Johnny (five) and his big brother Robert (seven), outside their nan's house in Erskineville. All he needed was family and Erko, the great training ground of his life.

Growing up, Erko was as every neighbourhood should be. Good friends, plenty of fun. Here a teenage Johnny is off the long run-up.

Johnny's parents, Marge and Alf Lewis, at a family wedding. Everything he learned about people he learned from them, and the people around them.

Johnny, aged about eleven, boxing at the old Railway Institute, near Central Railway Station. What would the experienced trainer now say to the novice boxer then? 'Retire.'

Where it all began. An 18-year-old Johnny coaching Newtown Police Boys Club boxing team, shortly after Snowy McFadyen returned. Back row: Snowy McFadyen, Steve O'Connell, Eddie McDermott, Frank Keane, Johnny. Middle row: Mario Azzopardi, Alan 'Bull' Parker, Joe Azzopardi, Desmond Locksley. Front row: Vic Ferraro, Simon Azzopardi.

Newtown Aussie Rules, where Johnny learned what was needed to be a winner. He is front row, second from right.

'If they say nothing … say nothing.' Johnny at a dance with his Aussies coach Arthur Dunningham and Geoff Sewell, the man he shared his paper run with. Sewell taught him many old-school tricks.

They needed a painter for a photo for a magazine story. Johnny, an apprentice with Sydney County Council, posed for the photo with an old lady. 'The start and finish of my modelling career,' he says.

Paul Hayward in 1976, with Bruce Langdale. Even though Hayward received a 22-year sentence for drug trafficking in Bangkok, Johnny has one clear assessment of Hayward: 'He is the finest man I know.'

When Newtown coach Warren Ryan complained that Tommy Raudonikis (left, in 1981) was getting the credit for the Jets' success, Johnny was succinct. 'But Warren, you only taught 'em how to play football. Tommy taught 'em how to win.'

In the old days, the old-timers used up all the bench at Newtown to watch the fighters train, but that disappeared as the game faded. With Fenech's emergence, though, they soon returned.

Jeff Fenech after beating Satoshi Shingaki, April 26, 1985, to capture the IBF bantamweight title. 'I love youse all,' Fenech told the crowd.

Seven weeks after taking the title from Satoshi Shingaki in 1985, Jeff Fenech beats John Matienza. Fenech's improvement was such he was a different fighter with each new fight.

Partners in crime. Johnny Lewis with Peter Mitrevski (left) and Jeff Fenech (right) in 1986. More family, and all that entails, than friends.

Coming back champion of the world … Referee Joe Cortez pulls Jeff Harding away after he knocks down Dennis Andries for the second time, about to capture the WBC light-heavyweight title in Atlantic City on June 24, 1989.

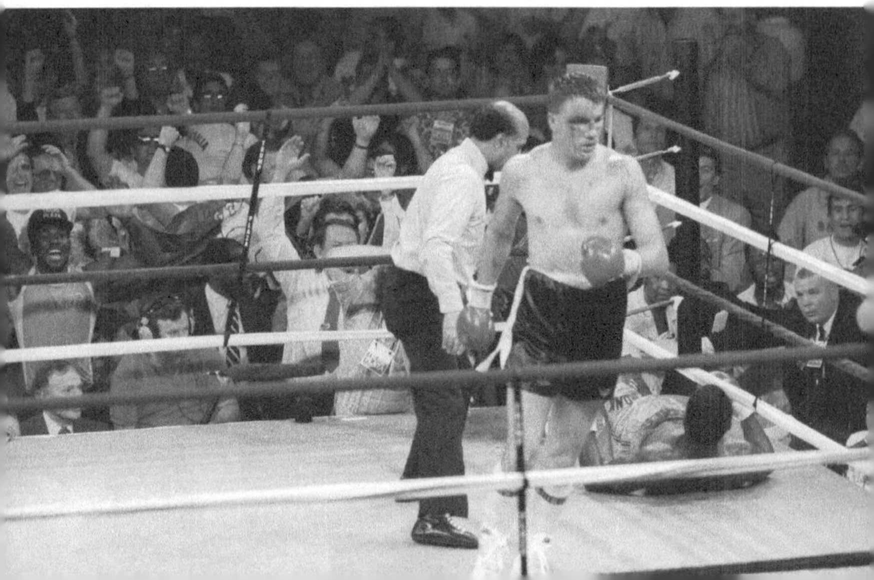

The tough guys know they're tough. Steve Roach at the airport with Johnny before leaving for the 1989 New Zealand tour.

Trainer of champions. Jeff Fenech and Jeff Harding pose with Johnny in 1989. He was the first Australian trainer to have two current world champions in his gym.

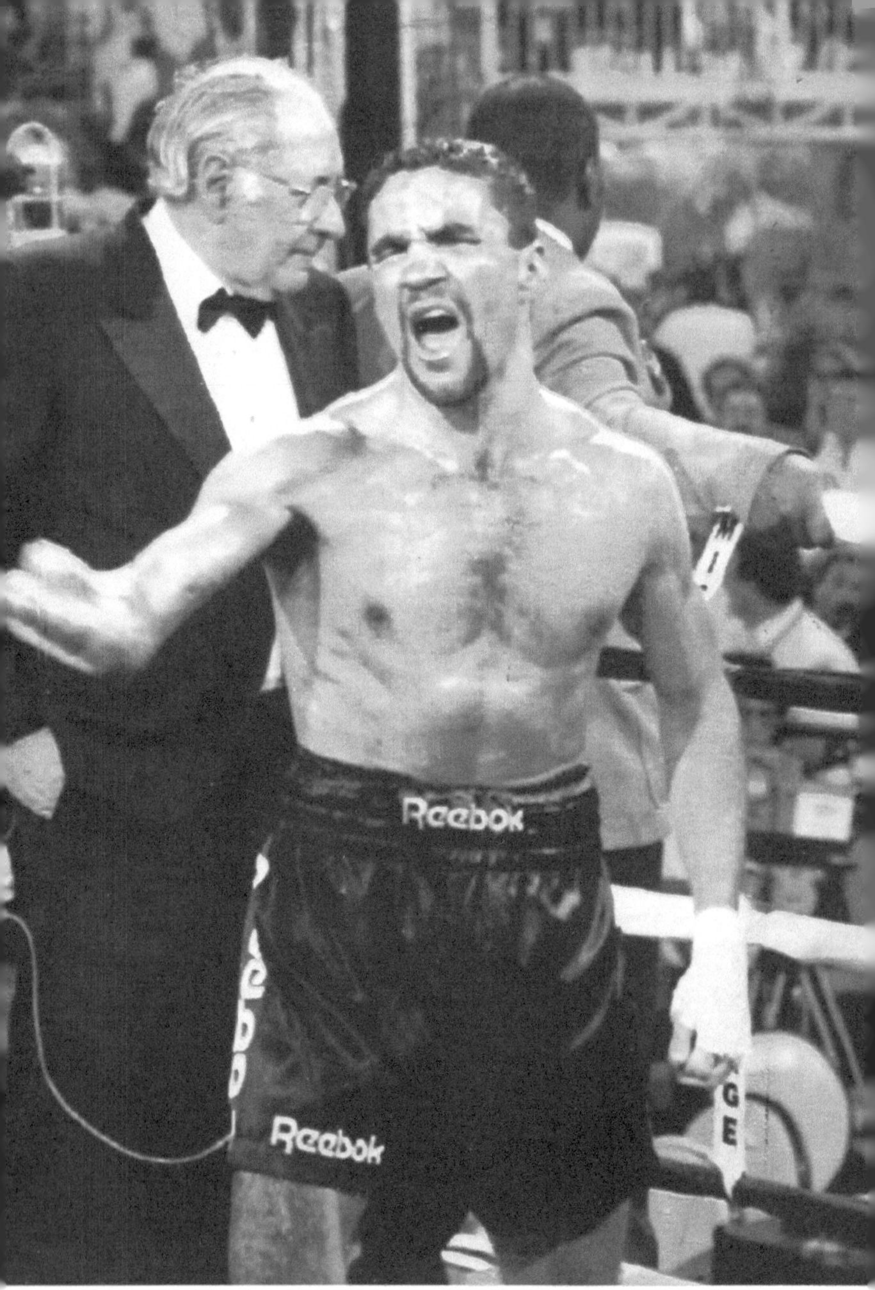

Robbery in Vegas. Fenech explodes after the draw against Azumah Nelson is announced, 1991.

CHAPTER 12

Six weeks before Fenech beat Shingaki in the rematch, Lester Ellis showed his brave fighter's heart by putting his title on the line against ageing Australian Barry Michael. There was no reward for Ellis other than a handsome local gate and the ego of shutting down Michael forever. Nearing the end of his career, Michael had taken to baiting Ellis in a bid to lure him into a fight and win the world title that had eluded him all his career.

It worked.

They had once been friends. A young Ellis had sparred and learned from Michael as he rose through the ranks. Now Ellis considered Michael old. But Michael had no doubt he still had Ellis's measure.

Michael won over fifteen rounds, losing no more than five of them.

The fight was live on ABC-TV. The government-funded broadcaster, noting the popularity of Jeff Fenech and the surge of interest in boxing in the wake of his title win, had gambled that the Ellis–Michael fight would grab a big audience.

It was a terrific time in Australian boxing.

Fenech was the poster boy for those old lines that boxing creates and Hollywood steals. A new man of wisdom was emerging in Johnny Lewis. He spoke quietly and with purpose. Not quite in the perceptive riddles of Jack Gibson, but his words were to the point and contained the wisdom of the streets he grew up in. People began picking up on his simple truths. And then there was Mordey. The gambler rolling the dice and pulling it off over a bourbon and hard-won luck.

It was terrific, and it was perfect.

Johnny knocked off work this day and headed to the gym, doing a little training on his own before his fighters began arriving. Yet his mind weighed him down. As he lifted dumbbells, he knew what he had to do, and that he really didn't want to do it. Why did it have to feel like this if you were doing the right thing?

The door swung open and Fenech walked in.

'Son,' Johnny said, calling Fenech over, 'See that door you just walked in?'

Fenech smiled.

'Turn around and walk out of it. Get out of here.'

'What's wrong?'

'You're getting a bit carried away with yourself.'

THEY'D never copped lairs growing up in Erskineville, and Johnny saw no reason to start copping them in the gym now. Around Erko there'd always be someone around to knock the lair out of anybody who started to get too full of themselves. Fenech was in need of a knocking.

It was the little things. Johnny had started noticing the way he treated friends, taking jokes a little too far, into territory where feelings were hurt. It happened sometimes with Jeff, he knew that, but until now he had been able to cut it off with a simple word here or there to pull him back into line. What irked Johnny was how his target changed depending on the company he kept. There was Peter Mitrevski, his best mate one day and on the end of a ridiculing the next. And with all these blow-ins starting to hang around, looking to bask in Fenech's glory, Mitrevski was becoming the patsy, just for their entertainment.

He understood that Fenech liked having people around him. But he was playing to the new crowd at the expense of those who'd stuck with him through the tough years.

You stuck with your mates first. Always.

Fenech was getting aggressive, too. Arrogant. Johnny would get calls saying he'd been in a fight at a nightclub, or that he was giving somebody grief.

Of course, there were times when Fenech was targeted. Some mug would pick him, just to show off. Look at me with the champion boxer, even if he doesn't weigh much more than your average jockey. But it was happening too often at too many places to always be somebody else's fault.

Johnny had had enough.

Fenech was shattered. Within five minutes he was on the phone apologising. He spoke in hurt tones, a castigated young boy. He'd do anything, he said, to come back.

You can only imagine Mordey's reaction if he had known. Lewis was breaking up the *team*? It would have killed him. It wasn't only Johnny's public image that was being crafted. For Mordey, it begins sometime after the Shingaki fight, when he is talking to the *Daily Mirror* about the cost of his new venture, saying, 'The second—the one in which Fenech won the world title—didn't come nearly as cheap. About $250,000, I'd reckon. We broke even on that bout.'

And there it is.

Break even.

In the recorded history of man, nobody broke even more often than Bill Mordey, which is some performance.

The first journalist to pick up on it was Ray Chesterton, he of the vivid red sports coat and with a wit equally vibrant. Soon, it began appearing in his copy. And then it wasn't long before barely a story about Mordey was written without him being mentioned as Bill 'Break Even' Mordey or later, Break Even Bill Mordey.

Fenech's banishment from the gym lasted one day. Johnny was everything in his life, much more than his trainer. He arrived at the gym and apologised again and, as Johnny had hoped, was humble and willing to make amends.

With Coffee scheduled for November, Mordey, blissfully unaware of the break, took the Fenech show around Australia to give everybody a look before the Coffee fight. Or that's how he put it to the press. A new city represented a new audience willing to fill its stadium, no matter how light the opponent. Brisbane got a look at Fenech in a non-title fight against the American Kenny Butts.

Butts's value was in his record. Before Fenech he had fought the Olympic gold medallist Steve McCrory, a name all of Australia knew. Behind Fenech's world title still hung the unfinished business of McCrory. Butts had lost to McCrory over six rounds in a unanimous decision. Johnny believed Fenech was far too strong for him and would finish him fast, whetting the public's appetite for a Fenech–McCrory fight. In the end, the fight was notable only for Butts's terrible performance. At one point he even hid behind the referee. After getting an early taste of Fenech's ferocity, he fled before quitting on his stool at the end of the second. He spent all six minutes of the bout fleeing from an actual fight. His purse was $6000, effectively a thousand dollars a minute.

Mordey was dirty. When Butts later invoiced him for airfares, accommodation and fees, swelling his purse to $17,000, Mordey groaned.

Coffee was next. The American marked the next level in Fenech's development. They'd seen his style before, but he was the best fighter Fenech had faced. The fight was booked for the Sydney Entertainment Centre, which held 11,000 people. Media interest was huge.

One morning Fenech went running in Centennial Park, somewhere different to do his roadwork. He was getting ready to drive away when he saw Coffee running towards him. He'd chosen the same place for his roadwork.

Fenech waited until he was near. 'You'll have to run faster than that.'

'Man,' Coffee replied, 'you'll have to go quicker to catch me.'

It was the first time they had laid eyes on each other. When Mordey heard of it he had only one instinct. He called the *Daily Mirror*.

Coffee tried hard to irritate Fenech. He gabbed away and even a few of Fenech's knockers came out in support of the American. Ern McQuillan let Coffee train at his gym and claimed he possessed the best jab since Freddie Dawson, which made the old timers wipe a tear from their eye.

At work, Johnny ran into a workmate that was always knocking Fenech.

'You want to back your fighter?' the bloke yelled.

'No,' Johnny said, 'but I'll put you on to plenty of blokes that do.'

'He won't win this one. He'll wonder what hit him.'

Fenech tried to stay calm before the fight by reading Johnny Famechon's biography but did a poor job of it. He was fighting his instinct.

Mordey organised a 'Parade of Champions' at Newtown Police Boys Club. Lester Ellis, Fenech's Olympic teammate Shane Knox, Jeff Harding and Billy Johnstone all stepped forward to spar after Fenech. More than a thousand people looked on, including former champions Charkey Ramon and Jimmy Carruthers—who Johnny had recently learned had cancer.

Later, in the foyer, Coffee's best friend, Waldorf 'Mookie' Coleman, tried to hand Fenech a poster of Coffee with 'Coffee knocks out Fenech' written on a glove. Across the middle was 'Dear Jeff, Thanks for the title.'

Peter Mitrevski grabbed the poster from Coleman and threw it, provoking a push-and-shove that Fenech leapt into.

Johnny jumped in quickly to separate them.

The press boys loved it. The pre-fight scuffle is often a piece of playful choreography designed to provide some colourful images for the nightly news. But as Johnny knew, Fenech is playful when it comes to fighting like wharfies are playful.

Finally pulling Fenech away he worked quickly to make him settle down.

'Cassius Clay did this all the time,' Johnny said. 'Ever since this bloke got here he's been mouthing off. He wants you to be rattled. He wants you as mad as hell and making mistakes. You do your talking after the fight.'

As well as selling this fight, Mordey was looking to see how well Fenech carried the big venue. He was hoping to match him with WBA champion Richie Sandoval there the next year. The press were already talking of it as a megafight. Sandoval was considered the best bantamweight in the world and the Australians, watching Fenech's improvement in each fight, were planning an ambush.

But first Fenech had Coffee to deal with.

Their fight featured head butts, low blows, biting and only the occasional thumb in the eye, at great pain to the recipient. In the fourth, Coffee turned to his corner and said: 'I've got him. I've got him. He's mine.'

Johnny, hearing it, stayed calm in the corner to keep Fenech calm.

'You're working off your jab, it's all working,' he said. 'You're outjabbing the jabber.'

Fenech kept jabbing. Another round ended.

'Keep your hands up. Keep tidy,' Johnny said. 'He's trying to bring you on to his right hand.'

Every time Fenech got up from his stool, Johnny sent him back with the same words.

'Jeff, I love you.'

'I love you, too.'

They went fifteen rounds. Shortly before the decision was announced, Coffee grabbed Fenech in the ring. 'You'll hold the title for a lifetime,' he said. Fenech was the winner on all three cards, 148–140, 146–141 and 145–140.

A couple of days later, Johnny was back at work when the workmate came up to him.

'Oh well,' he said, 'I'll admit it, I was wrong ... But how was I to know the other bloke couldn't fight?'

THREE WEEKS later, just after Christmas 1985, Johnny took Fenech and several other fighters to Parklea Prison. Fifteen months after the Milperra massacre, Phil McElwaine and his brothers were still inside, awaiting trial. Fenech sparred six rounds with Phil's brother Mark in a makeshift ring. Chicka Moore, the Newtown great, had started the Young Offenders Program in the police boys clubs. Johnny generally headed it up for him, taking his fighters into prisons across the state to show the inmates there was another way to use their aggression.

'I always think if you look for it there is good in everyone,' he told Fenech. 'And if you find it, well, then you can run with that.'

CHAPTER 13

It wasn't a bad end to 1985. Four years before, if Jeff Fenech had found himself at the Confederation of Australian Sport awards ceremony, it would have been to steal the silverware from the tables. Now he was receiving the Male Athlete of the Year award from Prime Minister Bob Hawke. His acceptance speech was about Johnny Lewis.

'I owe everything to Johnny,' he said, his voice catching. 'Without John I'd probably be in jail now. He changed my life. In fact, he built me a life. Every success I've had, in boxing and life, belongs to him …'

No one in the audience could have known it at the time, but Fenech's success or failure in boxing was literally in his hands. The break he'd never acknowledged had not healed. Now he was breaking bones in his hands in every fight. He had to ice his hands for twenty minutes after every training session, and he hated the ice. Each day they were just that little bit worse than the day before.

Hands, of course often trouble fighters.

Muhammad Ali battled brittle hands towards the end of his career.

The young Sugar Ray Leonard suffered from similar problems, and his trainer, Angelo Dundee, ended up cushioning his knuckles with feminine hygiene pads before wrapping his hands.

A long-ago street fight had left Fenech unable to fold his index finger into a fist, so the knuckle took the full weight of each punch. It was made worse because in training he refused to wear any more bandaging than necessary. At the same time, panty-liners weren't going to save him, either. Johnny tried early to make him pad his hands better, but Fenech resisted. As much as possible, he wanted to feel bone on bone.

And everyone wanted to see Fenech feel it. Locals, often veterans of the old Stadium fights, would wander into the gym and sit on the benches that ran beside the ring to watch him train. It was the cheapest entertainment in the city. Johnny felt proud to see them coming back—proud that he was playing his part in that.

But Fenech's hands weren't the only thing giving him grief. He was also finding it tougher to pull weight off as his body grew.

Even before the Coffee fight, Johnny had threatened to withdraw him for fear he was wasting too hard to make weight. Not long afterwards, WBA champion Richie Sandoval, *Ring* magazine's king of the bantamweights, was knocked down five times before being stopped by Gaby Canizales in the seventh. Sandoval started convulsing in the ring. They could not get his mouthguard out. For minutes they worked on him. It caused such a scare that Top Rank promoter Bob Arum offered Sandoval employment forever on the condition he never fought again. Sandoval took the job and retired. Somewhere far away, possibly in the direction of Mordey's Classic Promotions, somebody kicked a dog. Mordey's megafight was off.

Most blamed the loss on Sandoval's need to lose twelve pounds, about five kilograms, in the ten days before the fight.

Johnny and Mordey worried that something similar could happen to Fenech.

Mordey started manoeuvring, planning ahead. The goal was still

Steve McCrory, but for Fenech's warm-up fight Mordey organised a step up to super-bantamweight against a tough little Mexican, Daniel Zaragoza, a former WBC world bantamweight champion. It gave Fenech a needed break from boiling down to bantamweight. Fighting Zaragoza the Mexican, in the midst of a career that would take him to the International Boxing Hall of Fame, also gave him credibility.

In every other area the gym was humming. Mitrevski was improving. Jeff Harding continued his progress, making Australia's team for the Commonwealth Games in Edinburgh, Scotland. Harding was considered a strong medal chance. At Newtown he was sparring plenty of men from other gyms and performing strongly. Johnny watched him work with one boy from the Woolloomooloo Police Boys Club across the inner-city. Steve Dack was tough and game and just not quite good enough. It was like that for a lot that came up against Harding. He liked the way this other kid went, though.

Shortly after they arrived in Perth for the Zaragoza fight suspended New South Wales detective Roger Rogerson went on Channel Nine's *Willesee*, the national current affairs program, and named Neddy Smith, who still yells a big g'day whenever he sees Johnny at Redfern Oval, watching Souths, as a police informer.

The following day, Smith was in McEvoy Street, Waterloo, when a car jumped the footpath and ran him down. Police concluded it was no accident. The car tried to reverse back over him.

The next day Smith went on *Willesee* himself. He blamed police for the attempt on his life. He denied he was an informer.

Meanwhile, in Perth, Fenech beat Zaragoza over ten rounds. Zaragoza was not nearly as washed up as they were led to believe and fought hard all the way. When Fenech arrived at breakfast the next morning his head carried so many lumps he was almost unrecognisable. And his hands, once again, were broken.

'Bill might be a good promoter,' he said, 'but he's a fucking awful judge.'

On the plus side, Fenech had made weight comfortably and been strong throughout. It told Johnny where they were heading. It also got Fenech ranked among the super-bantamweights: the WBC put him at No. 10. Mordey booked the Sydney Entertainment Centre for August, hoping Fenech would step up a division to fight WBC super-bantamweight champion Samart Payakaroon.

They returned from Perth and almost as soon as they landed Johnny heard the whispers. The man that ran Neddy Smith down was Terry Ball. Johnny did all he could do, which unfortunately wasn't a lot. He hoped it wasn't true. Already at the White Horse Hotel, in Crown Street, Surry Hills, people cleared from the bar when Terry walked in for a beer. Nobody wanted to be in the general vicinity when Neddy Smith came through the door shooting.

Johnny didn't know if it was right or wrong. Instead, he goes back and it is twenty-seven years earlier, 1969, and Johnny is going to hospital to visit a friend that has been shot through the mouth. All his teeth, so big and so beautiful that he is known around town for his wonderful straight teeth, got blown clear across the footpath.

'You've got a hide,' another visitor says, seeing Johnny arrive.

'Why's that?' Johnny says.

'You know.'

'No I don't. Why?'

'You know.'

Johnny was frustrated. 'Why?'

The visitor looked at him. 'Oh well,' he says, 'the dogs'll be barking it tomorrow anyway. Your mate did this.'

'Who?'

'Terry.'

Johnny turned up his nose. Terry was one of his fighters at the Botany Street gym. 'Terry wouldn't do this.'

'Bullshit he wouldn't.'

Late that night Johnny's phone rings at home.

'Johnny?'

'Hello Terry,' says Johnny.

'I need to talk to you, mate. Can we meet at St Peters station?'

'What time?'

'Midnight.'

St Peters, an unmanned train stop in Sydney's inner-west, gets only a little business at midnight, and not for transport purposes.

'See you there,' Johnny says.

Johnny didn't ask why or what or anything else when they met. Terry just told him he had a fight in Melbourne coming up and that he needed to train for it. But there was this little situation he was in. He couldn't really be seen out at the moment.

Not to worry, Johnny says. He'll pick him up at twelve the next night and they'll go to the gym and train. Terry tells him where he is staying and Johnny and his mate, Loopy Hammond, pick him up the following night. They unlock Botany Street and train at midnight.

Every night after that Johnny and Loopy stop in front of Terry's hideaway house and wait for Terry to slip down the stairs, a hat pulled low and a coat pulled high, before heading off to train. When the fight arrives Kevin Gore leads car loads of friends from Sydney to Melbourne to support Terry against a pretty good Italian fighter, Jake Gulino, who has a mass of local support himself. The fight is at Festival Hall, and the Italians want to back their boy for plenty.

Gore, with connections to Melbourne's Painters and Dockers Union, as luck would have it, tells the Dockers Terry is only a little bugger, but he punches like a heavyweight. The Dockers look at the card and see they are fighting at lightweight, and figure that on this new information the odds look very good, so they say they will take that bet.

Fighting under the name Terry Wilson, Terry Ball was one of the bravest fighters Johnny ever stood in the corner for. He had extraordinary toughness, the courage of ten men, and whatever he heard from the corner he delivered without question.

The faith the Italians had in Gulino seemed well justified. He started strongly, working nicely off his jab. It went that way for one round, two rounds, and into the third, until Terry caught him with one of those big shots Kevin Gore mentioned.

There was nearly a riot after that. Nobody knows what quite started it. Maybe one of the Dockers was counting his money in front of the Italians. Terry was only 24, but he retired after that. And now all these years later Johnny was worrying about him again.

Terry was later arrested and charged with attempted murder. Smith, who knew Terry, was called as a witness. They had grown up on the same streets, around Redfern, Newtown and Erskineville. Smith walked into court and, in fine legal fashion, the prosecutor stood up and in his great courtroom voice asked Smith to identify the man that had tried to kill him.

Smith told the court he got a good look at the man that ran him down and he was certain it was not Terry Ball. Case dismissed.

Steve McCrory arrived in Australia nearly three weeks before the fight. He got off the plane, put his Olympic gold medal around his neck, and said he was ready to take Fenech's belt.

'I know he's a tough brawler and that he's not much of a thinker,' he said. 'But I never took much notice of him in LA, and I never really knew who he was until he won the IBF title.' This, we know, was not true. 'I know he's always crying that he lost in the Olympics, but you won't hear me doing that,' he continued. 'I got that gold medal and now I'll take Fenech's championship belt.'

McCrory was from Detroit, and trained at what was fast becoming the most famous boxing gym in the world. The Kronk gym was home to Emanuel Steward, who believed in having his fighters train and spar together, irrespective of weight. In the United States that was hailed as a revolutionary idea. At Newtown, by necessity, that's the only way they'd ever done it.

For all his confidence, McCrory got a shock. As he ridiculed the little brawler Fenech, somebody told him that Fenech actually stood several inches taller than him.

'No, he can't be that big,' he said.

Oh, yes.

'I thought he was only real short,' a clearly surprised McCrory said. 'I guess I'll just have to punch him down to size.'

Yet the size difference changed the whole dynamic of the fight. McCrory had believed it would be the age-old battle: the taller boxer with the reach advantage against the wild brawler, short and coming on. That Fenech would not only be more aggressive but have a slight height and reach advantage made him think more deeply. But McCrory was stuck with it. When he got his first glimpse of his opponent, he said: 'He looks more like a lightweight.'

Fenech's broad back was one of the reasons he found it so difficult to pull weight. He was probably the largest bantamweight in the world. Combined with his strength, this made him almost impossible for other bantamweights to handle. But Fenech was edging out of the bantamweight class.

And his hands were giving him so much pain that he couldn't punch. Forget about pad work with Johnny, he couldn't even hit the floor-to-ceiling ball. It was all shadow-boxing to avoid impact to his hands.

'His hand injury has been annoying, but it doesn't change our attitude towards the outcome,' Johnny said.

The hands, though, were compounding his problems with his weight. 'I would have preferred to bring Jeff's weight down by making him work hard in the gym,' Johnny said, 'lots of rounds punching the floor to ceiling ball and a lot of hard work on the punching pads. But with his hand in this condition he won't be hitting anything harder than air until he gets into the ring to fight McCrory.'

But punching air was frustrating Fenech. One day he cut loose, punching the pads with full power in the hope of getting in a full workout.

He broke a hand bone, again.

He got it X-rayed and told Mordey. Mordey said the only option was to cancel the fight.

Fenech went home and ate a bowl of pasta, his first proper meal in weeks.

Next morning, at 5.30, the phone rang. It was Mordey.

'If we cancel the fight, I'll do my money.'

Fenech put his head back on his pillow. 'OK,' he said. 'I'll fight.'

Now he had another problem. He had put on several kilograms overnight from the pasta. His body, starved for so long, soaked it up. Back to the starvation diet.

After several days back in the gym, though, Fenech wasn't shifting enough weight. Worried, Johnny spoke to Mordey. 'I can't push this kid any more,' he said. 'I'm not losing an ounce of it. The fight can still go ahead, but Jeff might have to weigh in heavy,' he said. Mordey knew what that meant. It meant forfeiting the title. He wouldn't hear of it. Forfeiting the title would kill the gate.

Some time later, Mordey called Fenech again.

'I'm going to send you to a health farm,' he said.

Not just Fenech but the whole team. They went in a show of solidarity.

It was torture.

Mordey hadn't been there a day before he was trying to get out. He had no weight to lose, and there was no drinking or smoking. All the food was health food. Even Johnny found it painful.

Second day in, Mordey ran into a couple of fat women and got playful. 'I weighed twenty stone when I first got here.'

'How long you been here?' they asked, filled with hope.

'A week.'

'How'd you lose so much weight so fast?'

'Well, you come up to my room tonight and I'll let you in on the secret.'

Johnny could hardly blame them for knocking him back. 'If somebody was coming in and they saw Bill walking out, they'd say, "Jesus, we're not going in there."'

They ate nuts and raw vegetables and food Johnny couldn't pronounce. Food he had never seen before. After two days he was nearly fainting. The solidarity was important, though. For Fenech's sake, they had to show they were in it together. So they all ate what he ate and suffered alongside him.

Fenech began each day with roadwork, running six to eight kilometres. Breakfast was diluted apple juice or a glass of carrot juice with chlorophyll. There was more juice for morning tea and more again for lunch. Dinner was a vegetable casserole.

He trained in the gym with Johnny, shadow-boxing, and worked a car tyre with a sledgehammer to raise his heart rate.

The press reported that Fenech was training at his 'country hideaway'. Nobody wanted the truth revealed; that Fenech was struggling to make weight. Nobody wanted to give McCrory that edge.

Johnny couldn't take it any more. One day he saw an old pushbike leaning against a wall and hatched a rescue operation. He called in Shane Knox, Fenech's sparring partner and Olympic teammate, who would be fighting on the undercard.

'Mate,' he said, 'get on that bike, and I want a meat pie, a vanilla slice and a carton of chocolate milk. Get out through the fence there.'

Half an hour later Knox was back and Johnny took off to his room. The pie didn't stand a chance. He walked out and straight into Fenech.

'How you going?'

'Oh, mate,' Fenech said, and that was all he needed to say.

'Don't worry about it, mate,' Johnny said, patting him. 'We're all going through it.'

THE SUNDAY before the fight, back at Newtown, Fenech worked the pads. His broken hand was sore and numb but would be 'two hundred per cent' by the time he fought McCrory. Jeff believed in understatement.

When the health-farm hell was over, Fenech was still overweight. The press, following every movement on the scales, said it was three pounds. In truth, three days before the fight he was nine pounds overweight. Four kilograms. It was all the more serious because Fenech had already sweated and boiled every spare ounce of water from his body. Johnny thought of Richie Sandoval and was worried.

The night before the fight Fenech still had four pounds to lose. It was a mountain. Johnny called Mordey and told him the battle was over. Jeff couldn't make it.

'He tried his arse off,' Johnny said. 'He's concerned you're going to lose your money.'

Mordey wanted Fenech to try again.

'Bill, it's impossible,' Johnny said. 'Mate, the fight can go ahead, but if we win, the title's vacant, and if they win they get the title. Either way, we'll have to fight him at about five pounds over the weight. He just can't do it. He tried, he done everything that had to be done.'

Johnny went to bed at peace with it. They had no choice but to surrender the title, for Fenech's health's sake.

Fenech didn't go to bed.

He spent most of the night in a sauna before having a small nap. As he sweated down he worried about Mordey doing his money. How would they draw a walk-up crowd if the title wasn't at stake? Most of all, after all that waiting since LA, he didn't want to surrender the title to McCrory like this. He didn't want to have to give McCrory an *excuse* for losing.

So at 4.30 a.m. on the morning of the fight, Fenech climbed out of bed.

He put on three tracksuits and walked out the front door of his Erskineville flat and started running the wet, empty streets with Peter Mitrevski. He ran for an hour, till the sweat soaked through all three tracksuits. They got home and dragged an electric heater into his lounge room and sealed the gaps around the door, then Fenech changed into a dry tracksuit and put a plastic raincoat over it, put on a beanie, and started shadow-boxing in front of the heater.

Johnny was due to pick him up for a trial weigh-in at 8 a.m. At 7.30, Johnny's phone rang.

'Johnny. Come over here.'

'What's up?'

'I made it.'

'What?'

'Johnny, I made the weight, I made the weight.'

When Johnny got there Fenech was grey and gaunt and his cheeks were hollow. Tears came to Johnny's eyes.

'Mate, I'm really disappointed in you,' he said. 'Don't you understand?'

Johnny thought about calling the fight off anyway. Maybe he'd made a mistake by not doing so already. The damage from this type of wasting could be permanent.

Indeed, every reputable boxing organisation would soon change its rules governing weigh-ins so they would be held the day before the fight. Doctors found that serious brain injuries were being caused when fighters got so dehydrated that they lost the shock-absorbing cerebrospinal fluid in which the brain floats, leaving no cushion between the brain and the skull. The new rules gave fighters twenty-four hours to eat again and, more importantly, drink.

'I wanted to make the weight,' Fenech told Johnny. 'I don't want to lose the title like that.'

Deep inside, Johnny's admiration reached new levels. The toughness of this kid. First with the hands preventing him from training and now pulling off weight like nobody he had seen before.

'Fenech's body is the same as ours,' he told a reporter later. 'He just gets himself above it. He's amazing. His hands are just absolutely swollen and bruised, battered, but he just says "Mate, put the bandages on and let me in there."'

They went to the weigh-in and, in true Fenech style, there was a blow-up. Fenech jumped on the scales, weighed in right on the 53.5 kg bantamweight limit, then jumped off and gulped down a forkful of his mum's lasagne. Emanuel Steward squawked, claiming he hadn't seen the scales. An official began yelling for Fenech to get weighed again.

'No, no,' Johnny said. 'He's made the weight.'

By then Fenech was raising the fork for a second bite. You could hardly expect a man to weigh in again after he had just eaten, right?

As the weigh-in broke up, with Steward unhappy and outfoxed, Johnny tried to quiet his own fears.

Something wasn't quite right.

The first job of any trainer, he reminded himself, is the welfare of his fighter. Nothing had changed since all those years ago at South Sydney Juniors. So far, Fenech had made Johnny's job as trainer the easiest job in the world. He did everything he was asked in the gym, Johnny never had to check if he had done his roadwork, Fenech was never in trouble in the ring. All Johnny did was press the go button.

In return, Johnny owed it to him to safeguard his health. This fight was at the Sydney Entertainment Centre in front of a sell-out crowd of eleven thousand. While the first bell was still some hours away, no matter how much Fenech drank in that time, it was likely he would still be dehydrated, and somewhat weakened, at fight time.

While the WBC had switched to twelve-round title fights in a bid to avoid the brain injuries that most often came late in a fight, the IBF had stuck with tradition. The fight was fifteen rounds when the belt was on the line.

Fenech started cautiously, as if aware of the risk. He stuck mostly to his jab, trying to beat McCrory the same way he'd beaten Coffee. Early in the fight his knuckle broke sending pain searing up his arm with each punch. Yet he was winning the rounds and, fuelled by adrenaline, he continued.

Towards the end of the sixth round they exchanged on the ropes.

McCrory came out of it the only way a fighter should come out of an exchange, which is with a left hook.

It landed flush on Fenech's chin and stopped him in his tracks. He didn't sag. He didn't begin to wobble. He simply stopped. Weakened and hurt, Fenech was a punch away from being stopped. He was on the edge of being counted out.

'No, no, he's gone,' Johnny said in the corner. 'He's gone.'

He reached for the towel. He was unsure how hurt Fenech was. He held up the towel, ready to throw it. One more punch and he was throwing it in.

And that was where Steve McCrory, Olympic champion, lost the fight. By the time he realised that Fenech was a punch away from the end, it was too late. He failed to find the punch to end it.

It was just seconds in real time, but that is all you get sometimes, and always in title fights. After those seconds, Fenech became Jeff Fenech. With Johnny still holding the towel in his hand, he somehow found the strength not just to fight back but to dominate McCrory.

The bell sounded and Fenech walked to his corner.

'Jeff, Jeff. Are you all right, son?' It was Johnny.

Fenech didn't answer.

'Tell me if you're hurt. Tell me the truth.'

Still no answer. Johnny wiped Fenech down. Mitrevski held an ice bag at his neck. He got a drink of water.

'Are you hurt, Jeff?'

It was the third no-answer. Johnny was on the brink of turning and stopping the fight. Then came Fenech's reply, and it should have been accompanied by trumpets: 'Don't be stupid, Johnny.'

In a perverse way, Fenech had found strength in Johnny's hesitation to toss in the towel. It had told him he was OK.

'You know you're safe because he's there,' he said later. 'You know he loves you to death, and that everything is going to be OK.'

Fenech used the seventh round to slowly get himself together.

Somehow, that round was cut short by thirty-four seconds. No one on the scene seems to have been aware of it. It was viewers watching at home who called radio stations later to complain.

Come the eighth, McCrory never even got close. Despite the wasting, the lack of sleep, the 4.30 a.m. run, Fenech was getting stronger as the fight went on. Now more at ease in the corner, Johnny was able to admire what he was seeing.

He saw Fenech drop McCrory with a body shot in the thirteenth, and while the challenger was able to climb to his feet and see out the round, he started wilting in the fourteenth. Fenech bullied him until referee Paul Moore stopped it.

'We have no excuses,' said McCrory's cornerman Prentiss Byrd. 'Steve would have beaten any other bantamweight in the world tonight. But not Jeff Fenech. He is awesome.'

Both Fenech's hands had swollen so much Johnny couldn't pull his gloves off. As they were cut off in the ring Fenech winced, his head tipping back. With the victory, the pain in his hands, he became overwhelmed with emotion and cried.

He had his Olympic revenge, and the bantamweights were over with, along with the struggle to make weight. They had gambled and won. Johnny was glad it was the last time. Mordey had already prepared for Fenech's transition to the heavier weight class. He would hang on to the bantamweight title until after he fought Samart Payakaroon for the WBC's super-bantamweight title.

The next morning, Fenech went to the Kings Cross Hotel to see McCrory off. He missed him by minutes. McCrory was already on his way to the airport. His corner had whimpered something about protesting the thirty-four seconds that went missing in the seventh, but it didn't have a chance of being upheld.

McCrory also missed the party at the Entertainment Centre after the fight. Johnny felt obligated to attend, but there were too many people for him. Dozens gatecrashed it.

Fenech arrived late.

He had sat in the dressing room for a long time, slumped in a chair. With his misshapen hands and bent in pain, he remained until a small boy bent down to tie his shoelaces so he could finally get up to leave.

CHAPTER 14

A DAY LATER, in a pub in Sydney, Joe Bugner watched Tim Witherspoon stop Frank Bruno at Wembley Stadium, in England. Bugner was no ordinary heavyweight. He was the former Hungarian contender by way of England, and his name comes with its own sub-clause. Whenever he was mentioned he was not just Joe Bugner but 'Joe Bugner, the only man to twice go the distance with Muhammad Ali'. It was said so often people even believed it. But Joe Frazier, Leon Spinks, Ken Norton and even George Chuvalo did the same. Regardless, Bugner was now living in Double Bay, Sydney, and absolutely enjoying his retirement. Until he saw the Witherspoon–Bruno fight for the WBA heavyweight belt.

'If I can't beat them …' Joe says to himself.

Not long after, Mordey called Johnny to say Joe Bugner wanted to make a comeback.

It would not be his first comeback, and Johnny was less than enthusiastic. Why can't these guys walk away? he thought. Still, Mordey was keen. He, at any rate, believed they could make it work.

Johnny spoke to several people about it. 'When the bloke was good he wasn't any good,' he said. But Bugner appealed to another side of Johnny. 'He wants me to train him, and he sounds pretty sincere.'

Nowadays, fighters age slowly, fighting well into their late thirties, even their early forties, and fighting as well as men ten and fifteen years younger. Bugner was thirty-six, but at the time that was considered old. And this was 1986, nearly three years since he last fought in the ring.

Impressed by Bugner's sincerity, and as a favour to Mordey, Johnny agreed. But he told Bugner that if he got even one sniff that the comeback was going to turn into a circus or a freak show he was out.

The first day in the gym Johnny worked him on the pads. It was the equivalent of a mechanic lifting the hood. He needed to see what he was working with. What he always tested for was how much a fighter could dig. Bugner's first right cross nearly threw Johnny's shoulder out. Johnny liked that. It said Bugner was serious. He was working hard.

After his first workout Bugner spoke to the reporters who'd turned up.

'For the first time in my life I've got someone in my corner totally committed to helping me realise my true potential,' he said. 'The cynics will say I'm just in it for the money, but I came back because I had seen the job Lewis had done with Jeff Fenech and because I watched the Witherspoon–Bruno fight and I knew I was as good as them.' He added: 'I know it sounds corny, but I want to win for Australia because I am so happy in my new country.'

Bugner joined the growing stable of fighters out of Newtown, trained by Johnny, promoted by Mordey, out to conquer the world and everything in it.

IN SCOTLAND, another Lewis-trained fighter, Jeff Harding, was in Australia's team at the Commonwealth Games. Ignoring official warnings, he wore a Canterbury Bulldogs football jersey into the ring, his thank you to the football club's sponsorship during his amateur days. He returned from the Games as the middleweight silver medallist and announced he was turning professional.

Shane Knox was undefeated after six pro fights, and Peter Mitrevski was the NSW flyweight champion. Well-regarded Tongan cruiserweight Tony Fulilangi also showed up. All these men recognised that the Lewis–Mordey partnership was not only moving fighters through the rankings but taking them to places other Australian fighters had struggled to reach.

As they had with Fenech, Johnny and Mordey moved Harding quickly. He fought four times in his first eight months as a pro. Caught between the middleweight limit which he was growing out of, and the light-heavyweight limit which he still hadn't grown into.

For a fighter campaigning in the heavier divisions, Harding had rare gifts.

As far as condition and toughness go, he was everything Fenech was, only bigger. In the gym Johnny would do whole rounds pushing up on Harding, forcing him to back away, and he would throw nothing but left rips, left hooks. Boom-boom, one after the other, the right hand never coming off his chin.

Harding loved the work, and like Fenech he would jump straight from the pads and onto the bag with barely a break.

Johnny knew it. He was blessed twice.

At the end of 1986 Harding won his pro debut, a fourth-round knockout of Tommy Roberts in the same ring where Fenech had made his debut, at Marrickville RSL Club. In his second fight, three months later, he scored a strong fifth-round technical knockout against Queenslander Emmanuel Otti at the Hordern Pavilion, and then declared he was just twelve months away from fighting Korean IBF super-middleweight champion Chong-Pal Park. But after Otti, Johnny moved him up to light-heavyweight for good.

Otti was a good amateur fighter from a pretty good stable, trained by

Reg Layton. As they walked to the dressing room after the fight Johnny heard a call from behind. It was Reg, carrying the bucket.

'I've got a bloke up here that'll fight your bloke if you want it,' he said.

'We'll do that one day,' Johnny said. 'Whenever you're ready.' He knew who he was talking about. Reg had a real good puncher named Doug Sam.

'He'll give it to your bloke.'

'All right, Reg,' Johnny said. He liked Reg. 'But you did just say that about Otti.'

Fenech's fight against Samart Payakaroon was confirmed, for May 8, 1987. His warm-up fight was at the fairly relaxed featherweight limit against Australian Tony (Mad Dog) Miller. Fenech won in a decision despite a recent operation on his right hand.

A win against Payakaroon would make him the first Australian champion to win world titles in two different weight divisions. But Payakaroon was the most composed, absolutely confident fighter that had come to Australia. Fenech, going up a division, was giving away height and reach for the first time in his pro career. And Fenech's hand troubles meant he no longer had a knockout punch. He had to rely on strength and work rate and a will forged in iron. He simply fought at a pace his opponent could not keep, chipping away until nothing was left to chip away.

Before both their fights, Coffee and McCrory watched plenty of tape and believed Fenech's earlier opponents had erred by not being fit enough. They were going to be different, they said. They were going to be as fit as Fenech and then defeat him with their superior skill. Only they couldn't. Fenech set off at a pace they tried to stay with, and when they expected him to tire he didn't. They did.

Johnny had Fenech so fit he often needed three sparring partners in the ring at the same time, rotating them every minute because Fenech wore them down so quickly.

Payakaroon was the first to recognise that Fenech's fitness was something greater than average. Seeing where Coffee and McCrory failed, Payakaroon didn't want to risk the fight going the distance and planned to take Fenech out early. And he had every reason to be confident. Two of his previous three fights had been against the tough Mexican Juan Meza and all-time great Lupe Pintor. He'd stopped Meza in the twelfth and Pintor in the fifth. As champion, he also insisted on the Reyes brand of glove which, with minimal padding over the knuckle, favour the bigger puncher in any fight.

The Thais were hardly secretive about their plan. They were happy to talk about how Payakaroon, a southpaw, would knock Fenech out with his left hand.

Mordey, meanwhile, had to sell the fight. To induce Payakaroon to Australia, he had promised a $300,000 purse. He was looking for a hook to promote the bout.

'Michael, find me a Thai restaurant,' he called out to Michael Dann one day.

'There's one up at Taylor Square.'

They invited Payakaroon there for dinner. As it turned out, Payakaroon knew the restaurant well. He already ate there most nights, and even did his own cooking in the kitchen. Best of all he knew a couple of the waitresses particularly well. He did not need to be asked twice.

Several nights later they were at the Thai restaurant in Taylor Square, Payakaroon flashing his bright white smile at the waitresses and Mordey welcoming the fighter's handlers to Sydney and the waitresses flashing right back.

Over dinner, Payakaroon's manager, Sombhop, said to Mordey, 'We want to have a bet.' There is no better man in Sydney he could have asked.

'OK,' said Mordey.

'We want to have two.'

'Two thousand dollars on Payakaroon to win,' Mordey said, making sure the terms were clearly stipulated.

'No, two hundred thousand.'

This pulled even Mordey up.

'Oh, we don't bet like that,' Mordey said. That was two-thirds of the purse.

Later, Michael Dann pulled Mordey aside.

'Why don't you hold the bet?' It was not so much a question as a request.

'Are you mad?'

'Look,' Dann said, 'if Fenech gets beat we're fucked anyway, but we're not going to get beat.'

'Michael, don't even talk like that,' Mordey said. 'Don't even talk like that.'

But the Thais kept at him, and so did Dann. Somehow, word leaked to the press that the Thais were so confident they were willing to bet their purse. It was all unconfirmed, though. A whisper went around that Mordey had accepted the bet. Mordey did not confirm the rumour but he did nothing to discourage it, either. This is not as dishonest as it might seem. If the track taught him anything, Mordey knew the perils of spouting about any newfound wealth.

For years, the rumour persisted that Mordey took their bet, but he didn't.

On the night of the fight, the SP bookmaker George Freeman walked into the Sydney Entertainment Centre with $100,000 in a brown paper bag. Other big punters threw in bets of five thousand and ten thousand and two thousand, whatever they could afford. Mordey put all the money in Freeman's brown paper bag and had Ron Casey hold it. Then he headed to the bar for a drink.

After a seven ounce of beer and a Jack Daniels to chase it down, he walked back into the arena to see that Casey had casually dropped the paper bag under his seat.

'Ron,' Mordey said, 'there's two hundred thousand in that paper bag you're minding.'

'Jesus,' said Casey.

For the rest of the night he sat on it.

As expected, Payakaroon went at Fenech from the bell.

Honours were shared until, with fourteen seconds left in the first round, Payakaroon bobbed back, Fenech hopped in to close the distance, and Payakaroon shot out a right jab. It caught Fenech with his feet off the canvas and, with nothing grounding him, he hit the deck.

Referee Arthur Mercante started an eight count, even though Fenech was quick to his feet.

At the bell, Johnny sat him down in the corner.

'Do you love me, son? Do you love me as much as I love you?' he said.

'Yes, I love you,' Fenech said.

It was an unusual exchange in the corner of the ring in between rounds of a fight.

Love …

What was he looking for?

It was trust.

Johnny knew Fenech was not suffering any effects from the knock-down. He wanted him to know that he was looking out for him, that he wouldn't let him be hurt. Just as he had felt many years earlier with Dick O'Connor in his corner, Johnny wanted Fenech to feel safe.

He wanted Fenech to know that he could go back for that second round and do whatever was needed to win the fight and that if it ever started to look bad, he would be looking out for him.

So Fenech climbed off his stool and took the fight to Samart Payakaroon. He stood and weaved and brawled, giving slightly better than he was getting, and by the third he was well on top.

Come the fourth, he knocked Payakaroon out.

As the crowd cheered the new super-bantamweight champion, Payakaroon slumped to the canvas unconscious. He was out for four minutes. While he slowly came round in his dressing room, Johnny and Fenech walked in to check that he was OK.

Fenech reached to shake his opponent's hand, but Payakaroon's fingers were limp. Soon afterwards, he was taken to hospital.

After the fight, Mordey pulled the money out of the paper bag and counted it out to return to those who'd backed Fenech. He boosted it with the money kept from Payakaroon's purse.

As he counted the money he realised one punter certain to go away a winner had bet $20,000. He could afford to be so certain because, as Mordey counted the money out, a sharp eye saw the whole $20,000 was made up of counterfeit bills. It wouldn't have bought Payakaroon a postcard at the airport.

A few days later, Payakaroon was ready to fly home. The loss was devastating for him. He returned to Thailand in near disgrace, openly accused of throwing the fight. He would eventually join a Buddhist monastery to escape the criticism. Johnny and Fenech went to Payakaroon's hotel room to farewell him. This is uncommon in the fight game, but they did it often. Fenech enjoyed seeing his opponents afterwards, when the fight had gone out of them and they could relax and even share a laugh. Johnny saw its benefit to Fenech. From the young kid, filled with the street, that first walked into his gym, this was as important a moment as any in the whole process. It was part of becoming a man. He was maturing. On this day, Payakaroon kept saying how strong Fenech was. Johnny told Payakaroon that Fenech had won the fight for all of Australia.

At this, Payakaroon's manager, Yingyong Parnichphol, stepped in.

'No, no, not just for Australia,' he said. 'No, no, he win for you. He win for you, Mr Lewis. He win for you.'

The trial of the thirty-one bikies accused over the Milperra Massacre finally ended a month later in June. During it, Johnny had been asked to take the stand. 'I'm just gonna speak the truth,' he'd said on the way to the court. Phil McElwaine's lawyer asked Johnny about his client's character and Johnny told the court, 'He's honest and a credit to his family.' Of the thirty-one bikies charged, nine were convicted of murder and twenty-one of manslaughter and affray. Mark and Greg McElwaine were sentenced to twelve years' jail. Phil McElwaine was found guilty only of affray, the only bikie to walk out of court. Johnny felt a small sense of victory. Hopefully, he thought, Phil can get on with life now. Hopefully, the bad luck is behind him.

Joe Bugner had been steadily working his way towards his own title fight. In September 1986, Mordey matched Bugner with James 'Quick' Tillis at the Sydney Entertainment Centre, a fight Bugner took on points over ten rounds.

Two months later, Mike Tyson set the heavyweight division alight by knocking out Trevor Berbick to take the WBC title and become history's youngest heavyweight champion. Suddenly, Bugner's optimism about the title seemed not quite so well placed. But Mordey had backed too many horses and walked home from too many racetracks to worry too much about that.

In the lead-up to a possible bout with Tyson, Mordey headlined Bugner with Greg Page, the former WBA heavyweight champion and a frequent sparring partner of Tyson's.

From the moment Page and his entourage arrived, they drove Mordey mad with requests.

To occupy them one night, Mordey slung Michael Dann and Brian Mills a thousand dollars and told them to take the Americans to a pub in Brighton. There was a lovely legs competition or something, they could go to that.

Afterwards, Page's entourage wanted more girls. They wanted a brothel. The only one Dann knew of was across town, a place called De Lorenzo's.

They walked into a dark reception room and the madam soon had a nice little parade going. Dann and Mills sat in reception for three hours before the fighter's entourage finally resurfaced.

'That was great,' one said.

One of the girls walked out with them. She spoke slowly and deliberately.

'Never bring them here again,' she said.

The bill was $2500. They had only a thousand on them.

'Sorry, ma'am,' Dann said. 'We're with Bill Mordey and these are some fighters from America and we've only got a thousand on us, but we're good for it.'

It must have been one of the few times a customer walked out of a brothel with money owing.

Bugner continued his comeback with a ten-round decision over Page.

It was a busy night for Johnny. Earlier on the same card, Harding stopped Johnny Taupau Sr in two, while Peter Mitrevski took a decision over Charlie Brown.

It was all going so well.

CHAPTER 15

Michael Dann and Brian Mills were too embarrassed to tell Mordey about the $1500 they were short at the brothel.

'Where are we going to get $1500 from?' Mills said.

Dann shrugged. Maybe if they said nothing it would go away.

A week later, the secretary at the *Big League* office answered the phone.

'There's a De Lorenzo's on the phone,' she said to Mordey.

'Tell 'em I'll call them back,' Mordey said. Mordey had no idea who De Lorenzo's was. He had no intention of calling them back. Dann overheard from the office next door. He still hadn't figured a way to get the money or, failing that, to tell Mordey.

A week later came another call.

'Who the hell's De Lorenzo's?' Mordey said. 'I'm not here.'

Again the call went untaken. Mordey stuck his head into Dann's office.

'Did you look after those bastards?'

'Yeah, we looked after them.'

Several more days went by, and several more unanswered phone calls. Finally the De Lorenzo's caller absolutely demanded to speak to Mordey. Mordey, annoyed, told his secretary to put the guy through. Dann, close enough to hear, felt like crawling under his desk.

'Hello? What are you, a hair dressing salon?' The pause was brief. Then there was a yell. 'Michael! What's this … a fucking brothel!'

'I didn't know how to tell you,' Dann said, walking into Mordey's office.

Mordey spoke back into the phone. 'The money will be there today.'

He hung up.

'Don't do that to me again. Brothels ringing here looking for money. Take the $1500. What were you thinking, did you buy the joint or something?'

Everything else was going so well. The fights came quickly, the wins equally so. Harding was looking at a possible world title shot. In September he knocked out Luka Sugar Joel in two to win the Australasian light-heavyweight title.

Fenech's hands were finally right, and he was about to face Mexican legend Carlos Zarate. Meanwhile, Bugner flew to England for a fight that could put him squarely into world title contention.

It was now fifteen months since Bugner had watched Frank Bruno lose his crack at the world title against Tim Witherspoon. After Bugner had beaten Greg Page, American promoter Don King promised the winner of Bugner–Bruno a title fight against the now undisputed heavyweight champion Mike Tyson, who had joined the King stable. Michael Dann and one of Johnny's trainers at Newtown, Brian Wilmot, flew out with Bugner to oversee his training. English promoter Barry Hearn picked them up at the airport in a Bentley and a Rolls and life was good. First night in London, Bugner and his wife Marlene invited Dann and Wilmot to dinner. It was a civilised start, nice wine and a meal cooked right beside their table. After dinner, Dann announced he was tired and going to bed.

Bugner said he might remain. 'We're going to have a little dessert,' he said.

Johnny had no option but to train Bugner by correspondence. He had stayed behind to handle Fenech's fight against Carlos Zarate at the Hordern on 16 October. While Zarate was considered past his best, he was twelve fights into a comeback that contained ten knockouts.

Johnny called Dann in London each day. 'How's everything going?'

'Oh, terrific here,' Dann said.

'What's Joe up to?'

'Well, today we're going to the Lonsdale Gym with that Danny Mancini, the trainer there.'

'Sounds good.'

Too right, thought Dann. With Mancini taking Bugner through pads and Wilmot overseeing, Dann had a wonderful time sightseeing.

Each day Johnny checked in, and each day got the same response about how well Joe was training.

'How far's he running?' he asked one day. Mordey was on the extension, listening

'Buggered if I know,' Dann said. 'He leaves at six and gets back at eight.'

'Aren't you going with him?' Mordey said.

'No, he runs by himself,' Dann said. 'I checked with the concierge and he said he leaves at six and gets back at eight.'

'Go with him,' Mordey said.

Happily for Dann, Bugner wouldn't let him. 'Nope,' he said. 'No one runs with me. I run by myself.'

For both Johnny and Mordey, the Fenech–Zarate fight could not come quickly enough. Zarate was an eventual Hall of Famer, and had lost only twice in sixty-eight fights. Fenech knocked him down in the first round and dominated the next two. Then an accidental head clash opened a nasty gash under Fenech's eye. Johnny patched it up between rounds, but it was going to be a problem for the entire fight. At the end of the fourth, the doctor stopped the fight.

Both Fenech and Zarate celebrated, which almost led to a fresh scuffle in the ring. Since the fight had gone more than three rounds, it would go to the judges. All three gave Fenech the fight 40–34, a technical decision.

Two days later, Johnny, Mordey and Fenech boarded a plane to London. It is not true they spotted Bugner while on approach, but they might have if they'd tried.

'Christ,' Mordey said to Dann after he saw Bugner. 'He's fatter than you.'

'I'm gonna call the fight off,' Johnny said.

Barry Hearn, the English promoter, yelped. 'You're bloody kidding.'

Bugner appeared in no condition to fight. Forget about those morning runs. He looked like he hadn't got up from the dessert table. Bugner eventually weighed in a kilogram lighter than he had for the Greg Page fight three months earlier, but they had hoped he'd be six to seven kilograms lighter.

On the morning of the fight Mordey called Dann aside and told him Makita, the power-tool company, was interested in sponsoring the fight, but there was a problem. The promotors were unable to get anything on television because the network had made its own sponsorship arrangements. However, if Mordey could do anything about it, they'd said, there would be £10,000 in it for him.

'You think we can come up with a way?' he said to Dann.

'Yep.'

They went to Selfridges, the department store, and found the prettiest salesgirl in the building. Dann approached her supervisor.

'Excuse me madam, we're here for a world title fight and we'd like that young lady there to carry the Australian flag for us. Would you mind if I ask her?'

'Go right ahead.'

Dann approached the young woman and they introduced themselves. 'Would you carry the flag? There's £500 in it for you. You'll just have to wear this Makita outfit.'

'Are you having me on?'

'No, I'm not.'

Ten minutes later, she climbed into Hearn's Rolls-Royce and headed for home to ask her mum if it was OK, before going to White Hart Lane, home ground of English football club Tottenham Hotspur.

Dann went to the production truck at the stadium and took the cameraman aside.

'We've got a young lady carrying the flag for us, an absolute stunner,' he said. 'Forget about Joe, and just put the camera on her. And here's £500.'

'If you want to give me five hundred quid for putting her on TV,' the cameraman said, pocketing the money, 'I'll have her on all night.'

In the dressing room, Bugner warmed up. Bruno was a beloved figure in English boxing, a flawed hero, loved all the more because of his acceptance of those flaws. He had an outstanding physique and had knocked out many men, but he was vulnerable to any punch in the vicinity of the jaw. It meant his fights usually ended spectacularly, whichever way they went.

After Joe was gloved and warmed up, a television producer knocked on the door and called him out. They could hear the crowd outside. There was singing and chanting at a volume they'd never heard in Australia. Just before they headed out, Johnny called the small Australian team together. Forming a circle, they put their arms around each other. He spoke of what this fight meant for Joe and what it meant to have all those that were closest to him there. When he finished, Dann felt ready to go out and face Bruno himself.

Bugner and Johnny and Brian Wilmot headed to the ring. Mordey and Dann went back to the grandstand and a private box.

'You having a bet, Bill?' British promoter Mickey Duff asked Mordey.

Mordey sort of shrugged. 'Yeah, I'm going to have a small wager.'

'I'll give you £3,' Duff said.

'Three pounds?' Mordey said. 'He's £3.50 with the bookies.'

'Okay, you can have £3500 to £1000,' Duff said.

'Are you fair dinkum, Mick?' Bill was playing with him now. 'I give the paper boy a thousand. I'll have £35,000 to £10,000.'

'You sure? That's a bit steep, Bill.'

'I'll have £10,000 on him.'

'OK, £10,000.'

Mordey turned to Dann, quietly pleased. 'We've got this running for nothing. That's the £10,000 from Makita.'

Unfortunately, that was about as competitive as the night got. Bruno, fitter and with a punch that was heavy if not explosive, dominated, and when Bugner began taking punishment on the ropes in the eighth round, the referee ended it.

Bugner's comeback was over.

CHAPTER 16

There was always an energy in the gym, even aside from the training. There was a sense of family, and a lot of laughs. Usually somewhere in the middle of the fun was Jeff Fenech, who needed to look no further than Peter Mitrevski for an accomplice. Jeff Harding didn't always see the humour involved.

Where Fenech had formed a bond with Johnny, adopting him as a surrogate father, Jeff Harding was a more difficult read.

In 1987 Johnny met Steve Crawley, a journalist with *The Sun*. Johnny is a sentimental man, and a sensitive man, and nobody wrote with more sensitivity than Crawley. Johnny saw it went beyond his words on a page, and they formed an immediate friendship. He pointed Crawley towards this kid coming through, Jeff Harding.

Crawley interviewed Harding before he fought Fijian light-heavyweight champion Mosese Vilia. The fight was the undercard of Mordey's final major promotion of the year, the headline fight being Fenech against Osmar Avila. He spoke about Fenech, and about himself.

'Jeff [Fenech] tends to have a lot of people around him … I don't have anybody. I live by myself. Johnny Lewis might say, "Come around and stay with me the night" but I don't like it. I like to sleep in my own bed. Apart from a sister I call every now and then, I don't even see my family. Not that I don't like them. It's just I'm a funny person.'

The one place where Harding did give his full trust was the ring. In the ring, he trusted beyond what Johnny asked. And after a win, he glowed. The happiest Johnny ever saw him was after a win.

Nineteen eighty-eight was a happy year for Harding. He stopped Vilia in two rounds, and three months later won the New South Wales and vacant Australian cruiserweight titles with a unanimous decision over Apollo Sweet. Every day Johnny worked him hard in the ring. Left rip, left hook, for round after round, and a lot of work on Harding's defence. Harding responded.

Next he fought Doug Sam at Rosehill for the Oceania-Pacific Boxing Federation's light-heavyweight title.

Sam was from the same stable as Emmanuel Otti, whom Harding had beaten the year before. Reg Layton was finally bringing his good one down.

Here he was.

And there he went.

Harding stopped Sam in five rounds. On the way to the dressing room afterwards, Johnny saw Layton in front of him.

'Hey, Reg,' he called out. 'You got anyone else up there?'

Harding beat Jorge Juan Salgado and then two months later fought the big-punching Don Lee at the Hordern Pavilion. At the end of the second, Harding sat down filthy. 'Johnny, he broke my fucking nose.'

'Fuck your fucking nose,' Johnny said. 'Sit down and shut up. Now listen …'

'But he broke my fucking nose.'

'Fuck your fucking nose. Get out there and break his nose.'

One of Johnny's seconds moved to give Harding a drink. By now disgusted, Johnny pushed the bottle away and instead picked Harding up under the arms. 'Get out there and stop whingeing.'

Lee banged away again but this time, the more he banged, the more Harding enjoyed it. At the end of the seventh, Harding came back to the corner.

'How's your nose?' Johnny asked.

'Fuck my fucking nose!' growled Harding. He stopped Don Lee a round later.

After more wins, over Charlie Dean Moore and Carlos Antunes Fonseca, Harding had moved up to No. 5 in the WBC's super-middleweight rankings.

Meanwhile, Peter Mitrevski captured the vacant Australian flyweight title, taking Charlie Brown in a technical decision in eight. Johnny couldn't have been more proud of a fighter. Nobody worked harder with what he had than Mitrevski. Mitrevski was limited, but through hard work and courage he had become an Australian champion. No one could ever take that away, and no one deserved it more.

But Johnny didn't think Mitrevski had any further to go in boxing. Maybe it was time to get out before he got hurt.

'No way,' Mitrevski said. His feelings were hurt. He thought about leaving Johnny and finding another trainer, but his friendship with Fenech and his obligation to Johnny after what he had done for him kept him at Newtown. Still, it was a question he began to wrestle with, unable to leave it alone. And he remained upset with Johnny for even suggesting retirement.

Fenech had now stepped up a division a second time to fight for the vacant WBC featherweight title. His opponent was Victor Callejas, a Puerto Rican with a formidable 24–1 record, including 20 knockouts.

Early in the first, Fenech leaned forward and Callejas ripped a left uppercut that straightened him up. Fenech wobbled briefly, then put his hands by his sides and looked at Callejas as if to say, 'Is that all you got?' But Fenech was hurt, more than Callejas realised. Boxing people believe conditioning helps fighters recover from big shots. It might have been the only thing that saved Fenech. Raising his gloves to his temples, he waded back in. All too typically, he not only recovered but was dominating by the end of the round.

'Is this guy human?' Callejas said to his trainer when he got back to the corner.

Johnny wasn't entirely surprised when he saw Callejas head-butt Fenech early in the second. It broke Fenech's nose. Fenech elbowed Callejas back and American referee Richard Steele stood back and more or less said, If that's the way you boys want to fight, then go right ahead. Johnny knew where this was headed. Callejas was taking the fight to the streets, and had probably found the one champion in the world more at home with it than him.

The fight was filled with head-butts, elbows and low blows. If someone had lobbed a tyre iron into the ring, either man would cheerfully have used it. What struck Johnny, crouched in the corner, was the noise, the thud, heavy and dull, of skulls banging together.

Fenech's hands went again, robbing him of the power to finish Callejas.

'Pick up the work rate,' Johnny told him on his stool. If Fenech no longer had the power for the big shots, he would have to work Callejas until he was done. Then Johnny pulled one of his favourite ploys. Before the minute break was over, he picked Fenech up and pushed him to the middle of the ring. When Callejas's trainer moved aside, Fenech was already centre-ring, waiting.

Between each round, Callejas began peeking around his trainer, his tired expression dissolving into disbelief when he saw Fenech waiting for him every time. Fenech eventually wore him down, and then out, in the tenth. He was now a three-time world champion.

■ ■ ■

A FEW months after the fight, Johnny heard that Russell Cox had been arrested in Melbourne with another prison escapee, Raymond John Denning, after a shootout with police. Johnny, who hadn't heard from Cox for some time, was worried about his welfare, but he eventually got word that Cox was unhurt. He would spend the next sixteen years in jail.

Now forty-four, Johnny still lived in the same house he had grown up in and still worked his eight hours signwriting for Sydney County Council before heading to the gym each day. But these days it seemed he was on the road all the time chewing up the holidays and long service leave he had accumulated. Though he missed home all the way, he had to go where the fights were.

In November 1988, he was appointed trainer for the Australian amateur boxing team.

It was a big moment in his life. 'It's something I've wanted for such a long time,' he told *The Australian*. 'It's every coach's dream to be made head coach for a Commonwealth Games or Olympic Games. Amateur boxing is my true love.'

Arthur Tunstall, secretary-treasurer of the Commonwealth Games Association as well as the boss of boxing in Australia, said, 'Lewis is an outstanding personality and coach, and he's calm in a corner. He reads a fight very well.'

They were nice words from Tunstall, but only four years before, Johnny had been banned for six months for taking Fenech to Fiji. What had changed in that time was nothing but public recognition.

Now his schedule was busier than ever. The team would fight at the President's Cup in Jakarta in February, the King's Cup in Bangkok in April, the Canada Cup in Ottawa in June, the World Championships in Moscow in September, and then the Oceania Championships in New Zealand. In January 1989, also in New Zealand, would be the Commonwealth Games.

But at Newtown, nothing had changed.

■■■

Fenech was scheduled to fight Marcos Villasana in November 1989, but the Mexican withdrew overnight with injured ribs and Mordey, in what he believed was a piece of inspired thinking, booked the American George 'Go Go' Navarro as his replacement.

Fenech detonated. He stalked the gym, talking out his frustration.

'Has that Mordey lost his marbles?' he said. 'Is he allowing those Yanks to lead him by the nose? Doesn't he know how good Navarro is? If he doesn't, I do. He is a completely different fighter to Villasana. I've been training for him for three weeks.

'That's all wasted now. I have to change my approach to get mentally geared for a much more difficult opponent. Mordey should have realised that.'

Mordey sat back, cool as you like.

'I don't care what featherweight it is, they can't stand up to you,' he said. 'That's the type of faith I've got in you. Anyway, if you don't want to fight Navarro I'll call the bout off. That's the easiest way, though it will cost me thousands. I'm trying to do the best for you, and all I cop is abuse.'

At this point Johnny stepped in. Nobody was calling off any fight, he said. Johnny knew how to play Fenech right. 'Either we forget Villasana and train for Navarro or we go our separate ways,' he said. 'We're wasting time going nowhere like this, so let's make a decision right now.'

He knew Fenech would not call off the fight. Fenech survived on drama before his fights. If nothing was happening, he made something happen. It kept his energy ticking over.

'I'll train on,' Fenech said, 'but get rid of these bloody black monsters,' he said, tossing away the sixteen-ounce gloves he'd been training in. Now it was the gloves, which he had been using to protect his fragile hands.

'Bill got those from the States for you when your hands got crook,' Johnny said. 'You have to keep using them.'

'That's ridiculous,' Fenech said. 'Here I am a featherweight and I'm wearing gloves heavyweights use.'

'Yeah, that might be so, but heavyweights don't have the same troubles with their hands you do. Anyway, don't tell me what gloves you should use. I know what's best for you.'

Later, when Fenech headed to the showers, Johnny spoke to his mate Ray Connelly, the ring announcer.

'He's never been like this before,' he said. 'The tension he's feeling is good, though. Come Wednesday week, he'll be ready with both barrels.'

A WEEK before the Navarro fight, they were in Melbourne heading to the Collingwood gym: Johnny and Fenech, Harding and Mitrevski, Mordey and Ray Connelly and Con Spiropoulos, Fenech's mate, who still travelled everywhere with them. Fenech leaned towards Con's ear.

Con looked at Johnny. 'Shut up baldy,' he said, 'or I'll knock your block off.'

Con has been brain damaged since birth. Four years earlier, Con could not put three words together. He was always around the neighbourhood, the big kid the other kids fled from. Who knew Con just wanted to play? Then Fenech began to understand. Then he reached out.

Now here they were on the bus, Fenech taking Con places he'd never imagined, and saying, 'Johnny Lewis is a baldy-headed old bastard.'

Johnny's head jerked up, 'I beg your pardon, Con?'

Fenech whispered again. Con said, 'Shut up baldy, or I'll knock your block off.'

Then Fenech whispered one more time. 'I love you Johnny,' Con said.

'I love you too, Con.'

■■■

Fenech stopped George Navarro in five.

In April 1989, they finally got Marcos Villasana. A day before the fight, in Melbourne, where Fenech drew his biggest crowds, Johnny received a big lift. News out of Bangkok was that Paul Hayward was being released from jail later that day.

Little Pauly.

After eleven years, he had been pardoned. Johnny felt a happiness he could not shut down.

The fight nearly succeeded in doing that. Fenech's hands went early, and he struggled to keep Villasana off him. He clubbed Villasana, but his eyes swelled and his nose was broken, and for the first time he was unable to dictate the fight in his usual way. He finally won a unanimous decision.

In the dressing room after the fight, in nasal tones brought on by his broken nose, he called Johnny aside.

'I'm going to announce my retirement,' he said.

Johnny had feared this might happen. On the one hand, it was fine. Fenech had done just about all he could have in boxing. He was undefeated, a triple world champion, and had just beaten Villasana who'd had two unlucky losses to the WBC super-featherweight champion Azumah Nelson. While Nelson had been their ultimate goal, Fenech would still be leaving with a record that stood up under the fiercest light.

But now was not the time to be making that kind of decision.

'Don't announce it now,' he said to Fenech. 'Just answer the questions about the fight and announce it tomorrow.'

But Johnny sensed that Fenech wanted to tell the world at the press conference after the fight. He thought that was a mistake. But that was also Jeff. Once he made a decision he went with it.

At the press conference, Fenech broke down as he spoke. He said he could no longer stand the pain in his hands. He had had enough.

The Fenech Johnny knew never worried about pain. He had the highest pain threshold he had seen in nearly thirty years of training fighters. Sitting beside the weeping Fenech, Johnny convinced himself that Fenech deserved all the rest that retirement would bring.

The announcement shocked the reporters. Only minutes earlier Fenech had told a radio audience that he now planned to fight super-featherweight Azumah Nelson and unify the division. Most of the assembled journos felt his best was yet to come. He still needed that big, defining fight, like Ali–Frazier, Hagler–Leonard, Dempsey–Tunney … He had done what he had done too easily.

But now that Fenech had decided, Johnny supported him with all he had. He told the press he really felt Jeff had done the right thing. His broken voice had shown he had nothing left. The pain had finally drained him, finally won.

CHAPTER 17

Jeff Harding bled for his fame.

He trained hard and fought hard. He lived hard. He never did a thing easy in his life.

After Fenech's retirement, men with notepads came walking through the door, their questions all the same. How would it affect Johnny?

'I'll carry the flag for Newtown Police Boys Club,' Harding said, working a heavy bag resting solidly on Johnny's left shoulder.

'Life goes on,' he said.

For Johnny the joy was never about titles and glory. When he told them that he got just as big a kick out of an amateur kid winning a trophy on debut as he did out of a Fenech winning a belt, nobody ever quite believed him.

He also had trouble making reporters understand that there were other fighters in the gym. Jeff Harding, for example. Harding was the new star of the stable, and Johnny had great hope for him. Harding did too, and he was prepared to train and fight as hard as anyone to get his own world title. 'If I can do a third of what Jeff did,' Harding said, referring to Fenech's three world titles, 'it will be because all roads lead to Johnny Lewis at Newtown.'

Whenever he spoke like this, a slight sing-song to his voice, you could be sure of one thing about Jeff Harding. Here he was at his best.

Harding kept working the bag as the reporters plied Johnny with their questions about Fenech, all looking right past the next real good one. With each whump on the bag Harding was taking himself closer to a moment that not even Fenech could quite rise to.

Before the end of the month, Johnny was in Bangkok with the amateurs for the King's Cup. Fenech had announced he wanted to play rugby league, and the Parramatta Eels offered him the opportunity, but first he went to Bangkok with Johnny to rest his hands. Johnny brought in an old mate, Manny Hinton, to train Harding while he was away with the amateurs. As he had earlier with Bugner, he would stay in touch by phone.

He felt a little easier about Harding, though.

Back in the *Big League* office, they were also coming to grips with Fenech's retirement. They had no choice. Mordey rang Don Majeski to discuss Harding. Who could he fight? Who was available? Who suited? He began looking around the world for opponents.

Harding was tougher to sell than Fenech. Fenech sold out venues, generating ticket sales of fourteen or fifteen thousand. Harding belonged in another era. He should have been fighting in the old Sydney Stadium days, when fight fans were educated and turned out for a fight, not an event.

Because Harding always gave a fight. He couldn't always sell one.

Before Harding fought the Argentinean Nestor Giovannini in Newcastle, on May 10, 1989, Mordey got on the phone to work up some publicity. Local television agreed to put him on the news. Harding was warming up as the television crew arrived and began setting up their lights.

'Johnny,' Harding said, 'are you going to tell this bloke, or am I going to have to shove that camera up his arse?'

The cameraman looked up, packed up, and was out the door before he learned the answer.

'Mate, what'd you do that for?' Johnny said.

'It's the day before a fight,' Harding said.

'But Bill sent that bloke along. You're struggling to sell tickets and you chase him away.'

Harding didn't care. Nobody would realise until much later, when it was too late, the hurt he suffered at the discovery of his father's identity. A quiet shift took place, with everybody now on the outside. Harding became more calloused, as if people could be trusted only so far. For years afterwards it would be spoken about in whispers, that the news of his father's identity changed him.

In his own way, Harding was deeply sensitive. He suffered injury, but nobody could tell because he carried his scars so deep.

It is often the way, the man looking for love is the man who won't let anybody in. As Frank Keane, one of Johnny's old fighters and a man that would become particularly close to Harding, said one day: 'Jeff's a good bloke, but he's afraid somebody's gonna find out.'

Not long after that, one of Mordey's *Big League* writers, Peter Peters, was talking to Manly and Australian rugby league coach Bob Fulton about rugby league things when the conversation leapt the rails and turned to Johnny.

Fulton should use Johnny on his coaching staff, Peters said.

Fulton, a man always after an edge, liked the idea immediately. Johnny intrigued him. He didn't know him, but he liked not just what he had done with Fenech but the way his fighters spoke about him.

There must be something to this bloke, he thought. He picked up the phone, and Johnny took the job.

Then in late May came an offer from American promoter Bob Arum. The previous year, Donny Lalonde had lost his WBC light-heavyweight title to Sugar Ray Leonard in a fight that was also for the vacant WBC super-middleweight crown. Leonard immediately vacated the light-heavyweight belt. Dennis Andries, who then won the title, planned to fight Lalonde until the Canadian abruptly retired with hand troubles. It left Andries without an opponent. As the No. 2-ranked contender, Harding was being offered the fight in Atlantic City, New Jersey, on June 24.

Johnny said no. Harding had only fourteen fights behind him. He needed more before challenging a seasoned champion of Andries's calibre. In the back of Johnny's mind was the thought that Harding had failed to improve in his fight over Giovannini. Mordey tried to argue it. Johnny still said no.

'I expect Jeff to improve in every fight. Last fight he didn't improve,' he said. Mordey accepted Johnny's decision. But then he spoke to Don Majeski.

'They reckon Harding's good enough,' Mordey said, going back to Johnny.

'Sometimes, Bill, you've got to wait a little bit longer,' Johnny said.

Harding, who is a fighter, said he hadn't performed so well against Giovannini because the Argentinean wasn't that good a fighter.

He told everyone who would listen: 'The better the opponent, the better I become.'

Johnny talked it over with Majeski. Majeski said that since Lalonde had pulled out, Andries had trained off and begun to put on weight. 'He's blown up. I reckon it's the best time to get him.'

The next day, Johnny walked into Newtown and grabbed Harding.

'Guess what, mate?'

'What?'

'I'm taking that fight.'

Harding rattled with excitement. 'I won't let you down, Johnny. Shit yeah, we'll beat him. The WBC title. I'll be the next Paul Hogan over there.'

They had just three weeks to prepare. If Harding hadn't been so superbly conditioned, Johnny would never have accepted the fight on such short notice. Even so, he felt uneasy. They needed quality sparring but had nowhere to get it.

Australia's only other world-class light-heavy was Guy Waters, from the Waters boxing family. A blood feud had long been going on between Waters, the established star in the division, and the rising Harding. Mordey had been trying to lure Waters into the ring against Harding, without success.

Then a young man walked into the gym with a mug that said he must have had a thousand fights. 'Michael Kariatiana,' he introduced himself. His record was 1–1. At once, everyone in the gym thought the same thing: it must have been one tough loss.

Then it emerged that Kariatiana was a tent boxer. He thought he was a middleweight, but wasn't sure. He just fought.

'I was born in a boxing tent,' he said. 'That's all I know—I travel all through Queensland and the [Northern] Territory with Roy Bell's tent show. I came down because you can't find any good sparring partners up there.'

Harding sparred two rounds with Kariatiana, whose blood splashed from his mouth and nose all over Harding's T-shirt. Then another young man, Guy Belbin, jumped in for two rounds. Belbin was the Australian amateur middleweight champion. He'd had trouble finding sparring partners at the opposite end of the country, in Tasmania.

While Harding sparred, a kid walked in, much as Fenech had eight years before, to watch. He said nothing until he saw Harding bounce a one-two off Belbin's headgear.

'Who does he fight?' the kid asked.

'Dennis Andries.'

'Where's he from?'

'England.'

'Is he any good?'

'He's the world champion.'

'Sheeeit.'

■■■

Johnny had to go to Ottawa with the amateur team for the Canada Cup. With his fight in New Jersey so close, Harding went with him. How would Jeff, the loner, go in a team environment? Johnny thought about it all the way across the Pacific.

Turned out it was the best thing that could have happened. Out of Fenech's shadow, Harding quickly became a mentor for the amateur fighters. His inherent decency found room to grow. At each fight he was the No. 1 cheerleader in the Australian corner. He got towels and made sure the fighters were comfortable in the dressing room between bouts.

He was responding to people in a way Johnny hadn't seen him respond before. Unlike many fighters, uncomfortable fighting away from home, he actually developed overseas. He felt he was on a mission, representing not just himself but his country. He sparred with the amateur team and the locals too. Good sparring. Of the Australians, Jamie Nicholson won a lightweight silver medal, Meldon Orr won gold in the light-heavyweights.

Johnny saw another potential world champion in Michael Akkawy, still the hardest puncher he has ever seen. A welterweight, Akkawy's punches lifted his opponent's feet off the canvas. Most cruiserweights would have swapped with him right there.

'Vicious,' Johnny said. He thought that right up until a car accident ended Akkawy's career, after just one professional fight.

Twelve days before the Andries fight, Harding gathered the Aussie team to watch Sugar Ray Leonard fighting Tommy Hearns in what was to become their controversial draw.

They got to Atlantic City with Harding improving at every session. As they headed from the airport to their hotel, they drove past a big billboard, all lit up: 'Andries vs Harding', with a picture of the Australian Hitman.

Harding could not mask his pride, and Johnny felt good that he felt good.

Almost all his sparring in Atlantic City was with former WBC light-heavyweight champion Matthew Saad Muhammad. It topped his preparation perfectly.

The fight was at the Atlantic City Convention Center in a big, twenty-foot-square ring. The night before, Harding and Johnny went to bed early, while Mordey and Fenech, who'd flown in to Atlantic City, took to the tables downstairs in the casino.

They pooled a couple of grand each and Mordey took it to the blackjack table.

He filled one tray. It was worth twenty-five thousand dollars. He filled another tray, another twenty-five thousand, then he filled a third and was a good way into the fourth.

'Let's pull out,' Fenech said.

'I'll just fill this tray and then we're done,' Mordey said.

It would have been a hundred grand neat. It would have been, but soon four trays became three trays, which became two trays and finally one.

When Mordey finally got up from the table not a chip was left in front of him. The sole good news was that, as the stack had diminished, Fenech had quietly secreted chips off the table and Bill's partner Gwenda had slipped them into her purse. They broke slightly better than even.

Some hours later, there was a knock on Harding's door. It was the early hours of the morning. Harding ignored it.

The bang came again, harder this time.

The third time, Harding raged out of bed and swung the door open.

'What?'

It was the police. There had been trouble in the casino downstairs, they said. An Australian boxer named Jeff had knocked out an abusive blackjack player.

Harding told them, in direct terms, that he had a world title fight tomorrow and that it wasn't him.

It's fair to say he was less than cordial when he saw Fenech the next day. Despite that, the dressing room was quiet before the fight. Johnny liked the silence. It was a good silence: the silence not of fear but of intent. Harding got ready with deliberate purpose, no wasted emotion, no false aggression.

Johnny wrapped Harding's hands and spoke quietly and infrequently, just giving him small reminders.

He wanted Harding to concentrate on his defence. Andries was a big puncher, he said. He had gone the distance plenty of times, so he could stay as well. And he had been in the ring against the very best, like Tommy Hearns.

He was dangerous. So Harding needed to be tight and perfect.

And brave.

From the first round on, Harding took punishment. He let go a left rip right on top of Andries's liver and the champion came straight back with an overhand right that split him over the left eye. By the second round, Alex Wallau and Dan Dierdorf, commentating for American ABC's *Wide World of Sports*, were already admiring the toughness of both men.

'This fight could be fought in an eight-foot ring,' Dierdorf said.

Harding bled, but kept on giving.

Sitting ringside, Fenech was next to Mike Tyson, now the undisputed heavyweight champion. Tyson, in red bib-and-brace overalls, sat next to Don King. A baseball-card signing session was being held next door to the Convention Centre, and two absolute legends, Ted Williams and Joe DiMaggio, had also sneaked in for the fight.

By the end of the third, Dierdorf and Wallau were wondering when the pace would slow. The two fighters couldn't possibly keep this up, they said. After the fourth, Andries's trainer, Emanuel Steward, told him to keep throwing the right hand. It was landing, he said, and no man could take it for long.

In the fifth, a short right put Harding down. He bounced up quickly, rolling his eyes when referee Joe Cortez started a standing eight count. It hurt him not a bit.

'He's a little bit tired,' Johnny told Harding at the end of the sixth. 'But Jeffrey, you've got to be tidy. Get off the ropes and put him on there.'

Johnny wanted his boys not only to play the part but look the part, clean, disciplined, precise.

At the end of every round, he sat Harding down and cleaned the blood from the cut over his eye, treating it with Vaseline mixed with adrenaline. Manny Hinton towelled off the sweat and water. When Harding took a drink and it spilled down his chest, they wiped him again.

At the end of the seventh, another sip of water mixed with the blood in his mouth and stained the white band on his trunks. The bloody water was immediately wiped up. Every time Harding stood up from his stool, he looked fresh and ready to fight.

In the eighth, Harding ripped Andries with a left. From the corner Johnny heard Andries groan. His body was betraying him. Johnny could see Harding was starting to break him up inside.

When Harding came back to the corner, the instructions were simple.

'Jeff, listen to me, mate. We're coming home. We're fighting to plan. Keep working the body, rip him up the guts.'

If there was one great quality about Harding, he gave himself completely in a fight. He responded to every instruction. And whereas Johnny normally doesn't like his fighters talking between rounds, Harding was his exception. He knew that this fighter fed off his own emotion.

The momentum began to shift.

Of the first six rounds, Harding had won perhaps one, the third. Now, with his tenacity and 'God-given chin', as Dierdorf put it, keeping him in the fight, he started coming home.

Andries's problems were compounded by bad advice in his corner. Emanuel Steward kept telling him he was behind. Kept telling him he had to lift his already improbable work rate. Kept saying he had to knock Harding out.

'How you feeling?' Johnny asked at the end of the ninth.

'Bit tired,' Harding said.

'You can't get tired,' Johnny barked. 'He's the one getting tired.'

He sat Harding down and ran the towel over him.

By the tenth, Andries was just about physically gone. Every movement was made in quicksand, slow and laborious. Right before the end of the eleventh round, Harding moved in and started digging at him again.

'Tremendous body punching by Jeff Harding,' said Dierdorf. By now the commentators were in full yell. Again and again they shouted it: they could not believe the stamina. Harding, after all he had taken, was not only still going, still on his feet, but was now the one dishing out the punishment. As the bell to end the eleventh rang, Harding turned and jogged back to his corner. And raised his arms.

'Look at the spring in the step of Jeff Harding at the end of the eleventh round,' Wallau said, yelling over the crowd. 'He threw his hands up.'

It was a performance beyond courage.

For eleven rounds Harding had taken punishment, and he had one round left to try to win the fight. Johnny had one tactical instruction in the corner. Jab hard, and come in after it. While Harding had suffered for most of the fight, Johnny knew that he was now in a position to win. He spent the rest of the break finding the kind of words that make men do what men can't often do, and as the end-of-break buzzer sounded, he picked Harding up and said, 'Jeff, go out and come back champion of the world.'

Harding turned. 'I love ya, Johnny.'

Andries started the twelfth on empty. He was stiff-legged and shoulder weary. A Harding jab sent him backwards towards the ropes. Harding followed and threw two more jabs, then alternated rights and lefts as Andries crumpled to the canvas.

He rose before the count, and Harding moved in and knocked him down again.

Harding again retreated to the neutral corner. Not only was he now cut above the right eye, but after being held together for the best part of eleven rounds the cut near his left eye sprang open. 'Look at Jeff Harding!' cried Wallau, and there was the Hitman, blood streaming down his face, bleeding for his fame, moments away from the greatest moment of his life.

Of two men's lives.

Harding moved in again after the standing eight, Andries wobbled, and after more blows the referee moved in and stopped it. Jeff Harding spun out of his grip and, gloves raised, ran into the arms of Johnny coming through the ropes. He was the new WBC light-heavyweight champion of the world, and one of the Australians shouldered him up centre ring.

'On the shoulders of his countrymen ...' Dierdorf said.

Harding kept pumping his fists. 'Champion of the world! Champion of the world!'

In the ring after the fight, Wallau interviewed Harding. He described it as not the best fight of the year, but one of the best fights he had ever seen. 'Your reaction to your unbelievable performance?'

'I'd like to, first of all, thank everybody from Australia that came out with me,' Harding said, high on adrenaline. 'My trainer Johnny Lewis, who I love so much, and everyone else that helped me. I'd like to thank Matthew Saad Muhammad for giving me such a good sparring session in the preparation for this fight and also I'd like to thank everybody else that was involved in Jeff Harding's success. And also, I'd like to say hello to my mum and dad at home—and I'll be home, because I'm the champ.'

'Jeff,' Wallau said, 'when you got this shot because Donny Lalonde retired, you only had fourteen pro fights. In your mind was there doubt whether you were ready to win a world championship?'

'Johnny Lewis took the fight, and that was good enough as a win for me. He's my mentor, he tells me what to do. I just do the boxing. Johnny

Lewis, I love this guy. Because of Johnny Lewis I'm here today. And Steve Cansdell, I love you too, brother.'

Steve Cansdell had been Harding's first coach in Grafton.

Wallau told Harding he had been behind on all three scorecards, trailing 106–103, 107–105, and 104–103.

'You needed a knockout to win it,' Wallau said.

'I got the knockout. I was there to the end. The knockout came. That's boxing.'

For all the greatness of Fenech, Harding's win holds a special place in Johnny's heart. It was a performance in courage.

Ringside, Donald Trump was so impressed that he announced a party at his Trump Plaza afterward. After a performance like that, Jeff Harding needed a party.

But first he needed stitches. As he was being sewn up in the hospital emergency room, Johnny sat in the waiting room alone—and at a wonderful peace. Waiting by himself, he had time to think back on it all, back to the offer of this fight coming through and how he'd knocked it back, back to the short preparation, back to the way Harding had blossomed once they got off the plane. He sat back, sick people waiting around him, and absorbed all that had happened in the past few weeks, and in that strange setting there was not a more content man in the world.

Harding was like him in some ways. Back in Australia, they would have left the venue and gone to a little café in Newtown for a coffee and a little peace to reflect on their work. So the wait at the hospital was almost therapeutic.

Eventually Harding emerged and they drove to Trump Plaza. Tyson, Ted Williams and Joe DiMaggio were all there. When Harding walked in with his face stitched up, one eye shut and the other half shut, those who noticed him first fell silent. Others, noting the silence, turned to see what was happening and went quiet, too.

And then, all at once, the applause started.

CHAPTER 18

He was on the committee at Newtown and Warren Ryan, the coach, was steering the Jets to their unlikely grand final. Midway through the season, they lost a game.

At the leagues club afterwards, Ryan called Johnny aside.

'All right,' he said, 'Tell me what you think.'

Johnny named three or four changes he thought Ryan should make to the team.

'I can give you all but one,' Ryan said.

'And one other thing,' Johnny said.

'What's that?'

'You've got to stop being jealous of Tom Raudonikis.'

'Fucking Raudonikis,' said Ryan. 'Whenever we win it's because of Raudonikis, and whenever we lose it's because of Ryan.'

'Yeah, but Warren,' said Johnny, 'you taught 'em how to play football. Tommy taught 'em how to win.'

Winning was important to Johnny. He loved rugby league because of the winners, men like Tom Raudonikis.

It didn't take long for Australian rugby league coach Bob Fulton to recognise just how smart he'd been in hiring Johnny. Just days into the tour to New Zealand in July 1989, Fulton knew he had done exactly the right thing. It wasn't because Johnny said or did anything in particular, it was because everything he said or did was perfect.

Officially, Johnny had been hired as a trainer. Fulton was one of the early innovators in the game, the first to recognise the benefits of boxing as a form of cross-training. Already doing it at his Manly club, he now brought it to the national team. Johnny took the players through pad work and other drills.

But his great value was away from the training paddock.

Fulton began to rely on Johnny's people-radar. Problems can begin on tour when a player is dropped or is unable to break into the starting team, and whingeing escalates into backbiting or worse. Johnny sensed when this was happening and knew just how to head it off. He'd find his way next to a player at breakfast and get him to go for a walk with him, or he'd talk with the player after everyone else had drifted off. Almost casually, he would explain what the player needed to do or stop doing. He headed off trouble before it began and, the whole time he was there, Fulton never really had a problem.

Early in the tour, Johnny spoke to Australian prop Steve Roach. Roach was a tough guy with the ability to back it up, but he was too proud to ever back down. Johnny never told him he had a problem. Instead, in relaxed conversations, he spoke to Roach about tough guys, and how the toughest didn't really have to show others how tough they were at all, for they knew it themselves. Roach understood what was not being said.

Throughout the first Test, New Zealand fullback Darrell Williams baited Roach, even took a few swings, and Roach refused to retaliate. He played football instead, and he led Australia to victory. After the game he walked into the dressing room and caught sight of Johnny. He winked.

Nothing more needed to be said.

■■■

While Johnny was in Rotorua with the Australians, Jeff Fenech announced his comeback. Fenech claimed that Mike Tyson had told him in Atlantic City that he'd retired too young. Tyson had convinced him to see a specialist about his hands.

Harding had been allowed to enjoy being Australia's lone champion only three weeks before the press went mad again for Fenech.

The Australian reporters following the tour chased Johnny for comment.

'I don't believe in comebacks,' he said. 'I'll be having a long talk to Jeff about his decision when I return to Sydney.'

When they got back and Fulton offered Johnny the job through to the Kangaroo tour of England and France the following year, which would last three months, Johnny needed a full second to accept. Aside from boxers, he believes footballers are the toughest athletes alive. He enjoys just being around them.

His next piece of business was to meet Fenech. They talked it out over several days, and agreed to go ahead with the comeback. Johnny would be in Fenech's corner. Fenech was still the WBC's featherweight champion, but the intention was to fight at super-featherweight. Azumah Nelson was the WBC champion in this division.

Before Fenech chose his first fight or Harding began his defence, Johnny left Sydney with the Australian amateur team for the World Championships in Moscow. Australians have never fared strongly at the World Championships, and he believes they never will until the association invests in some of the Aboriginal boys growing up in the Outback, where they have everything but opportunity. If the association is patient and works at spotting and developing talent in those areas, he says, it will find a bus-load of potential champions.

As he sat watching the fights in Moscow, the scene lit up. A little Russian boxer, a lightweight, came out fighting for the strong Soviet

Union team. Watching him work the ring, Johnny saw a poise and ring savvy that would make this fighter a great pro. It wasn't power or even a devastating performance that stood out. The kid just punched correctly. He had good skills. Smart.

When Johnny saw him again two nights later, he was eliminated by an East German fighter, but the performance only convinced him that this kid was the real deal.

After the fight Johnny found the Russian doctor, who spoke passable English.

'D'you think that kid would be interested in coming to Australia?' he said. 'The lightweight?'

'He's a good boy, that boy,' the doctor said.

'A very good boy?'

'Outside of boxing, very good.'

'That's what you want.'

'I think he would be very interested in coming over,' the doctor said.

His name was Konstantin Tszyu. Johnny stored it away.

On his return, somebody was waiting for him. Dean Waters, the heavyweight, was headed to court on a murder charge brought against him and his father Ces, a venomous little man of spite and ill-will. Ces was an old English bare-knuckles fighter who would give his opponents a kicking with steel-capped boots. He passed all his pain on to his boys. The murder charge against Dean was soon dropped.

Waters told Johnny he was thinking about leaving his father and needed a trainer.

Johnny was shocked. For years Ces, driven by jealousy, had railed at Johnny and all his fighters. His sons had been dragged into the battle by association.

'Get the blubber off, Dean, and we'll start from there,' Johnny said.

He didn't see Waters as a heavyweight, he wasn't big enough. Heavyweight had been Ces's ambition. Waters was a cruiserweight. So first Johnny sent him to his mate Bobby Lanigan, who now trained the footballers at Parramatta. The instructions were simple: get the excess off.

HARDING's first defence was against Briton Tom 'The Bomb' Collins.

When Mordey signed the fight, British promoter Danny Mancini asked: 'Was Collins a mandatory fight?'

'No,' Mordey said.

'Then you're all crazy,' Mancini said. 'If he hits Harding on the chin, they'll be counting out ten minutes, not ten seconds.'

Harding dropped Collins in the first, but come the second, Collins wound up and went boom with his big right hand. It landed flush, as perfect as if he had asked God himself to throw it. Harding's momentum barely slowed. He brushed his nose with his glove and waded back in. Those sitting ringside swear they saw the Caribbean-born Collins turn white.

Tom Collins refused to come out for the third round. When the bell rang he stayed down as if glued to his stool. He claimed a shoulder injury. The WBC held back his purse while it investigated.

Fenech made his comeback a month later, beating Mario Martinez on points in a WBC super-featherweight eliminator. In a bid to solve, or at least hold off, Fenech's eternal hand problems, Johnny asked Martinez's crew if he could put extra tape around his knuckles. They knocked him back.

The next day Martinez weighed in heavy, even after he stood naked on the scales. Given that Fenech was already stepping up a division, Johnny refused to let Martinez fight over the weight and gave him two hours to sweat it off. Martinez spoke to his advisors and walked out. They weren't fighting. Mordey chased after them and came back to Johnny in a small panic.

'He's not going to make it. He said he's going home,' Mordey said. Mordey had fifteen thousand seats already sold. A cancellation would cruel him.

'I can't do it,' Johnny said. 'It's too much on me. Any more and they'll laugh at us.'

Mordey turned to Fenech for support.

'John's the boss,' Fenech said. 'If he says the fight's off, it's off.'

Of course they eventually fought, and Fenech won, earning him a shot at Azumah Nelson's title.

As Mordey tried to work out how he was going to get Nelson, who was contracted to American promoter Don King, he and Johnny started talking about an exit plan for Harding.

Johnny wanted Harding to retire.

On the surface it sounded absurd, and he knew it. Harding had just won a title. The first rule of boxing is make the money while you can, and the title makes the money. But Johnny was increasingly worried about the punishment Harding took in each fight. Victories won at such cost made for a spectacular career, but not a long one. Every fight, he wore the scars of victory, and Johnny's job was to protect his fighter, no matter what. Harding had a rematch against Nestor Giovannini coming up. Johnny told Mordey to get Harding two more fights, the second against Donny Lalonde. The Canadian, known as the Golden Boy long before Oscar De La Hoya adopted the name, was making a comeback. If Harding gave Lalonde a shot at winning the title he'd lost to Sugar Ray Leonard it would pay millions.

That, in Johnny's view, should be his last fight. Harding always spoke well on television. Johnny believed he could make a career as an after-dinner speaker. People paid to listen to—even just to be near—toughness like his.

Harding took the idea badly. He took it personally. He was upset.

Johnny tried to explain that he had forty, fifty years to live after boxing. He wanted him to be healthy and enjoy it.

Harding wouldn't hear of it.

In December Johnny was named Coach of the Year at the Sport Australia Awards. He was the only Australian trainer to ever have two current world champions in his gym, and his record in world-title fights was 13–0.

In January 1990, soon after Johnny returned with the Australian team from the Commonwealth Games in Auckland, he got a call.

'Johnny, I gotta see you,' Harding said.

They met at the café in King Street, Newtown, that they liked to go to after a fight.

'Is everything all right?' Johnny said.

'Yeah, it's good,' said Harding. There was hardly a pause. 'Mate, I'm gonna go with someone else.'

Johnny's head popped back, his forehead screwing down in disappointment, confusion. 'Why?'

Harding gave several reasons. Johnny was training so many other blokes, he said, the amateurs and what-not. He hinted at problems in the gym with other fighters. There had always been an unspoken tension between Harding and Fenech. Harding complained often to Mordey that he was not earning the same money as Fenech, to which Mordey replied that Fenech was drawing fifteen thousand to a fight and Harding was drawing a thousand. Fenech, for his part, believed profits from his fights were bankrolling Harding promotions.

'Jeff, look,' Johnny said. 'I really don't want to do this, but you could come into the gym after they leave, or something like that. I really don't want to lose you.'

'You want me to retire,' Harding said.

'Mate, I do,' said Johnny.

'Well, I don't want to, and other people reckon I shouldn't, either.'

Johnny realised Harding was gone. Once his mind was made up, you couldn't change it.

'Mate, then you go with them,' Johnny said. Those were the last words they exchanged for a long time.

WHAT bothered Johnny was that Harding was clearly hurt. In many ways Harding could be an acquired taste, but Johnny loved him. He went home and sat in his little Erskineville flat and thought about mates and how mates treat each other. And his mind drifts back to his teenage years and his mate Robert 'Loopy' Hammond. Johnny loved the way Loopy carried himself. He had a touch of class about him.

They are in Hyde Park this night and Johnny knows he is seventeen because he wasn't drinking, he was too young, but some of the others were. Johnny and Loopy and two other mates, Maxie Dean one of them.

Johnny went to grab a drink from the bubbler. As he bent down, a dozen or so young blokes walked past. Johnny overheard one of them talking. 'Remember,' this bloke says, 'once it starts it's one in, all in.'

Johnny stood up and wiped his mouth and walked casually back to Loopy and the other two. He was terrified. He'd been fighting for near on four years now, but you could fill his pockets with rocks and he still wouldn't tip the scales much over seven stone. Besides, four against twelve is poor odds no matter how you frame it.

As Johnny told Loopy what he'd heard, the dozen young blokes found them and formed a half circle around them. The script is always the same. Words were said. They were finding a way to start it.

'Who's the best out of you?' Loopy said.

'I am,' said one of them, stepping forward.

'Well, me and you,' Loopy said. The words weren't out of his mouth before he knocked the kid cold.

'Who's the second best out of you?'

'I am.'

This bloke, too was out cold the moment the words spilled from his mouth.

'Is there a third best?'

There was no third best.

Loopy Hammond had stepped up and defended them all that night. That took courage. That's the way it was around Erko. Look after your own.

Around these streets, Johnny thought, still trying to understand Jeff Harding walking away, there were a thousand situations where people could have turned on each other. Down the road was a bloke who sold suits as hot as a two-dollar pistol, but nobody ever gave him up. Everybody knew Snowy Robbins's gym was turned over to SP bookmakers on weekends. Yet the community shielded them from the police who, truth be told, more often turned a blind eye anyway.

No matter how tough the situation, you stuck solid with your mates. That was the Erko way.

Times were changing.

Now Harding was walking away. They also had a way of dealing with that in Erko. You don't speak to him again.

Harding left and started training across town, at John McColl's Glebe Estate Gym, across the road from the Wentworth Park dog track. Manny Hinton, Johnny's old mate, went with him as trainer. He and Johnny had been close since before the time Hinton's son Mark started fighting and Hinton brought him to Johnny to train.

'Hitman Split', read the *Daily Mirror*'s back-page headline three days later. The break was portrayed sympathetically: nobody's fault, no anger.

'No one's the bad guy,' Harding's manager Tim Pickup, the former Canterbury rugby league player, told the *Mirror*. 'John has so many ongoing commitments with the Australian rugby league team and the amateurs that things reached an impasse as far as Jeff was concerned. It was a hard step to leave a big family situation like they have at the Newtown Police Boys, and Jeff will love Johnny to the day he dies.'

There was no quote from Harding, though. Or Johnny.

'The split won't affect Harding's relationship with promoter Bill Mordey,' the last paragraph read.

Johnny understood why Harding had left. He just struggled to accept it. He was hurt. Something happens when you work a fighter's corner, when you train him in the gym and break him down and build him back up again.

When the fighter walks away after six years of that, it's like a relationship break-up. Before long Johnny's hurt and bewilderment turned to dull anger.

Harding repeated the no-hard-feelings line to the *Sydney Morning Herald* the next day, though he admitted that he'd been frustrated by the amount of time Johnny gave to other fighters.

'I'm like the apprentice becoming the tradesman,' Harding said. 'It was time to move on. No one has been in my ear. No one has told me what to do. I've made my own decision.'

Johnny was quoted in the same story. 'The fight game is bigger than Jeff Harding and Johnny Lewis, and I'm not prepared to devote all my time to one fella,' he said. 'I've got a couple of amateurs who are just as important as Jeff Harding and, as I've always said, the most important person in this gymnasium is the one who is fighting next.'

Later, Johnny learned that Harding told a few people how Johnny wanted him to fight just a few more times and then retire. 'Tell him to tell Fenech to retire,' they'd said. It was enough to sway Harding, given his preoccupation with Fenech and supposed favouritism in the gym.

What frustrated Johnny most was his whole intention was to look after Harding's interests. He didn't want him to retire because he favoured Fenech. It was because Harding took three times as much punishment as Fenech did in every fight he fought. Now he was fighting at the top level, he couldn't finish a fight without swollen eyes and a busted nose from the kind of blows square in the face that shook the sweat from his shoulders. Johnny was simply acknowledging what everybody loved about Harding: he was too tough for his own good.

Fenech, out of loyalty to Johnny, immediately cut Harding off. 'Out of sight, out of mind,' he said.

It suited Harding fine.

In the February 1990 rematch with Nestor Giovannini, he ground out another tough win.

Mordey still promoted Harding as well as the rest of Johnny's fighters, and was about to take over Dean Waters and his brother Guy, a light-heavyweight, who'd also joined the Lewis stable. But Fenech, battling a series of viral infections, did not fight at all in 1990.

Johnny was watching on TV in July when Harding fought Dennis Andries in their rematch at Rod Laver Arena in Melbourne. When Andries knocked Harding out in the seventh to reclaim the title, he got quite emotional.

He hadn't expected this. He thought Andries was gone and that Harding would account for him even more easily this time. His reaction surprised him too. It showed him that he still had a lot of love for Jeff Harding.

Later, while Johnny was in New Zealand on tour with the Australian team, an Australian television reporter grabbed him.

'Would you like to talk about Jimmy Carruthers?'

'Yeah, mate, what about?'

'He just passed away.'

Johnny stopped. He felt cold inside. Only weeks earlier, Jimmy's wife had called and asked if he'd like to go and see him. Jimmy was getting sick from the cancer, she said. But Johnny had no idea he'd been so close to death.

'Tell him he's not gonna like what he sees,' Carruthers had yelled from the background while his wife was on the phone.

'No, that's all right,' Johnny had said. 'I'll come anyway.'

Later, though, he thought again. He had seen people at work waste with cancer. The last image of them stayed with him. He looked at the big photo he kept at home of Jimmy shaping up in his prime, and he thought about the day he'd farewelled him at Snowy Robbins's gym with his dad and his brother.

'Listen, I'm not gonna go,' he said calling back.

Jimmy's wife understood.

Johnny wanted to remember him at his best.

Looking at this reporter now, he was so in shock he hardly knew what he was saying. Jimmy Carruthers was gone, the man who, so long ago, had given him the confidence to believe he could make it as a trainer.

CHAPTER 19

At first Johnny had felt unsure about getting involved with the rugby league boys. He worried that, at forty-six, he might be a bit old. But when he went with the Kangaroos on the tour of England and France, his hotel rooms soon became like George Street. Walk in any day and there might be Brad Mackay and Laurie Daley. Or Mal Meninga, Kevin Walters and Gary Belcher. Reports came out of the tour that Allan Langer, the champion little halfback, had got in a blue with his Brisbane teammate Mick Hancock.

The next day Langer was in Johnny's room, flicking playful jabs towards Hancock sitting on Johnny's bed.

'How am I doin' Johnny?'

But it was a long tour, three months, and after the Kangaroos had gone through England undefeated, Johnny told Bobby Fulton he needed to go home. The French leg was minor, and back home his new fighter Guy Waters was in training for a big fight.

Mordey had matched Waters with Dennis Andries for the WBC

light-heavyweight belt. The winner would fight Jeff Harding. Andries, who couldn't draw a breath in America, had hit an unexpected goldmine in Australia and was working it for all it was worth, benefiting directly from the Harding–Waters rivalry.

Waters had the style and defence to beat Andries, and everybody grew excited about what that meant. For years Waters and Harding had been the country's top two light-heavies, but nobody had been able to make the match. Now, with a title as the bait, all that had to happen was for Waters to beat Andries. If he did later go up against Harding, Johnny would be opposing the fighter who'd left him.

Back in Sydney, he put Waters straight on the pads. By now the Sydney Swans, the Australian Football League team, had started training at Newtown. The gym sang with the rhythms of the fighters. Peter Mitrevski had suffered a knockout loss to Manny Melchor before Johnny left on the Kangaroo tour and had finally taken Johnny's advice and retired.

'I didn't want to admit it,' he said, 'but you were right.'

So much was going right, but Johnny was still bothered about the Harding split.

Waters and Andries fought at the Memorial Drive Tennis Centre in Adelaide. Fenech, in his first fight in fourteen months, fought on the undercard, stopping Canada's John Kahlbenn in four.

What happened next Johnny found hard to explain.

Waters had the fight, but he didn't want it.

From the opening round he fought within himself. He fought cautiously. Too defensive. Johnny still thought Andries was shot as a champion, that his legs were gone. He had deteriorated a lot since he'd last seen him, in Atlantic City eighteen months earlier. Between rounds Johnny told Waters to step up the pace. He wanted him to extend Andries, push him into places where he wasn't comfortable. He'd weaken, Johnny said.

For round after round Waters ignored him.

Behind their corner, big brother Dean kept yelling, 'Stick and run.'

Guy was doing plenty of that. On the one hand, who could blame him? His whole life, he'd been taught to fight that way by his father Ces.

'Stick and run,' Dean yelled again.

Johnny turned to Bobby Lanigan, sitting beside him: 'I wish he'd shove that stick and run up his arse and throw a left and a right. Maybe a hook at the end of it.'

They bled in the corner like this for nine rounds, watching Guy stick and run and waste away the world title he had fought all his life for. No amount of talking in the corner could convince Guy to change tactics.

At the end of the ninth, Johnny got desperate.

'Guy,' he said, 'come on, mate. Keep the pressure on him so he gets tired and you can be the world champion at the end of the night.'

Maybe it was because Johnny had not had enough time with Waters. Maybe the trust ingrained in Fenech and Harding and even little Peter Mitrevski just hadn't had time to develop. Or maybe years of abuse from his father had made it hard for Guy Waters to trust anybody. But as Waters sat on his stool, Johnny's instructions fell dead to the floor.

His frustration grew. It went the whole twelve rounds. The scorecards were announced: 115–114, 116–112 and 117–113, all to Andries.

In the dressing room afterwards, they sat quietly. Others stood looking at their shoes. Guy Waters wept, crying for lost opportunity.

'I guess I just didn't work hard enough,' he said after gathering himself. 'I didn't put enough pressure on him.'

Guy Waters's corner was the most frustrating corner Johnny had ever worked.

At the King's Cup in Bangkok in April, Johnny saw this kid Konstantin Tszyu fighting again. This time Tszyu easily beat the East German who'd beaten him at the 1989 World Championships in Moscow. The manner he did it justified everything Johnny first thought he saw. The amateur

World Championships were coming up this year in Sydney. Johnny told Mordey they should go along and make their move.

For now, though, Mordey had done a deal with Don King, making the match Fenech had returned to boxing for, against Ghana's Azumah Nelson. At thirty-two Nelson had thirty-six fights. His only losses were against all-time great Salvador Sanchez, who died in a car accident three weeks after they fought, and Pernell Whitaker, like Sanchez a Hall of Fame fighter.

Fenech would fight Nelson in Las Vegas in June, on the Mike Tyson–Donovan 'Razor' Ruddock undercard. It would be his first fight in the United States. To secure the deal, Mordey had to concede promotional rights for Fenech's next four fights to King. For those rights, King paid $6.5 million.

'Fenech is a fighter's fighter,' King said. 'What you see is what you get. He gives his all in the ring, just like Tyson does. That's all you can ask of a man.'

Fenech had a simple philosophy on the fight. It went down brilliantly with the American audience: 'I'm very much looking forward to punching Nelson's face in on June 28.'

What impressed the Americans were not the tough words. What impressed them was Fenech's total lack of bravado. He was stating this as fact.

In many ways, it was what Johnny and Fenech had been building towards their whole careers. This was the mountain.

The day after they arrived in Vegas, Fenech resumed training—and ran into trouble. Out that morning doing roadwork with Peter Mitrevski, he spotted Mike Tyson on a track field, doing sprints. Tyson was training under Richie Giachetti, his new trainer, who'd trained the likes of Larry Holmes and Aaron Pryor.

Fenech jumped the fence and started working out in front of them. They got the full show. Fenech pictured these guys going home to tell everyone about the bloke from Australia: 'You should see this kid Fenech!'

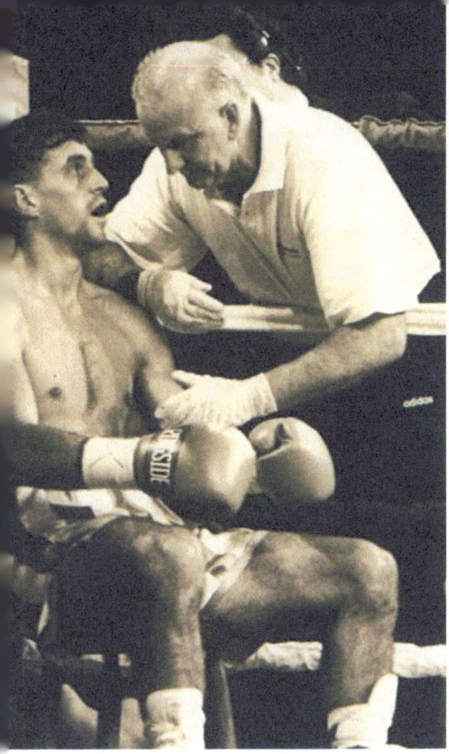

Together they could have been anything. Virgil Hill moved to Australia to train with Johnny in 1992, and while they would win back Hill's WBA light-heavyweight title eight months later, personal reasons forced him to move back to the States.

Justin Rowsell remains the one great regret of Johnny's career. One of the greatest boxers he trained, politics and fate saw to it Rowsell would never win the title he deserved.

Making good on a promise. When Steve Dack told Johnny he wanted to fight, Johnny told him to get his law degree first, then he'd put him on a Kostya Tszyu undercard. Steve took the decision in six before Tszyu beat Hugo Pineda at Parramatta Stadium in 1995.

Boxing politics. After the Kostya Tszyu–Bill Mordey split, many careers suffered. Here the pre-fight press conference for the Justin Rowsell–Lovemore Ndou fight erupts. Rowsell (blue jeans, black cap) and Bill Mordey (suit and tie) are thinking of ducking under the table. Note the guy on the left, concealing a glass. Federal police later took away vision of those involved, including persons of interest in other matters.

Johnny watches his fighters, led by Justin Rowsell (right), spar at Newtown Police Citizens' Youth Club. Who knew that a year later the gym would be closed forever?

Johnny first saw Kostya Tszyu at the Amateur World Championships in 1989, his Russian trainer describing his skills as a 'gift from god'. Three years later, Tszyu moved to Sydney to train under Johnny. Here, Tszyu is captured at the weigh-in before his title fight against Sharmba Mitchell in 2000. In the background are promoters Vlad Warton and Don King.

Kostya Tszyu entranced Australia. He looked exotic, had dynamic power in the ring, and training methods such as this—sharpening his reflexes with a tennis ball attached to his head by a rubber band—added to his mystery.

Bill Mordey is kissed by partner Gwenda at Singleton pub after being awarded $7.3 million in damages against Tszyu in September 1999. Like everything with Bill, the money came, the money went.

Johnny with Peter Mitrevski and Kostya hours before Tszyu's step-up fight against Zab Judah. Despite their problems, both Johnny and Tszyu had no problem keeping their preparation for a fight on focus.

Ricky Hatton, brave and honest and undefeated, kept coming at Tszyu all night. In the end, Tszyu lacked the power to keep him off and Hatton took the title in his hometown of Manchester when Johnny stopped Tszyu from coming out for the final round. It was Tszyu's final fight.

Gairy St Clair took a title fight on a few weeks' notice and then did what few fighters were capable of doing. He trusted. He gave himself completely to Johnny, who gave him the strategy to win. It means Gairy can now call himself a world champion.

Johnny with Ronny Nash while in America for the Oktay Urkal fight, while Nash contemplates going to the hardware store to buy himself a shovel to 'hit [Tszyu] over the fucking head with it'. Nash wasn't a fan.

You can take the jersey out of Newtown … Almost 30 years since the Jets were kicked out of the competition, the Jets gets a run-around in Nice, France. Johnny is holidaying.

Every year the people of Erskineville hold a reunion. Whoever heard of another suburb doing that? Here, more than 50 years after they first met, Johnny (far right) is with Max Dean (left), Frank Keane (a former fighter), and his son Brent. Jimmy Brooks is in the backgound.

The start of everything. Johnny outside Erskineville Oval, the ground where he used to run on at quarter-time to listen to the coaches rev up their players. Johnny distilled the essence of what was being said and, years later, used it many times between rounds.

When Russell Cox was on the run from police in three states, Johnny used to go visit him—as he did when he was later imprisoned. 'John gave me a sense of family,' Cox said. Here, Russell (far left, with partner Helen) is at the christening of Johnny's son, little Johnnie, who is being held by Johnny's partner Ingreed, with their eldest son Jackson in front.

Johnny with his mother Marge and his four children. Brent (back), Little Johnnie (nursed by Brent), Leisa and Jackson (nursed by Johnny). Marge told Johnny, 'Always look for the good in people.'

He tripled his intensity, cut down his recovery. Boy, did he put on a show. And boy, did he feel burned out after it.

When Fenech told Johnny about it at the gym that afternoon, Johnny made very little of it, although inside he was dying. The fight was three weeks away. Fenech, given all his wasting, would take weeks to get back to where he'd been just the day before.

The next day Johnny started working him differently. When Fenech got going on the pads, he often threw three hundred punches during his three-minute round, nearly two a second, all the way. Today Johnny got him to do a couple of combinations, move around, nice and easy on the pace.

'That's good, Jeff,' he said.

He had him hit the floor-to-ceiling ball, lay off the bag.

'We might only do a couple of rounds sparring today.'

It was going to be a job to bring Fenech back, but what else could he do?

Each day Johnny was reminded how much that first run had taken out of him. Fenech was at a quarter of where he should be. Instead of training him hard, every day Johnny pulled back, so he finished the session with a little more in the tank than he had the day before.

The whole time, Johnny never mentioned the problem. Instead, he encouraged Fenech, praised him for the precision of his punches, the power. Forget the fact he was throwing half as many punches as usual—if that. Focus on the positives.

Inside, Fenech knew. But so long as Johnny wasn't saying anything, he wasn't saying anything either.

After training one afternoon, Mitrevski said he wanted to go and watch Virgil Hill train in a gym on the other side of Vegas. Mitrevski had met Hill at the World Cup in Rome in 1983. 'He's a real good bloke,' he told Johnny.

Johnny suggested they put it off. The World Cup was eight years ago. A lot had happened since then. Hill was now the WBA light-heavyweight champion, had been for four years, and he was about to fight Tommy Hearns in a superfight. In truth, Johnny didn't want Mitrevski turning up to the gym to see his old friend and Hill not remembering him. He wanted to spare him the embarrassment.

Eventually he relented, though. Mitrevski was a persistent little bugger.

Hill greeted him just as he thought—like a long-lost friend. He invited them all to the fight, at Caesars Palace a few days later.

Johnny, Mitrevski and Fenech went along, and watched as Hearns took the title from Hill in a close but unanimous points decision.

The next day, a disappointed Hill found Mitrevski at the gym. He mentioned to Johnny that he wouldn't mind going to Australia to fight. He was thinking about relocating. Would Johnny train him?

By fight day, Johnny had brought Fenech a long way back. He still wasn't at his best, but Johnny was confident that Fenech would be able to keep up the pressure. 'We'll see if Azumah can cope with that pressure,' he said. 'We've got plenty of options open to us, but Jeff will certainly be testing out his body early in the fight.'

It was a big fight night. With Tyson headlining, it couldn't be otherwise. Ringside at the Mirage Casino were Bruce Willis and Demi Moore, Chuck Norris, Michael Jordan. Hearns added a touch of boxing royalty.

Though Tyson was the headliner, Don King told everybody that Fenech–Nelson would be the fight of the night. Showtime network commentators Ferdie Pacheco, Muhammad Ali's former doctor, and play-by-play commentator Steve Albert, repeated the spin. They admitted they did not know a lot about Fenech, but said they were looking forward to the fight. Few did know the Australian. The sign on the door of his dressing room at the Mirage said Jeff French.

From the start, Fenech surprised everyone. Pacheco described Nelson as having 'Howitzer hands' and was surprised that Fenech elected to stand directly in front of him and trade. 'Nelson cannot complain that he doesn't have a guy standing in front of him,' he said. 'I keep repeating, it's awesome to see a guy standing right in front of Azumah Nelson.'

Nelson bombed away in the first, engaging Fenech and landing the bigger shots.

'Azumah Nelson has a great many more tricks and techniques than does Fenech, who fights on courage and raw power,' Pacheco said.

Such was the power of Nelson's shots the commentators made the call early—the fight would not last the distance.

When the bell rang for the end of round one, Fenech bounced back to the corner. Johnny said nothing, just wiped Fenech down and got him ready for round two. After a long silence, he said, 'How do you feel, mate?'

'Good.'

'As you can see,' said Pacheco, 'precious little coaching in the corner of Fenech.'

Then Johnny went back to his old tricks. Before the warning call to signal the end of the break, he stood Fenech up and pushed him to the middle of the ring.

When Nelson looked up, Fenech was waiting.

When Nelson looked up for the third, he found Fenech waiting again.

It began to turn then. The third was fought almost entirely in one small corner, right above the commentators, and Fenech wobbled Nelson for the first time.

'What punishment each man took,' Pacheco said at the end of the third.

Fenech savaged Nelson in the third, fourth and fifth, and hurt him only slightly less in the sixth.

The snap went out of Nelson's punches. But it was there in the sixth round that Fenech lost the fight. Without that first day's run, and the toll it took, Fenech would have run right over Nelson in the next few rounds. Instead, he got to the top of the hill but didn't have it in him to push over it.

Instead, Nelson stayed in the fight.

Johnny knew Nelson was fading when he started swinging more wildly.

'Mate, this bloke is going to put everything in a big left hook this round, OK?'

Fenech listened.

Right before Johnny picked him up, Johnny said, 'Feeling good, mate.'

It was not a question.

Fenech seemed to dominate the rest of the fight.

'I think if they had him in Gallipoli they might have won down there,' Pacheco said in the ninth. He and Albert called Fenech ahead in the fight, going away.

'Fenech looks like one of those wind-up dolls,' said Pacheco.

In a bid to turn things, Nelson reached into his trick bag. At the end of the ninth he hit Fenech after the bell. Fenech erupted. Referee Joe Cortez jumped between them just as he moved to retaliate.

Johnny saw Nelson's foul as nothing but a positive, so long as Fenech stayed cool.

'You've got him, mate,' he said. 'Just go to work, mate, the next two. Don't let him bring you onto a big one in temper, OK?'

By the last, Pacheco had Fenech well ahead. He was surprised that the Australian continued to take the fight to Nelson instead of moving and protecting his lead.

'Somebody hasn't told him he's way ahead here. He's fighting as if he's behind.'

'All he has to do is stay away,' said Albert.

'This man knows only one thing. What courage, what determination and what force from Jeff Fenech.'

With twenty seconds left in the fight, Fenech nearly dropped Nelson with a big right hand. A second one wobbled him again.

As Johnny jumped into the ring and ran across to Fenech, celebrating at the bell, Pacheco reminded the viewers that Las Vegas was built on larceny.

'Certainly you have to think that if you did keep score the winner has to be Fenech,' he said. 'One never knows in Las Vegas, but even here you have to think it has to be a clear cut win for Fenech, who has covered himself with glory. It figured to be an exciting fight, and it was an exciting fight.'

Ring announcer Jimmy Lennon Jr grabbed the microphone and announced a split decision. Fenech shook his head. A sickness welled in his guts. He walked to the ropes and rested his arms on them, hanging his head as he listened to the judges' scores.

Johnny, still in their corner, started preparing himself.

Jerry Roth scored it 115–113 to Fenech. Miguel Donate, who should have worn a mask when he handed in his card, scored it 116–112 to Nelson.

When Lennon read that Dave Moretti scored it 114–114, making it a draw, Fenech threw his hands down. A howl came from somewhere inside. It turned out that Fenech had needed that final round to save the fight, after all.

Johnny grabbed him and put his hands on Fenech's cheeks, trying to calm him.

'Why?' Fenech said.

He pulled free and stalked across the ring in small rage. Don King walked across and slapped Fenech on the back: 'Return, man,' he said.

'Get fucked,' said Fenech.

'No way, he says,' said Albert, still calling from ringside.

WBC president Jose Sulaiman climbed into the ring, trying to console Fenech.

Pacheco was in the ring now, interviewing first Nelson and then

Fenech, whom Johnny was trying to calm in the corner. Fenech was crying.

King was already talking about a rematch: 'This is too good a fight. There's no loser.'

Pacheco asked Fenech if he wanted to fight Nelson again.

'I'll do it now. Put the gloves on, I'll do it now.'

'You thought you were ahead?' Pacheco said.

'I knew I was ahead.'

'In the last round you fought as though … You looked like you were desperate to win.'

'I'm desperate to throw punches,' Fenech said. 'All the time. That's my plan. I don't taper off, I don't slow down because I'm winning, I'm not like that. I want to win right to the end, and I thought I won that.'

King interrupted. Addressing Fenech, he said loudly, 'You were a Tasmanian devil, a thunder from Down Under, and you were coming for a war and a war you brought. Can't nobody question that. Twelve complete rounds of fighting.'

Fenech could hardly stand to look at him. When King had finished, Fenech turned back to Pacheco and said, 'I'll come back and fight him in two months. As long as I'm the main event here, I'll fight him. No problems.'

On the way home, Fenech said he would never fight under King again. He also believed that because the fight was a draw and he had not won, his four-fight contract with King was obsolete.

Johnny was reluctant to sound half-smart after the event; he'd always been uneasy about fighting in the United States under King. To the reporters waiting at Sydney Airport he admitted he had been 'cushioned' for a result like this. 'Why the hell we wanted to go over there in the first place has got me stumped.' Turning to Ray Connelly, he said, 'We knew it'd happen, didn't we?'

Connelly nodded.

'People kept saying he had to fight in America, and we kept asking, Why?' Johnny said.

Fenech, drained, could not do much more than shrug.

'For seven weeks Johnny Lewis emphasised to me we had to win clearly. He was scared about what might happen over there,' he said.

CHAPTER 20

SOMETHING BROKE inside Jeff Fenech that day in Las Vegas.

Oh, he came back. He beat Miguel Francia comfortably over ten rounds at the International Tennis Centre in Melbourne in September, and then he started focusing on the rematch with Azumah Nelson, about to become the biggest fight in Australian history. He came back from the fight, but he didn't come back whole.

At first it looked OK. Fenech said all the right stuff about fighting the rematch and really doing a job on Nelson this time, and everyone nodded and stole glances at each other. This guy was serious.

But Johnny noticed something altogether different. Fenech now started arriving at the gym late. He left early. He still did his work, and perhaps that's what made it so difficult to pin down, but he wasn't the same. Johnny noticed the difference but tried to focus on what was there, not what was missing.

Perhaps Fenech was just maturing. He was 27 now, maybe he was just listening to his body more. Johnny eased his concerns with that.

Fenech noticed a small difference, too. But he would not admit it until years later. Sparring one day for the Francia fight, he had walked into a shot and thought, 'Geez, that hurt.'

He had never thought that in sparring before.

He had never been hurt in sparring. Now it was happening more days than not.

EIGHT weeks after Fenech beat Francia, Virgil Hill spoke to Bill Mordey on the phone. He was relocating to Australia. He wanted to train with Johnny.

Everybody knew at once what that meant. Harding had gone to England and, two days before Fenech's Francia fight, reclaimed the WBC light-heavyweight title with a majority decision over Dennis Andries. Two judges had scored it his way, one even. (Guy Waters had since moved on to trainer Bruce Kennedy.)

The prospect of Hill fighting Harding interested many. That Mordey now promoted both fighters made it almost a certainty.

FOUR days later Bill Mordey phoned Johnny. 'Come on, mate. Let's go and take a look at this bloke you've been talking about.'

The 1991 World Amateur Boxing Championships were at the State Sports Centre at Homebush, in western Sydney. Over four fights, Konstantin Tszyu put together one of the more dominant displays at the championships. He stopped Mexican Albertano Caballero in the third round of his first fight, beat Puerto Rican Anibal Acevedo 29–10 in the second, and Nigerian James Moses went down 25–4 in the semi-finals. Of his 269 amateur fights Tszyu had lost only eleven. In the final he took on American Vernon Forrest, the gold-medal favourite, and won 32–9.

Mordey was smitten. He could not believe Tszyu's eye. 'He could have stood on a handkerchief all night and that other kid still wouldn't have been able to hit him,' he said to Michael Dann.

His style was unusual for a successful amateur. Close to a professional style, as Johnny saw. At this his coach, Vladimir Chernia, issued one of the great quotes: 'His style is a gift from God. We dare not change him.'

Mordey was not quite so poetic. 'He's something special, this kid.'

'I told you,' said Johnny. 'I'll organise a meet.'

They moved covertly, this time. At the first meeting with Tszyu and his trainer, Mordey said, 'I'd like you to come to my place. When are you flying out?'

'Two days.'

'Meeting tomorrow,' Mordey said, in pidgin English, so Tszyu's interpreter could not get it wrong.

Mordey wrote down his address in South Coogee.

'I have someone pick you up.'

'Only if I bring my trainer,' Tszyu said through his interpreter.

It was agreed.

When Tszyu had left, Mordey turned to Johnny and Michael Dann. 'Righto. Let's get the best vodka, the best coffees, prawns, the best oysters.'

And they went into action.

Mordey rang a bunch of friends, and invited them to dinner the following night. When Tszyu arrived with his trainer, the drinking began. '*Salut*!' and they would down another vodka. Tszyu alone drank water. At some point, after they had all had a thousand drinks, Tszyu's interpreter got around to why they were there.

'I would like you to come back to Australia and fight professional,' Mordey said.

'I speak to my father and my mother,' Tszyu said. 'And I have a girlfriend.'

It wasn't much harder than that. The dinner went beyond evening and into the early hours. Ring announcer Ray Connelly was asked how he might introduce Tszyu at his first pro fight.

'From the Ural Mountains in Siberia, Russia,' Connelly began, standing up at the table. 'Wearing white trunks with red bands and piping. Gold medallist at the Goodwill Games in the United States. Twice European champion. Climaxing a magnificent amateur career with a gold medal in the World Championships. In ten years of boxing he has won 259 out of 270 contests. About to be baptised in the professional sphere. Destiny's protégé of celestial grandeur. Fistic treasure—Konstantin Tszyu!'

So it went until Tszyu, with four hours until his flight home to Russia, had to leave.

Mordey walked him and his trainer and the interpreter to the door.

'You ring me,' Mordey said, and he put out his hand to shake. He slipped five thousand dollars into Tszyu's palm.

When the door shut, Dann was waiting.

'What did you do that for?'

'It's a bet,' Mordey said.

'You might never see him again.'

'I back plenty of losers,' Mordey said. 'It's just a bet. If I don't see him again, so what? It might make him think about coming back.'

A couple of days later Mordey's phone rang. A wonderful sound when you are hoping for good news.

'I'm going to come back if I can bring my trainer,' Tszyu said from Russia.

'Good as gold,' said Mordey.

Several days later, Mordey got another call.

'I am coming back with my girlfriend,' Tszyu said.

'What happened to the trainer?' asked Mordey.

'No, he is not coming.'

'Don't worry, we have a good trainer here, Johnny Lewis.'

Mordey announced Tszyu's signing a week after the championships.

The move shocked everybody, not least Russian boxing officials. The Soviet Union was in its death throes, but Russian officials had expected Tszyu to continue fighting amateur at least until the following year's Olympic Games in Barcelona.

Now he had won the amateur world championship Tszyu had no desire for Olympic glory.

'I have been offered more money to become a professional in Korea, but my aim is to be champion of the world,' he said through an interpreter. 'I believe I have a better chance of achieving that in Australia. To train with Jeff Fenech will be fantastic. I wouldn't have taken this step if I didn't think I could become world champion.'

Mordey promised he would debut on the Fenech–Nelson undercard along with Virgil Hill. He wanted to make Tszyu Russia's first professional world champion.

Apart from that the championships were a disappointment. Justin Rowsell, who Johnny trained at the Commonwealth Games a year earlier, was now training fulltime with him at Newtown, but faced disappointment when he was beaten, controversially, in the light-welterweight semi-finals. It meant a bronze medal, but Johnny truly believed he won the fight and should have been fighting for gold. Stefan Scriggins also won bronze in the welterweights. Three more progressed as far as the quarter-finals. Under Johnny's coaching, the Australians were finally making an impact in international competition.

Tszyu arrived in Australia with his girlfriend, Natasha Anikina, and was picked up and driven to the flash Quay West apartments overlooking Sydney Harbour. Mordey's mate Graham Goldberg was the general manager. He promised Mordey a room on the twenty-fifth floor provided he could generate publicity for the hotel. He might as well have asked a dog to scratch.

The next day, while cameramen and reporters from Channel Ten and Channel Seven were setting up to interview Tszyu, Dann took the couple to the fish markets to stock up on food. Tszyu couldn't believe it.

Before leaving Russia he had lined up to buy bread.

'You know,' Mordey said to Dann later, in the *Big League* office, 'I've never had a contract on anyone. But I'm going to get a contract on this bloke.'

Mordey rang his solicitor, Dann found a translator, and a contract was drawn up between Tszyu and Mordey's Classic Promotions.

Mordey insisted on six fights in the first twelve months. Fine, Tszyu said. They went through the rest of the contract, and Tszyu said it was all OK.

'But he wants three things,' the interpreter said.

This came as a surprise.

'What's he want?'

'First, he wants health insurance for him and Natasha.'

'Not a problem. HCF, we'll get that,' Mordey said.

'Next, he wants a microwave oven.'

'Not a problem, we'll add that in. What's number three?'

'That he never be asked not to win a fight.'

Mordey loved it. Mature, practical, honest. Everything Tszyu was doing impressed him. Before the meeting was over, Mordey told Tszyu he should learn to speak English. It would help sell him to the Australian public. Of course Tszyu agreed. Appeal means money. So the next day Brian Mills picked up Tszyu and Natasha and drove them to English lessons at Bondi Junction. He took them every day for months. Tszyu also wanted a dog and a bird.

Natasha began to call Mills, a gently spoken man with short hair growing white by the day, 'Papa'.

They got him the dog and the bird.

CHAPTER 21

Bill Mordey was putting together the biggest promotion in Australia.

Fenech–Nelson II was the biggest fight since Jack Johnson had rattled loose the heavyweight belt from Tommy Burns at Rushcutters Bay in 1908. A big fight needed a promotion to match. Mordey knew it. What he didn't know was how he was going to maximise his turnover.

It was a problem solved at *Big League* headquarters, in the hours shortly before they headed to the pub for lunch.

'Michael,' he said to Dann, 'You know how we're going to make money out of this? We're going to show this fight live,' he said.

This was in the days before cable TV.

'How are you going to show it live?'

'Get a satellite.'

'A satellite?'

'I'm telling you, they do it in America. I'm going to hire a satellite and put it in the sky here and we'll beam the fight to venues around Australia. We'll make a fortune.'

'How are you going to do that?'

'Never mind, it can be done. It's going to be done, and you've got a job. All you've got to do is get off your arse and sell the sites.'

Mordey had tried satellite broadcasting in 1988, when he bought the rights to the Mike Tyson–Michael Spinks fight under the banner of his company King Vision. Halfway through the fight, the signal dropped out. This was going to be different. They renamed the company Fight Vision.

Dann went to what he knew. He called Johnny Holloway again and got a copy of the AJC racing calendar. As he looked at the listings, he realised he was looking at the answer. Racecourses and registered clubs.

It was an idea of genius. Few venues in Australia that would hold the audiences they expected were equipped to televise this fight. Race clubs were. Dann sold race clubs around the country on the idea of buying the rights to screen the fight on the big screens in their betting rings. It would be on a Sunday afternoon, so it could also be televised into the United States in Saturday night prime time. Sunday was one of the few days when there were no race meetings, so the fight would be a source of extra revenue for the clubs. As well as ten per cent of the gate, they would get the full bar and concession-stand takings. So he and Mordey's son Craig 'The Clone' sold the fight to 126 venues around Australia. Each would charge fans twenty dollars to walk on track and watch the fight. Scribbling down the figures, they estimated twenty million would come in.

This opened a new concern. How to make sure the money made it back to them and wasn't diverted into the pockets of the clubs. After all, they were dealing with experts.

'There's only one way. You can't trust family. Family rob one another,' Dann said. 'But you can trust the Lions Clubs and Rotary.'

'What are you talking about?' said Mordey.

'We'll bring the Lions Clubs and Rotary in and we'll give them five per cent to collect it. Five per cent of twenty mill is a million dollars. We won't tell anyone that, but we'll get Terry Smith to write in the *Tele* that

Fenech is going to donate a million dollars out of his purse to the Lions Clubs and Rotary.'

Mordey looked at him as if he'd just promised to flap his arms and fly to the moon.

'*You* might be a millionaire,' he said. 'You give them a million of your dollars, not mine.'

But Dann insisted it was a good idea. Two months earlier, Fenech had appeared in court charged with interfering with a witness to an alleged assault. The charity donation would be good public relations for him.

Three days later, Mordey called Dann into his office and pulled out a letter from Brambles Security. The company proposed to put three guards at each venue, at eighty dollars an hour each. After it was over, the guards would take the money back to the Brambles offices, count it, and within forty-eight hours Mordey would have a cheque.

'Now, eighty dollars an hour for five hours, that's four hundred each person. That's about a thousand dollars a place, across a hundred or so venues. That's one hundred thousand dollars. And you're talking a million.'

'But you're not going to get the publicity that way. And people aren't going to think Fenech is not the arsehole they think he is.'

'But my way, we're going to be nine hundred thousand better off. See you later.'

From the start they ran into small problems. One of Mordey's cheques bounced, a small cheque for four thousand dollars.

'Leave it with me,' said Dann. He got back to Mordey shortly after: 'It's going to cost you four airfares.'

Dann arranged to fly Mordey's bank manager, plus three, to Melbourne and give them prime seats for the fight.

In Melbourne, Johnny was having different problems. Fenech's training was still off-key, but he had Kostya Tszyu in the gym right on the mark for his professional debut and Virgil Hill ready to go. Fenech still couldn't finish training each day fast enough.

And he was chasing women at a furious pace.

One day, Fenech spoke to Johnny about his sparring partners. He spoke quietly. He didn't want anyone else to hear.

He thought they were sparring a little more heavily than sparring partners should. A five-bell alarm rang inside Johnny's head.

The Jeff Fenech he knew wouldn't have noticed such a thing. He would have walked through anyone who got a bit heavy, and squared up just so they'd remember who was paying who.

That night, Johnny rang Mordey.

'I don't think we should go ahead with this,' he said. 'This bloke's not giving me what he used to. I think we should call it off.'

'I'll come down a bit earlier. I'll be down there in a few days,' Mordey said.

Johnny said nothing to Fenech. He didn't want him to know he was concerned. You don't plant doubt in your fighter. It was Johnny's job to figure out what to do and how to do it.

Johnny thought about it. And again he decided he believed in Fenech.

Three years earlier, he had dominated Marcos Villasana, winning ten of their twelve rounds. At the time there was hardly a struck match between Villasana and Azumah Nelson. And he and Fenech still thought they had excuses from the Las Vegas fight, even if they had never come out and explained them. Now, fighting at home, Johnny figured Fenech didn't need to be one hundred per cent to win. Less than that would mean a tougher fight, but he would still win.

A few days before the fight, they walked the venue, Princes Park.

With the ring in the centre, it could hold 40,000 people.

Johnny looked at the ring and up at the sky and back at the ring again.

'Which one's Nelson's corner?' he said.

They pointed to the red corner.

'Where's the sun going to be when we get into the ring?'

'Over there.'

This wasn't good enough.

'I want Nelson looking into the sun,' Johnny said.

They pulled the ring down and rebuilt it. This time, the red corner faced the afternoon sun.

Johnny's first fight was the second of the day. Virgil Hill walked into the ring an hour before midday—an early start timed for Showtime's American audience. Johnny had found Hill a treat to train, and a real good bloke, too. He easily beat American Aundrey Nelson, taking all ten rounds on each of the judges' scorecards. Johnny raced back to the dressing room after the decision.

Tszyu was coming out next. He was fighting former Australian Olympian Darrell Hiles, a lightweight that had given Australia's Olympic silver medallist, Spike Cheney, a tough fight almost a year earlier. As an amateur, Hiles had also put up a tough fight at the 1989 world titles against Andreas Zülow, the East German who went on to beat Tszyu.

While Tszyu had had an exceptional amateur career, Johnny knew better than most the difference between the amateurs and pros. Given this, he wanted Tszyu to start early and establish his dominance, get some respect from Hiles to stop him getting braver.

Speaking to Tszyu's interpreter, he said, 'Make sure we win the first round.'

Tszyu listened and nodded.

He knocked out Hiles in seventy seconds.

Tszyu climbed out of the ring and started towards the dressing room. From one of the golden ringside seats, a man stepped out, a tall man with a deep voice.

'*Molodets*,' he said. It was a Russian expression, kind of like, 'You beauty.'

Tszyu stopped, startled.

They spoke briefly and the man introduced himself.

'Vlad Warton,' he said. They arranged to meet later for dinner.

Warton said he'd introduce Tszyu to Sydney's Russian community.

When they got back to the dressing room, with one fight to go before Fenech hit the ring, Tszyu spoke to his interpreter, who turned to Johnny.

'Kostya say, Why did he have to win *in* the first round?'

Mordey said three hallelujahs when he heard that.

It was less successful around the country. While all was well inside Princes Park, the race clubs were going into meltdown. Operating out of the control centre, a caravan at Princes Park, Dann nearly lost his voice on the phone trying to solve small emergencies. A woman called from Orange, in country New South Wales. Nobody had turned up, she said. At Canterbury racetrack, in Sydney, they pulled down the fence so they didn't have to pay the twenty dollars.

Other clubs were calling with similar problems. Few of them were manned. Nobody was paying. While clubs were getting ten per cent of the entry fee, they soon realised that ten per cent of nothing was nothing. Money was flying out of Mordey's pocket, and Fenech's, too. Fenech, via publishing billionaire Kerry Packer's financial advisor, Theo Onisforou, had become a silent partner in the whole promotion.

On top of that it rained. The rain kept the crowd in Melbourne to about 37,000, four to five thousand less than a sell-out. Finally, the clouded wet skies meant that when Azumah Nelson took his stool in the ring there'd be no sunlight shining into his eyes. He wouldn't even squint.

For the first time, Johnny was in a Jeff Fenech dressing room without feeling total confidence. They warmed up on pads, Fenech walking around, thumping his gloves together, lightly shadow-boxing.

Motivation is a funny thing. For years, Fenech had been the most motivated athlete Johnny knew. Now, well …

But Johnny knew there was nothing more he could do now. If an athlete is not motivated minutes before he has to perform, it's out of the coach's hands. Fenech was gearing himself for the fight but Johnny wondered if, inside somewhere, Fenech was asking himself if he'd really done the work.

The knock at the door came. It was time.

For a while, it seemed like old times. Fenech went to the ring with his hands perched on Johnny's shoulders and the crowd cheering 'Fen-ech, Fen-ech'. A crackle went through the crowd. Kerry Packer was there, moved back to the third row to clear a seat for Mordey's bank manager. Mordey sat perched in the rain about twenty rows back, next to Dann and his son Craig 'The Clone'.

Fenech walked up the steps and climbed through the ropes and bounced around, acknowledging the crowd. But he didn't bless himself. Johnny tensed up. Every time Fenech had ever fought, right back through the amateurs, Johnny had watched him get in the ring and walk to the neutral corner and bless himself. Here was the most focused athlete Johnny had ever seen forgetting his lifelong ritual.

What was going on?

As they waited for Nelson, Fenech walked around and stood next to Johnny.

'Look at that over there,' he said.

At the back of the park, across 10,000 heads, some blokes had written F-E-N-E-C-H-R-U-L-E-S across their bare chests. Fenech had never noticed anything like that in thirty-seven fights.

At ringside, Pacheco was back with the Showtime team, talking about Hall of Fame qualifications. It was simple, as far as he was concerned.

'If he knocks out Fenech,' he said of Nelson, 'he gets in. If Fenech knocks him out and wins his fourth title, he gets in.'

Nelson dropped Fenech with a short right hand in the first round.

It stunned the country. After Fenech's robbery in Vegas, everyone had considered a win for him in Melbourne a formality.

'Ah, shit,' Johnny said.

Fenech rose, still cloudy. He fell again in the second from what appeared to be a slip but which referee Arthur Mercante ruled a knockdown. After two rounds, he was behind two 10–8 rounds.

Johnny went to work on him in the corner. He wiped him down, smeared Vaseline around his face, freshened him up.

'Are you all right, son?'

Fenech nodded.

Somehow, he clawed back from the two knockdowns and began taking rounds. Johnny started to relax. Enough rounds were left that they might be able to steal this on points.

That would be beautiful. Then Jeff could retire and it would be over.

And then it changed forever. Nelson landed a couple of nice shots towards the end of the sixth and Fenech was gone, probably saved by the bell from being knocked out.

It was back to battle stations in the corner.

At the bell after the seventh, Johnny realised he needed to get Fenech back into the fight. He stepped up the urgency in the corner, speaking briefly and directly.

'He wants a big hook at you, mate, or a big right hand. Jab. When you get him in close, punch the shit out of him, mate.'

Then a funny thing happened.

Fenech tilted his head and raised his eyebrows as if … he wasn't convinced.

In that small gesture, he revealed that he not only knew he was losing, he was probably struggling to stay in the fight.

Still he walked towards Nelson with his guard high and did what his trainer wanted. He backed Nelson into the red corner and started working him, exactly like he had in their first fight. But this time he was chest deep in Nelson's trap.

As Fenech ripped Nelson's body, the entire right side of his face was exposed. The moment his head lifted, Nelson swung the wild left hook Johnny had said he wanted. It landed flush, and Fenech wobbled. Another two full-blooded left hooks landed before a right hand crumpled Fenech. He fell to the canvas with Nelson still punching. Then he rolled onto his hands and knees and picked himself up.

Johnny jumped up the stairs and stood on the ring apron, ready to throw in the towel. How badly was Fenech hurt? He couldn't see because Mercante was in the way. He was still trying to get a good look when Mercante waved Nelson in. Fenech's guard again went high. Two more solid blows and he sagged into Mercante's chest. The referee didn't see the towel fluttering into the ring behind him.

Peter Mitrevski, working the corner with Bobby Lanigan and now also up on the apron, was in tears. By the time Mercante got control of Fenech, Johnny was already halfway across the ring to wrap his arms around him. To keep him safe.

To some extent Fenech had fought his way back. Despite the two knockdowns, two judges had it level 66–66 at the end, while the third had Nelson ahead 68–65. That didn't matter now. Nelson had won.

The crowd was stunned.

Fenech was humble and gracious and even a little apologetic in defeat. As he stepped out of the ring, the crowd rose to its feet. Here was a fighter. They cheered once more. 'Fen-ech, Fen-ech …'

Johnny walked with him, upset for Jeff and upset at himself.

He should have stopped it earlier, he thought, two or three punches earlier, and spared Fenech that last bit of punishment. He consoled himself with the fact that Fenech recovered quickly in the dressing room. The extra punches didn't seem to have done him lasting damage. Still, he thought, when they got home he would send Fenech off for a precautionary brain scan.

The silence in the dressing room was broken only by Fenech's sobs.

He felt he'd let everyone down.

When the press were finally admitted, Fenech told them there were no excuses. 'I feel champions have to accept defeat as well as winning and hopefully I've accepted it right tonight,' he said.

What about his reported breathing problems?

'No excuses, no excuses. I've done my best. I met a better fighter on the night. He's to be congratulated. He's a great fighter. Hopefully I can prepare better if it happens again. I'm proud, I definitely want to be champion again. I think I didn't do the right thing early. I had my head up, I got hit … Anyway, that's life.'

Fenech's private pain was that he knew he had not prepared as well as he could have. Johnny knew it, too.

Days later, in Sydney, the attendance figures at all the TV venues were coming in to the *Big League* office. Dann looked at them, then phoned a friend who had watched the fight at the local racetrack.

'How was the fight?'

'Mate, it was terrific,' he said. 'Except you couldn't get a beer at the bar. I reckon there must have been three thousand people there, but gee it was terrific …'

Dann looked at the figures he'd received for that venue.

A statement for four hundred and twenty-five people, with a cheque for $8500. The payment was about fifty thousand short, and that was at just one track. He and Mordey knew what this meant.

After a fight, Harding would be in the *Big League* office the next day without fail, looking for his cheque. Mordey would send Johnny's cheque to his accountant. Fenech would normally wander in a week or ten days later, whenever he happened to be in that part of the city and had finished celebrating. He wasn't celebrating now—and he would be even less happy when he saw his cheque.

'You fucking robbed me,' he said when he got it. They tried to tell him they'd been robbed themselves.

The twenty-million dollar fight had brought in nowhere near that. But Fenech was in no mood to listen.

'A lot of the venues weren't manned,' Mordey said, his voice sounding hollow.

Fenech was paid well, enough to put him on the road to a comfortable retirement. But it wasn't anything like he'd been promised. He had to accept it.

Afterwards Fenech went over to Newtown to see Johnny.

'I think you should retire,' Johnny said. 'I think it's time.'

Something had been missing since the draw in Las Vegas. In truth, he wished Fenech had stayed retired after Villasana, but now here they were.

Fenech admitted he'd made mistakes but said he wanted to continue. He thought he could beat Nelson if they fought again.

OK, Johnny said finally. He agreed for one reason.

Fenech didn't deserve a sad ending.

CHAPTER 22

MORDEY ALWAYS had one standing request for Brian Mills when they travelled for a fight: Nice and early the next day, take Johnny to the airport. By the time a fight was over, he couldn't get home quick enough.

He missed his family too much.

And he missed the gym. Getting back there rejuvenated him. Jeff Fenech might have lost, but back at Newtown some young kid would be getting ready for his amateur bout, and another one would have his eye on the state titles. Other pros would be training away. To all of them, their next fight was every bit as important as the one Fenech had just lost.

He needed the gym more than ever now. Fenech's loss was a tremendous shock. They questioned themselves for weeks about the reasons. They came up with this, mostly: the signs were there and they had ignored them.

Slowly they began to move on.

Johnny went to the footy to watch Newtown play. The Jets were back in senior footy, no longer in top-level competition but surviving in the second division, and Johnny still liked to watch them play. How could you ever fall out of love with the royal blue jumpers? By now he had been going to the footy nearly fifty years. In all that time, he said, he'd never seen a better football jumper when thirteen of them were on the field at once.

Up came Frank Farrington, the old club secretary. Just like old times.

'How y'going, Frank?'

'Do you know anything about Pauly?'

'No.'

'I heard he passed away.'

Johnny felt a hole explode inside. A sickness poured into it.

He got home to find his answering machine choked with messages saying Paul Hayward had died.

Paul was the most decent man Johnny ever knew. When he got arrested his baby daughter Kelly stopped talking. For months she didn't speak at all, until the day her mother took her to the dentist and, for some reason, the dentist pulled out a photo of her father.

'Daddy,' she said.

The sadness of that.

Paul's price was that by the time he returned home she had trouble understanding that this new man in their house was her father. There was never an easy day for Paul once he returned.

Johnny sat at home alone, thinking about Paul. He thought of Paul's son Bradley, his godson. He thought of the waste of a life that should have been filled with love and joy, and he began to cry. For all of them.

Hayward had died of a heroin overdose. He was thirty-nine. His habit had started in jail, an antidote to the suffering there. The speculation suggested it was suicide. Some said it was a simple mistake.

Johnny didn't focus on the manner of Hayward's death. He focused on the Paul he knew.

In all the letters he received while Paul was in jail, he said, 'I never once sensed weakness in him.' When he speaks of Hayward, he speaks softly, because a tear is only ever a sentence away.

MONTHS after Fenech's defeat and Hayward's death, Justin Rowsell was training in the gym. The 1992 Olympics were over, and Justin had moved to Sydney to turn pro under Johnny. Justin had established himself as one of Australia's best amateurs, not just now, but always. He won a bronze medal at the 1991 World Championships. A Commonwealth Games silver medal. Gold and silver at the Canada Cup. He had beaten some of the best amateurs in the world. Johnny was convinced he was a future world champion as a pro.

'Do you want to come and do some pad work with a couple of blokes?' Johnny asked. He was heading to Long Bay jail to visit the inmates.

Justin had moved from the small country town of Casino. Along with Tszyu and another good amateur, Eddy Younan, the Newtown stable was being replenished after Fenech's loss and Harding's walkout.

A couple of days before they went, Rowsell came to Johnny. Why did he need to go into a prison? he asked. Some of his mates didn't think it was a good idea. Johnny was a little disappointed he'd listened to them.

'I don't know who told you, mate, but you've got to make your own mind up on that,' he said.

A day later, Justin said he would go.

It pleased Johnny. His early memories of Erskineville are filled with the images of many good men who went to jail. It didn't suddenly make them bad.

They'd first started visiting prisoners in the mid '80s, under the Young Offenders program Chicka Moore started. At first they sparred the inmates, as Fenech had done against Mark McElwaine at Parklea. When that program was stopped, they sparred exhibitions for the inmates to watch but that too was stopped. Now they were doing pad-work exhibitions for the prisoners.

Each time Johnny visited a prison, three or four times a year, he'd take a few *Big League* magazines to hand out and a video of Fenech's or Harding's lastest fight.

As they moved through the series of gates and steel doors this time, there was a shout. 'Hey, Rowsell! What are you doing in here?'

It was a mate of Justin's, an Aboriginal kid from Kempsey he once boxed with. A little further on, Justin ran into another kid he knew from his amateur boxing days. This prison wasn't as bad as he thought it would be. He was among old friends.

As their workout began, a young man came up and put his arm around Johnny.

Johnny had met Jason Loughnan inside and grown enormously fond of him. Loughnan was a former junior surfing champion, the kind who would head out into the big surf to ride the waves when they closed the beaches. His adrenaline addiction soon had him stealing Porsches and tearing past police so they would chase him. His first prison stretch was eighteen months for car theft. Then they put a pervert in his cell one night who tried to touch him up and that ended badly. A judge put a further thirteen years on his eighteen month sentence.

For years now, he and Johnny had been swapping letters, Loughnan writing how he wanted to get out and help Johnny train fighters and Johnny saying the moment he did there'd be a job for him.

'Just be a good boy,' Johnny said to him. 'Work on getting your parole.'

It was not a promise Johnny made a lot. The only other promise was made some years later, when Johnny was visiting prisoners at the John Moroney Correctional Centre, near Windsor. He noticed a fit, hard young bloke looking at him.

For a good while he said nothing.

'Hello, Johnny,' he said after a while. 'I'm a friend of Jason Loughnan's.'

That was good enough for Johnny. He introduced himself to Tony Hines, and after Hines was released Johnny got him a job as a handyman at Newtown.

They remained friends until Hines was murdered in 2003, shot in the back of the head and tossed off a cliff.

Still in 1992, Virgil Hill had his third fight under Johnny. In his home town of Bismarck, North Dakota, he won back the WBA light-heavyweight title in a unanimous decision against Frank Tate. He became Johnny's third world champion, and they returned to Australia thinking about ways to capitalise on the title. The partnership was short-lived, though. Hill was soon forced to return to the United States for personal reasons. That's the way it goes sometimes.

Johnny rolled with the punches. He went back to work signwriting for the council, the same job he'd had since he was fifteen. In thirty-three years, he had accumulated months of long-service leave. He'd been using that to attend the overseas fights and, now, tour with the Australian rugby league team. The Kangaroos were in the middle of a busy year that featured an Ashes series in Australia and then a World Cup final in England.

In June Johnny headed to Townsville, where the Aussies defeated Papua New Guinea 36–14. Several days later he was back at work.

'A bloke in the office is gunning to get rid of you,' one of his workmates said. 'He reckons you haven't got the joint at heart.'

Johnny walked to the office to front the bloke, who just happened to be showing another colleague a scrapbook of newspaper clippings about all Johnny's travels.

'Are you going to take a redundancy?' the bloke said. Apparently, the council was going to start offering them in a year or so.

'I'll certainly take a look at it,' Johnny said. He was doing nothing but call his bluff.

'D'you want to go now?'

'Yes, I do,' Johnny said.

'Sign here.'

Once he'd started, he couldn't back down. It had taken more than thirty years, but from that day forward Johnny was a full-time boxing trainer.

It was lucky Kostya Tszyu followed up so well on his first-round knockout of Darrell Hiles. Tszyu fulfilled his obligation of six fights in his first twelve months, and he did it in some manner. He knocked out Nedrick Simmons in one round, so savagely that many ringside wondered if he'd killed him. After the fight Mordey, his nostrils twitching at the smell of money, pushed towards the ring apron and yelled out to Michael Dann, who was standing near Tszyu.

'Tell him to announce he's fighting Juan La Porte next,' he said. He wanted Tszyu to capitalise on his momentum by announcing a top-line opponent. It'll be on all the networks, Mordey thought.

'No,' Tszyu said. 'I need a holiday.'

Mordey looked at Dann in disgust. 'Doesn't take them fucking long.'

Tszyu beat Tony Jones in two rounds next, then did ten hard ones against Juan La Porte, the Puerto Rican legend and former WBC featherweight champion, in Sydney. For just his fourth fight, it was a staggering effort.

Tszyu knocked out Daniel Cusato in seven and closed the year by finishing Sammy Fuentes in one round.

He was knocking them all out, and Australia was falling in love with the little Russian with the pigtail that speared from the back of his head. Two months later Tszyu knocked out Steve Larrimore in two rounds in Memphis, Tennessee.

It looked to be going so well. It looked like there might be some bounce back after the Fenech loss.

But soon Johnny would be questioning everything, and wondering if he'd finally had enough.

CHAPTER 23

Kostya Tszyu entranced Australia. He was exotic. He was devastating. He had Bill Mordey selling him. It was easy.

Mordey liked to talk about Kostya Tszyu's eyes. They were big, brown and innocent, he'd say. But when he entered the ring, they turned black like an assassin's. Bill wrote the story himself. To get an angle the reporter needed to do no more than keep accurate notes.

In the gym, Tszyu pulled out training techniques nobody in Australia had seen before. He wore a headband with a piece of elastic tied to it, a tennis ball attached to the other end. He would put the headband on after his bag work and start punching the tennis ball as it snapped back. That done, he would fold a towel, drop it on the ground and pop up into a headstand, slowly extending his arms so he was on a solid tripod, and stay there, upside down, for minutes at a time. Everyone in the gym stopped and looked. Some even tried it.

His English was poor, but he was learning quickly. Vlad Warton had begun managing him, getting him a car, introducing him to Sydney's

Russian community and finding him sponsors, stuff Mordey didn't feel was part of a promoter's job.

All the while Tszyu was dropping opponents with knockouts that were highlight reel stuff.

Early in 1993 Johnny was preparing Tszyu for a fight in Newcastle when a friend approached and asked if he was interested in taking over Harding's training again. Johnny thought only briefly before saying no. He couldn't bring himself to do it. The bloke said Harding needed him. He was having trouble finding fights.

No, Johnny said. 'It'd be like getting back with one of your old sheilas.'

He concentrated on Tszyu's fight. But first Eddy Younan, who'd won the Australian featherweight title in 1991, had a fight at Newtown RSL Club against Indonesian Teofilo Tunacao. It was tough.

In the fifth, Younan's eye was cut after an accidental head clash. The doctor ruled the fight over.

Under the New South Wales Boxing Authority's rules, any fight stopped under doctor's orders after three rounds went to the scorecards. As the ring announcer collected the scores and they were tallied, Johnny sat Younan down in his corner to clean his eye, pushing adrenaline-soaked cotton buds into the cut to stop the bleeding.

Younan won the decision, but the Indonesians in the crowd didn't agree. A chair sailed across the hall in a small, aggressive arc, and the auditorium went *whump!* It was as if a match had been dropped in a kerosene tin. Chairs began sailing through the air. Everywhere men were fighting.

Bob Lanigan and Peter Mitrevski leapt the stairs and went through the ropes into the ring. It wasn't a whole lot safer there. Tunacao's people were in the ring and about as angry as those scuffling and tossing chairs outside it. They came aggressively towards Younan's corner.

Afraid Johnny was in trouble, Fenech jumped through the ropes to push himself in between Johnny and Tunacao's men. As Fenech got between them one of Tunacao's men pulled a gun, a small black piece that from the dangerous end looked as big as a cannon. Fenech hit the brakes.

There was no security. Only one other man saw the gun pulled on Fenech—Loopy Hammond. Johnny's old mate and protector was already heading in to help out when he saw it. He climbed through the ropes and went straight past Fenech to the gunman and needed to throw only one.

They'd won the fight, and the fight after it, too.

THIRTEEN days later, they weren't so lucky. Calvin Grove knocked out Fenech.

It shocked everybody. Fenech got hit with a clean right hand, his lip splitting with such velocity blood spurted down his chest.

It was over.

The Grove fight was supposed to be the beginning of Fenech's return, but it revealed that everything they'd feared was true. Fenech was still not right. The drive, the intensity, no longer there. And something had gone from the chin as well.

After the fight he announced his retirement. This time for real.

After resting for several weeks, Fenech returned to the gym, not as a fighter but to help Johnny train the boys. He took them through pad work himself, offering advice when it was needed and sometimes when it wasn't.

Johnny kept his distance. Maybe now, looking back, it was a mistake. He feared that once the bruises healed and the hands felt better, Fenech would convince himself he was right and want to make another comeback. He didn't want to see that, and he knew no amount of argument would make Fenech change his mind. So he tried to discourage Fenech from coming to the gym. He kept him at arm's length.

Soon enough, Fenech sensed the change in Johnny's attitude. He began coming less. Soon he stopped coming at all. Not long after that, he and Johnny just stopped talking.

As Fenech drifted away, Tszyu beat Livingstone Bramble over ten rounds in August, lifting him to No. 3 in the IBF rankings and No. 4 in the WBC rankings. A few days later he returned to Russia to marry Natasha. Vlad Warton house-sat for him, looking after his dog and his bird.

Mordey wanted to keep Tszyu busy. He rang Warton to say he had a fight booked in November.

Warton phoned Tszyu in Russia. No way was he returning now, Tszyu said. He had just got married. Two months became three. Mordey started getting itchy. Warton rang Tszyu again and said he had to be back by December. Tszyu held out, but told Warton that if Mordey was going to make him a fight, make it for the New Year.

Warton rang Johnny to tell him. Good, Johnny said. Tszyu needed to get back in the ring.

The fight was with Hector Lopez, a Mexican who could stay like Phar Lap, and was going to be a step-up fight for Tszyu.

By now, Mordey had fallen out with the American matchmaker Don Majeski. It happened after Jeff Harding, frustrated by inactivity, made his own fight in France. The fight was canned, but Majeski got his share. Mordey got stiffed, and blamed Majeski for not collecting his money for him. Their deal, and friendship, was over.

Harding was having his own problems. He did not fight at all in 1993—in fact, in the twenty-seven months after he won the title back from Andries he had only two fights. Too often he would make a match with an opponent, start to train, then have the opponent withdraw for any number of reasons from illness to injury.

Harding's long inactivity prompted Don King to petition the WBC to strip him of his title. Harding's manager Paul Hotz argued, justifiably, that the inactivity was not Harding's fault. Some in the Harding camp muttered that the repeated withdrawals by opponents might be part of a strategy to strip Harding of the title. With no outstanding light-heavyweight around and Harding fighting out of a boxing backwater, maybe that was the only way the American promoters could slip the title loose from him. They needed the title in play, of course, to make money.

The split with Majeski meant Mordey matched Tszyu with Lopez himself, which was no great problem. Lopez had won his previous fight for the North American Boxing Federation light welterweight title against David Santos but was later disqualified after tests revealed marijuana in his system. He had lost to Miguel Angel Gonzales before that and drawn with Guillermo Cruz the fight before. To both Mordey and Johnny, this showed he was vulnerable, a perfect route for Tszyu to take to genuinely world-class opposition.

Tszyu was being brought along nicely. With so many early knock-outs on his record, Johnny and Mordey were now giving him a fighter with a good chin and who could mix it up but lacked the big punch to seriously worry him. It was a fresh style to look at while taking Tszyu safely into deeper water.

They fought in Tampa, Florida. Aside from his debut on the Fenech–Nelson undercard, it marked Tszyu's return to American television. Justin Rowsell, also on the undercard, took a split decision against Patrick Simeon.

Johnny worked Tszyu's corner calmly. Round after round, he put gentle advice in Tszyu's ear. But as the fight progressed, he became concerned. Lopez still seemed to have a lot left. More, he had marked Tszyu's face considerably, and while Johnny believed Tszyu was winning, they were also back in America. By the start of the ninth, Tszyu's face was swollen and tired. Johnny realised a mischievous judge might score this Lopez's way.

Two such judges would be a disaster.

Fearing an upset, he urged Tszyu to finish the fight. Tszyu rallied and gave him what he could in the ninth. As he sat down before the tenth and last round, Johnny's thoughts went back to his childhood, sitting on the scoreboard at Erskineville Oval and running onto the local football field at half-time and three-quarter time to listen to the coaches revving up their players for one final effort. He loved those speeches. Guts and determination were the themes, and he remembered the impact they had on games.

'One round,' he said to Tszyu. 'You've got to win this round, son.' His voice was high, animated.

'Give us some water … Spit this out, son, spit it out.' He kept working as he spoke. 'Kostya, we must work under and bring the upper-cut. You feeling good? You feeling like a champion? You've got to win this round. You're a champion, understand? That's what you are, you're a champion … Come on, Kostya. The round of a champion, that's what I'm asking from you … Kostya, we must win this round, mate, you've got him out on his feet … Big right upper-cut in close, jab him hard. We must win this round.'

Tszyu went out and gave it everything he had. He took the fight on all three cards, but he was so spent that when they announced the decision he had very little left for celebrating.

Vlad Warton practically carried him from the ring.

Next morning, about 5 a.m., Johnny checked out of the hotel and stood waiting for his taxi to the airport. In the driveway, Hector Lopez was kissing a pretty little air hostess goodbye. He turned and saw Johnny watching him. Johnny said nothing as he watched. Lopez clearly hadn't recognised him. But as Johnny looked at Lopez laughing along with this woman he was aware his own fighter was upstairs, unable to get out of bed. Mordey had extended his stay so Tszyu could stay in bed for a couple of extra days and recover.

'Your boy got lucky last night,' Lopez said.

'Yeah,' Johnny said. 'Very lucky.'

Yeah, right, he thought.

All the way home, though, Johnny went over the fight, and what it took out of Tszyu. He'd lifted when he needed to. He gave Johnny the last two rounds when he called for it. But the toll was heavy. Fenech or Harding would have come through much better, he knew. He thought about Tszyu's amateur career, which spanned 270 fights, and his short explosive knockouts so far as a pro. Seven of his eleven wins hadn't gone beyond the second round.

We're going to have to be careful, he decided. He was unsure whether Tszyu was a stayer, a true twelve-round fighter. He suspected not.

Back in the hotel, Tszyu believed he had his excuses for the fight. He returned from Russia married, fat and happy, but unable to spar until far too late because he had teeth missing from dental work. His first spar was on Boxing Day, just sixteen days before the fight. He also felt Mordey had pushed him into the fight, and he wasn't happy about it.

Tszyu didn't think he was earning enough, either. Nor did Warton, who spoke to Mordey about getting Tszyu a better deal. Mordey explained that Tszyu's deal worked the same way as those of Fenech and Harding and whoever else he promoted.

It is here where the first piece of string in their relationship had come loose.

Small issues started becoming big ones. When Tszyu wanted to buy a new house, Mordey told him to be cautious. 'What happens if he gets hurt?' he said to Warton, who replied that he hoped they would all pitch in to help.

Mordey, for his part, was frustrated by the increasingly lengthy breaks Tszyu was taking between fights. He wanted Tszyu to snowball the momentum his knockouts generated. But the first thing Tszyu looked for after a fight was a good rest.

Johnny stayed out of all of it. None of his business, he thought. Tszyu still did not speak great English, but they communicated just fine. Each day in the gym they would smile and go to work. What else did they need to do? It was wonderfully simple.

Soon after he got back from Florida, Johnny was there in the gym one afternoon when Frank Keane walked in to ask a favour. Jeff Harding was training with Jimmy Withers now, Keane said, but he wondered if he could come to Newtown to spar.

'Of course,' Johnny said.

'There won't be any problems?'

'Not at all.'

Harding had finally got a fight, against American Mike McCallum. It was a dangerous fight. McCallum was just as tough and brutal as Harding. Johnny was actually looking forward to having Harding back in the gym, if only to spar his fighters. During his months of inactivity, rumours had started circulating that Harding had been drinking. If he was back in the gym, Johnny thought, no matter whose gym it was, at least he wouldn't be drinking.

And that's how their feud ended.

Despite the increasing frustration with Tszyu, Mordey played the game with the ruling IBF perfectly. Jake Rodriguez was the IBF light-welterweight champion and nobody doubted that if Tszyu could get him in the ring he would take the belt. But Rodriguez was contracted to Don King, so before that fight could happen, Tszyu would have to sign over future options to King.

Instead of going for it, Mordey waited King out. He put Tszyu in against Angel Hernandez and then saw him stop Pedro Sanchez in four. While this was happening, the No. 1 and No. 2–ranked light-welterweight contenders blew their chances and, thanks solely to patience and attrition, Tszyu assumed the IBF's No. 1 ranking. The top-ranked contender automatically had to fight the title-holder. Since this fight was mandatory, King would be cut out of any options if Tszyu won.

It worked a treat.

Before long, the deal was done. Tszyu would fight Rodriguez for the IBF light-welterweight belt at the MGM Grand in Las Vegas on January 28, 1995.

Before leaving for Las Vegas, Tszyu and Warton held a meeting about whether to leave Mordey. Fenech went to the meeting to support Tszyu as a mate. He also introduced Tszyu to Theo Onisforou, the man who'd helped him negotiate his deal with Mordey for the Azumah Nelson fight. Pay television had recently started in Australia, and Mordey was negotiating a deal to showcase Tszyu on Galaxy's Premier All Star Sports network. He took Tszyu aside and told him he was putting a deal together. 'Don't tell anyone,' he told Tszyu. 'We'll talk more when we get back.'

Tszyu said nothing.

And so they all flew to America, not realising this would be their last fight together, or that when it was over men who'd been close for more than a decade would no longer be speaking to each other.

Premier sent two executives to Las Vegas to talk to Tszyu but they were blocked from doing so. Tszyu needed to concentrate on his fight, they were told, which was only half true.

The unspoken tension between Fenech and Johnny, between Fenech and Mordey, was there in all the days before the fight. Where Fenech had sat at the tables with Mordey the night before Jeff Harding won his title, they didn't share anything this time.

Though Johnny didn't grasp the big picture until later, he kept noticing Fenech pulling Tszyu aside, whispering to him, then Vlad Warton doing the same. He thought maybe they just wanted to share in the glory now that Tszyu was about to become a world champion.

'They're plotting to take this kid off us,' Mordey said to him the day before the fight.

'No,' Johnny said. 'Kostya wouldn't be part of that.' He was too good a kid.

'No, you're wrong,' Mordey said.

Mordey was right.

When he told Tszyu of the Galaxy deal, Tszyu hadn't told Mordey that Warton and Fenech were already working on a deal with rival pay-TV network SKY Channel, owned by Kerry Packer. Theo Onisforou, an advisor to both Packer and Fenech, had lined it up.

Tszyu's potential defection wasn't the only problem they faced.

The night before the fight, Don King called Mordey to his room.

'We got a problem,' King said.

'What's that?'

'We got no fight.'

Mordey had no clue what he was talking about. 'What do you mean?'

'We got no fight. I need to see your boy's contract.'

'You can't see his contract,' he said.

'Then we got no fight,' King said.

It went like this for many minutes, back and forth. Mordey was reluctant to give King the contract for one reason: he knew King's reputation too well. He also knew that despite being champion, Rodriguez had little chance against Tszyu. King clearly recognised Tszyu's financial potential. The Russian kid was made for the American market. King needed Tszyu. Had Mordey understood the television side of it better, he could easily have told King to shove it. There was no way the networks would have stood for a cancellation this close to the fight, especially on such flimsy grounds.

But Mordey didn't understand the TV side. Besides, Don King was big and intimidating. He had served time for manslaughter after beating a man to death over unpaid gambling debts.

'All right,' Mordey said, 'I'll send the contract up.'

Accompanied by King's bodyguard, he returned to his room, put Tszyu's contract in an envelope and gave it to the bodyguard to take to King.

Next day, as he walked along the corridor towards the arena, Mordey saw King approaching. King walked right up on him, into his personal space. 'You think you're smart, don't you, white boy?' King said.

'Don,' Mordey said, 'you asked to see his contract. You got to see his contract.'

Mordey had sent King the Russian version.

Tszyu dominated the fight from the start. Only briefly was Johnny concerned, when he saw Tszyu start to look tired. But he quickly resumed control and stopped Rodriguez in six.

Under IBF protocol, Rodriguez wore his belt into the ring and kept it for all time, even though it was ceremoniously wrapped around Tszyu's waist when the decision was made official. But having had the belt wrapped around him, Tszyu wanted to wear it out of the ring. It took some time to get across to him that he would be given his own brand-new belt later.

As they argued over the belt, Fenech said, 'Kostya, Bill's incompetent. He should be getting the belt for you.' Eventually, Rodriguez relented and told Tszyu to keep the belt; the IBF could send the new one to him.

Finally resolved, they headed to the press conference where Tszyu took the stage and instead of Bill, Warton took the spot next to him.

Oh god no, Johnny thought, Bill's right.

At the post-fight celebration in Tszyu's suite, the whispers continued.

'You're not silly, Kostya ... you're not silly,' Fenech said at one point. A Channel Ten cameraman and his reporter also overheard Fenech say, 'Don't worry, Jamie will be with you in your corner next time.' They took this to mean Jamie Packer, though they had no inkling yet about what it meant.

Just over a week after they got back to Sydney, Johnny was woken by a call from radio broadcaster Alan Jones.

'Do you want to say anything about Kostya leaving you and Bill?'

Johnny was stunned.

'What?'

'The story in this morning's paper.' Steve Crawley had broken the story in *The Australian*.

'No,' Johnny said finally, 'I don't want to say nothing about it.'

He got a copy of the paper. The story said Tszyu was leaving to fight under the SKY Channel banner. Warton would be his new promoter. It looked like Fenech would train him.

Later that day, Johnny heard a knock. At his door were Tszyu and Warton. They stayed on the doorstep. Tszyu had a contract in his hand.

'Johnny, I want you to train me,' Tszyu said. 'And I want you to sign this.'

Johnny took the contract.

'I won't sign it,' he said, 'but I'll continue to train you.'

'Johnny, please sign the contract.'

'I won't sign it. I've never signed a contract with anyone. It's better that way. If you want to go, you can go, and if I want to go, I'll go. I'll never sign a contract with a fighter.'

'Can we shake hands on it?'

Johnny put out his hand.

Johnny's father was visiting at the time. Johnny put the contract on the kitchen counter and sat down next to his dad.

'What are you going to do?' his dad said.

'I always like to do things properly, so it's whether I remain fair dinkum to Bill or whether I should remain loyal to Kostya.'

Johnny started thinking aloud. Would Warton and Fenech be able to manage Tszyu properly?

'You want my opinion?' his dad said.

'I do.'

'I think you're doing the right thing.' Johnny listened. 'Bill's established in life, but you're responsible for this kid leaving his family and coming over here. If you stick with him you can always make sure his interests are looked after.'

An hour later, Mordey called.

'What do you make of all this?' he said.

'He was just here this morning,' Johnny said.

It dropped on Mordey. 'He wants you to stay on,' Mordey said.

'Yeah.'

'What are you going to do?'

Johnny told him he thought he was going to stay.

'That's all right,' Mordey said. 'I understand.'

Mordey promptly threatened to sue Tszyu, Warton, Fenech, Onisforou and SKY Channel for breach of contract. The following day, for the first time in more than thirty years, Johnny didn't go to the gym. He stayed away the next day, too, and the next, and the next.

Fenech called a press conference to explain his side of the affair. Mordey called a press conference to explain his. 'I always knew I was a bad judge of racehorses, but I thought I was a good judge of people,' he said. 'Maybe I'm just a bad judge.'

Everyone was speculating about which side Johnny would take. But he didn't call a press conference or attend one. As Mordey and Tszyu circled each other, he was caught in the middle. Now all Australia waited to see which way he would go.

CHAPTER 24

JOHNNY QUIETLY returned to work with Tszyu.

He never signed the contract, just turned up and started working. His father had been right, he decided. Tszyu had crossed the world to be with Johnny. He needed his help.

Johnny's decision to remain with Tszyu carried weight far beyond the gym and the world of boxing. Much of the Australian public thought Tszyu had behaved badly. He'd walked out on his promoter the moment he got the title, leaving him with nothing after all Mordey had done for him.

The only thing that tempered their outrage was Johnny's decision to stay with Tszyu. Perhaps, people started to think, it wasn't a black-and-white issue. Perhaps there were shades of grey.

If Johnny had sided with Mordey instead of Tszyu, a great majority of the Australian public would have turned on Tszyu forever. It was because Johnny was still in his corner that many of them chose to give Tszyu the benefit of the doubt.

Tszyu's camp privately recognised as much. It was important to keep

Johnny for reasons beyond his training talents. He was the link not only to the Australian fans, but to old-school values. Their agreement, after all, was on a handshake.

The split stayed uneasy, but everyone appeared to be moving on. Then, on Friday afternoon, March 17, Johnny got a call from Mordey.

'Mate, I just wanted you to know that you'll read a little story in the paper tomorrow about Mordey not using Lewis's fighters any more,' he said.

'What? Why are you doing that?' Johnny said.

'It's nothing really. You made your decision, you're going to stay with Kostya, so I can't use any of your fighters. You're with the Russians.'

'I'm not with the Russians, I'm with one. In due time I'll be knocking on your door with him and we'll be wanting to get straight back on the tracks again.'

'That'll never happen.'

This irked Johnny big time.

'Bill, I want to ask you a question. When Jeff Harding left me, did I ever ring you up and say that if you continue to promote him you won't have Fenech or any of my other fighters?'

'This is different.'

'What's different about it, Bill?'

'No, no,' Mordey said. 'Nope …'

'Bill, you tell me why. A bloke who won a world title, had one defence, left me and you continued to promote him. But you're telling me this is different?'

'That's all right,' Mordey said. He was trying to calm Johnny, that's all. 'I'm just telling you so you don't get upset when you read it,' he said.

'I will get upset because it's the act of a scorned woman. I thought more of you, Bill, than to do this.'

'It's not personal,' Mordey said, hanging up.

They never spoke again.

The next day a small headline at the bottom of page 142 of the *Daily Telegraph* read: 'Mordey Bans Lewis Fighters'. A small headline, announcing an earthquake.

The shock waves went beyond just Johnny and Mordey. All Johnny's fighters, all Mordey's new fighters were eventually affected by it. The destruction was widespread.

Mordey launched legal action against Tszyu in the Supreme Court and began planning to bring him down in the ring as well. He no longer called him Kostya. He called him simply the Russian. Warton, a former used-car salesman, was now Oil-Can Harry. Mordey had always called Johnny 'Lewie'. Now he was referred to as Lewis. None of Johnny's fighters would ever again get a start on a Mordey card.

Mordey's plan for Tszyu involved a young light-welterweight he had recently contracted to Premier. Shannan Taylor had fought Tszyu in the amateurs. He had a good punch and was already rearing for a shot at Tszyu.

'What I'm going to do is get Taylor and sit him on the Russian's bum for twelve months,' Mordey said. 'Move him up to No. 1 and then the Russian will have to make a mandatory defence.'

At Mordey's first promotion for Premier, Tszyu—to the surprise of many—turned up at the door of Parramatta Leagues Club with a small entourage and, once they got to the door, expected free entry. Mordey waved them in. During the night, several of Mordey's more colourful acquaintances came up and tugged his sleeve and made the offer. His choice, he could have one leg broken, or two. Mordey waved them all away. Among those in the crowd, one of Mordey's guests was Stan 'The Man' Smith. Sydney's most notorious hitman.

Johnny got caught in the crossfire. His phone started ringing at night.

'You weak dog,' an anonymous voice would say. And hang up.

One afternoon at the footy, a staffer of Mordey's tugged at his shirt, over his heart. Johnny went for him. As he chased the man around the corner of the grandstand, he ran straight into Australian Rugby League chairman Ken Arthurson.

'Hello, Johnny,' Arthurson said.

'Hello, Ken.'

The bloke got away.

Justin Rowsell stuck solid with Johnny, testimony to his character, since he was caught in the middle worse than anybody. He managed to train with Johnny and stay friends with Mordey, though he had yet to convince him to put him on one of his cards.

Johnny took Rowsell to Boston in early March 1995 to fight Alberto Alicea. He says he never saw a more beautiful performance in the ring. Rowsell hardly got hit before taking out Alicea in three.

Mordey still wouldn't use him, though. Rowsell was forced to survive as best he could. Another promoter, Barry Raff, offered to put him on his cards. After Alicea, he fought Darren Miller in front of a small crowd at Marrickville Town Hall. The momentum was running out of his career.

Everybody felt for Justin.

'It's a terrible situation,' said Craig Mordey. 'There's a place for nice people in this sport, but not many. We'd all like to go to Justin's fight on Friday night but we can't.'

The reason was simple.

'Jeff Fenech will be there.'

Johnny worried a lot about Justin and what was happening to him. They needed not just fights, but direction. In the meantime, Tszyu powered on, scoring a solid but dull win against Roger Mayweather in Newcastle in June 1995. Not long afterwards, Fenech knocked on Johnny's door. He was making a comeback.

It was a courtesy call. Fenech was going to train with Terry Lewis (no relation), and when he fought, the bloke in his corner would be Emanuel Steward, the American trainer who'd once handled Steve McCrory. Now considered the best in the world, Steward had agreed to oversee the final stages of Fenech's preparation.

'I don't like comebacks—I'm paranoid about them,' Johnny told the *Sunday Telegraph*. 'I don't care which fighter it is ... If I can help Jeff in any way, I will. But I don't want to be part of a comeback.'

Mordey, meanwhile, was getting mischievous.

Tszyu's next fight was a mandatory IBF defence against Colombian Hugo Pineda. With the two fighters' camps unable to agree on a purse, a purse bid was held. Warton wrote a guarantee for $800,000 and put it in an envelope. The guarantee Colombian promoter Bill Chalms had put in his sealed envelope was $801,000.

There are only two ways Chalms could have won by bidding just enough. The first is that he got very lucky.

Mordey phoned Chalms in Cartagena, Colombia, where the fight was to be held. He made him an offer for the Australian television rights. On Galaxy.

When Chalms accepted, Mordey laughed to himself and took his whole staff down to the pub, his shout. Let's see how the Russian's contract with SKY Channel goes now, he said.

'If you're going to go into the deep end of the pool,' he told Tszyu through the papers, 'you should be able to swim.'

A week later, he called a promoter in America and bought the Australian rights to the Pernell Whitaker–Jake Rodriguez fight. He wasn't after the main event. Jeff Fenech, whose major sponsor was SKY, was making his comeback on the undercard.

SKY had been trumped again.

Tszyu threatened to withdraw from the fight to get out of Mordey's coup. The IBF said it would strip him if he failed to make the mandatory defence. Tszyu stuck solid. He would not fight in Cartagena, he said. He was willing to forfeit the title rather than fight on Galaxy. Mordey was delighted. Shannan Taylor could fight for the vacant title, he said, after which they would be glad to give Tszyu a chance to win it back.

Then Warton, until now underestimated, showed great genius. Speaking for Tszyu, he told the press they were reluctant to fight in Colombia for fear that Tszyu would be nobbled. He noted the murder rate there. He struck at just the right time. A year earlier, Colombian defender Andres Escobar had been shot dead after returning from the soccer World Cup, where he had scored an own goal in his team's crucial 2–1 loss to the United States. How could anyone expect a fair go in such a place? Warton argued.

Eventually the IBF relented. The fight was delayed, then relocated to Parramatta Stadium in Sydney, and scheduled for January 1996 on SKY.

WHILE the fight business got uglier, Johnny focused on the little things. His great joy remained working with Justin Rowsell. Like Johnny, Justin was more comfortable away from crowds. One night at No Names Italian restaurant, Johnny ran into Steve Dack, Jeff Harding's old sparring partner.

'I'm thinking about fighting,' Dack told him.

'Didn't I hear a little whisper you were doing law?' Johnny said.

'That's right.'

'Well, mate, you concentrate on the law and give the fighting away.'

'Righto, Johnny.'

Johnny left him to his dinner. Later, Dack dropped by his table to say goodbye.

'Thanks for looking out for me, Johnny,' he said.

'Mate, don't mention it, it's just common sense.'

'Yeah, you're right.'

'Steve, I'll tell you what,' Johnny said. 'You finish your law course, and when you've got your degree we'll train for one fight, and I'll put you on a Kostya Tszyu undercard.'

'Serious?'

Justin Rowsell fought three more times before the year was out, with three knockouts. Early in 1996, he won again on the Tszyu–Pineda undercard. Rowsell was doing everything Johnny wanted of him. Johnny started thinking a world title was not far away if they could manoeuvre their way through the higher rankings.

On that same undercard, as promised, was middleweight Steve Dack. Steve never missed a session once he started training, and during his time in the gym he would make two great friendships. He would never go more than a couple of days without speaking to Johnny the rest of his life. And every day he would speak to Julian Stewart. In his late teens in 1996, Stewart was still watching the fighters from his wheelchair and still had the ability to lift people's spirits by his presence. Steve called Julian 'Sunshine'. Steve took a six-round decision against Glen Baragry, then donated his purse to the Matthew Talbot Hostel.

The tall, rangy Pineda became the first man to knock Tszyu down. Twice. It took Tszyu time to work Pineda out but Johnny was pleased with even that. Tszyu figured out his style and stopped him in eleven, showing Johnny what an intelligent fighter he was. He had come up against a new kind of opponent, and he had solved the puzzle.

By now, Russell Cox had transferred from the Victorian prison system to New South Wales. Over the past several years he had been in Goulburn, Long Bay, Grafton, Lithgow and Maitland. Johnny tried to visit him every two to three months or at least see him when he went into prisons with the Young Offenders Program. New regulations meant that now, instead of boxers, Johnny took young kids in minor trouble with the law to talk to the prisoners. Where the boxing had been meant as a diversion for prisoners, now the prisoners were being used to steer away kids on the verge of going bad.

Cox was one of the prisoners Corrective Services put forward to talk to the kids. When Johnny arrived, he'd nod him towards a certain young bloke and Russell would sit down alongside him. Cox's reputation still carried weight, even among the young ones.

'This is it,' he'd say, it was boring, and it was dangerous, and it wasn't a place you wanted to be.

The jail visits continued until one day, in the late '90s, they headed to Lithgow's maximum security jail.

After a short time in the main yard, they were let into a segregated area. Anybody that has been in a prison can feel the shifts between yards.

'Hello, Johnny.'

Johnny turned to see a man with a tear-drop tattoo under his left eye. It was John Travers, the leader of the murderers of Anita Cobby. He and four others had raped and beaten a young nurse. Travers then slit her throat. All were sentenced to life, which under truth-in-sentencing laws meant their whole lives. They were segregated to keep other prisoners from getting at them.

Johnny turned back to the warder in charge. 'Mate, I think you've got us in the wrong section here.'

'No, this is the right place.'

'No, mate, we're not doing anything here,' Johnny said. 'Put us out in the main yard.'

'What? You've got a problem? Are you treating these blokes differently?'

'No mate, you did that when you put them in here.'

The prison guard was as big as the badge he wore. 'If you don't do it here,' he said, 'then I'll see to it you never come in here again.'

'Well we're not doing it here,' Johnny said, and that was it. They were never asked back. The program was over.

It was now a year since the split with Mordey. Things with Tszyu were changing. He would come into the gym and Johnny would pull him into the ring and tell him they were doing six rounds on pads, then four on the bag. No, Tszyu would say, four rounds on pads, then three on the bag. Johnny wanted him to concentrate more on body punches. All good pros are good body punchers. Tszyu resisted. He preferred head punches, a throwback to his amateur style. Johnny was the boss, but Tszyu was refusing to listen.

The shift was subtle, but Johnny felt his control fading.

While he battled this front, Johnny pushed for more for Rowsell. It was no longer good enough picking up fights on small cards, grabbing a fight here and there. They needed a strategy to chase down a world title. Rowsell wanted to stick with Johnny, but without a promoter backing him it was difficult.

Warton came up with a deal for five fights, starting with American Mark Fernandez, ending with a title bout against South Africa's IBF lightweight champion, Philip Holiday. Shortly after the deal was signed, Fenech announced that he had a title shot at Holiday's lightweight belt.

Johnny and Rowsell ignored that and concentrated on Fernandez. Weeks before the fight, Johnny ran into trainer Scott Audrey.

'That fight with Fernandez is a dangerous one,' Audrey said. 'That kid can fight. You want to be careful fighting him.'

It concerned Johnny. Audrey was a good judge.

The Fenech fight was in Melbourne, and despite the unspoken tension between them, Fenech called Johnny and asked him to the fight. Johnny flew down. Fenech's request to have Johnny there was not as unusual as it might at first seem. Neither was Johnny's decision to go. Even when they were at odds, a bond remained. Something was created in all those hours in the gym, intangible and unbreakable.

They might barely be talking, but it just wouldn't be right if Johnny wasn't there.

It did not go long. Almost exactly as he had with Calvin Grove, Fenech walked into a straight right hand and was knocked out in the second round. He flopped on his back, gone. Immediately, the towel came in from the corner. As Holiday's arm went up in celebration, Johnny's eyes remained on Fenech. At first he was looking to make sure he was not seriously hurt. But Fenech, still stunned, got to his feet and, running on nothing but instinct, picked up his gloves to show the referee he was ready to resume. At the same time he tried subtly to kick the towel under his feet behind him and out of the ring before the referee saw it and stopped the fight.

Of course, the referee had already stopped the fight. But Johnny was in awe of Fenech's instinct to keep fighting.

Six days later, Rowsell stopped Fernandez in the tenth, winning the World Boxing Organisation's intercontinental lightweight title. He was on track for a world title. While Holiday's demolition of Fenech made him look like a killer to many boxing fans, Johnny knew Rowsell had more than enough skill to deal with him. For one thing, he wouldn't stand in front of Holiday the way Fenech did.

Nearly an hour after the Fernandez fight, Tszyu beat Corey Johnson of the United States in the main event. In Johnny's eyes, this was Tszyu's real birth as a pro. His body punches broke Johnson down. They had venom. Most of all, he revealed a body punch to the liver, delivered at just the right angle, that crumpled Johnson.

The decision to produce the body punches was his own. Tszyu was still improving. He really was going to be anything as a fighter.

Rowsell started moving quickly also. He had three good wins and was working along nicely. Then, in a bout against Ahmed Santos in Las Vegas, the fighters' heads clashed accidentally. Both were cut, and the bout was ruled a technical draw. Johnny was filthy. Justin was about to do a job on Santos, and the win would have announced him to the American audience. A draw was an opportunity lost.

Santos was the fifth fight in the deal with Warton. Holiday had recently won against Ivan Robinson, yet weeks and months went by, and Rowsell was still waiting for his promised title shot. Again the momentum was fizzing out.

Finally, Johnny called Warton, Tszyu and Rowsell to a meeting at the gym. What had happened to the Holiday fight? he asked Warton.

'We don't think Justin is ready for it,' Warton said.

'Well I do, and I'm his trainer,' Johnny said.

Warton asked Johnny where his loyalty was—with Tszyu or Rowsell. Johnny, of course, had always maintained that whoever had a fight coming up next was the most important fighter.

'If they were both fighting on the same night, who would you choose?' said Warton.

'I'd go with Justin,' Johnny said.

'Can I ask you why?'

'Yes. I really feel Kostya's had his chance and done very good, and it's very important that Justin gets his chance.'

'Very interesting,' said Warton. He looked at Tszyu, who said nothing. Shortly after, Tszyu went upstairs to start training.

'I want to thank you for your honesty,' Tszyu said when Johnny joined him.

Slowly though, Rowsell began to understand. He and Johnny could protest all they liked. Without a promoter, there was nothing they could do. It didn't matter how good your trainer was, he decided. What mattered was the promoter.

Until that day, Johnny had kept relations with Warton civil. As he saw it, they were working together to push Tszyu's career. Now Johnny basically stopped talking to Warton. He was getting sick of it all.

He went home and, not for the first time lately, thought seriously about retiring.

But he went back to work.

Over the next few months, Tszyu beat Jan Bergman and Leonardo Mas. Both opponents were accepted without Johnny's approval. That had never happened under Mordey, not with any of the fighters Johnny trained. Then one day Warton told him he had arranged a bout against Vince Phillips.

'He's been fighting welterweights,' Johnny said. He thought Warton had picked Phillips because, a year earlier, Ike Quartey had knocked him out in three rounds. Clearly they thought Tszyu could do the same. But since then Phillips had beaten the highly rated Jerry Smith and Juan Carlos Rodriguez, stopping them both, and at welterweight. If those wins weren't reason enough to be wary, Phillips was renowned for his intense work rate. Johnny thought back to Tampa, and Tszyu recovering in bed while Hector Lopez kissed air hostesses goodbye. If the strategy with Mordey was always to avoid big punchers until absolutely necessary, Johnny had added hard workers to Tszyu's list.

Making it even worse, Tszyu dropped off his training. One day he brought a bloke to the gym, known only as Max. Max was a vegetarian and a martial artist, who had fought at temples all across Thailand. In well over a hundred fights, he had never been beaten.

If Max had only fought in Buddhist temples, of course, his record could never be checked. When Johnny mentioned this, Max insisted he was telling the truth, and Tszyu apparently believed him.

Soon Tszyu started doing less pad work with Johnny. After a few rounds, he would pull the gloves off and head into the wrestling room to work with Max. He was doing less work on the heavy bag and the floor-to-ceiling ball as well. More and more of his training time was spent with Max.

It was now more than two years since the split with Mordey, and for Johnny, nearly all the fun of training Tszyu was gone. Initially he had felt that he owed him, and he'd stuck solid with him on that basis. But Tszyu wasn't listening anymore. It seemed Tszyu didn't need him.

His father, Boris, who had migrated to Australia, was also helping to dictate Tszyu's training routine. Johnny wasn't doing much more than holding pads.

They flew to Atlantic City to fight Phillips, Tszyu and his dad in business class, Johnny and Mitrevski in economy with Max. Where trips with Fenech, Harding and Rowsell had been fun, with walks and practical jokes and kidding around, Tszyu preferred to spend the days with his father or in his room. Apart from training and at dinner each night, Johnny hardly saw him.

One night Johnny and Peter Mitrevski took their nightly stroll along the Atlantic City boardwalk.

'As soon as this fight's over, I'm out,' Johnny said. 'I've had enough of this.'

Mitrevski didn't even have to ask why. 'If you're out, then I'm out, too,' he said.

They decided to tell Tszyu they were finished when the fight was over.

At breakfast a couple of days later, Johnny saw Ronny Nash, Warton's man for all jobs, looking tired. Nash got on well with Johnny but had never taken to Tszyu.

'How could you be tired? You've done nothing,' Johnny said, winding him up.

'I've been doing stuff at that business centre. I was down there till three o'clock this morning,' Nash said.

'Ronny, you're full of shit.'

'Don't call me a liar,' Nash said. 'Every time I'm there I see your mate Max in the bib-and-brace overalls.'

'He isn't my mate,' Johnny said.

'Every morning I have a cup of coffee and he has a big steak.'

'Ronny, you're a liar, he's a vegetarian.'

'Well, come and we'll see him.'

Johnny was bored, so why not, he thought. They knocked on Max's door. Max opened it naked.

'Mate, put a towel around you,' Johnny said.

'Mate,' said Nash, 'do I see you every morning?'

'Every morning,' Max said.

'And what do I have?'

'A coffee.'

'And what do you have?'

'Steak and eggs.'

'See,' Nash said, smiling at Johnny.

The night before the fight, Tszyu asked Johnny to his room after dinner to watch tape of Phillips.

'Just me and you?' Johnny said. He had had enough of this rule by committee.

'Yes.'

Shortly after Johnny arrived, Max knocked on the door.

'Sorry I'm late,' he said.

They sat and watched Phillips's last fight.

'What do you think?' Tszyu said at the end.

'Same as before. It's going to be a very, very hard fight,' Johnny said.

'Do you think he can punch?'

'Yeah, he can punch.'

'No,' Max said. 'You see him? When he punches, he's like this, with his elbow in. You must punch like this.'

Johnny and Tszyu watched Max demonstrate, with his elbow out, exactly how not to throw a punch. Johnny looked at Tszyu, and Tszyu looked back at Johnny, and Johnny was sure Tszyu was thinking the same thing he was thinking. He wondered what else Max had been telling him all those times in the wrestling room.

But Tszyu didn't start taking any more notice of Johnny.

Like many fighters, Tszyu preferred his dressing rooms quiet. He often liked to sit and read a book. When the time came to get ready, Johnny plonked down two chairs and placed a towel over the back of one for Tszyu to rest his arm on as he strapped his hands. He put a small white cross on the back of each fist, then began taping the left hand.

'Kostya, I need you over here.'

It was Max.

Tszyu looked at Max and back at Johnny and, a little uncertainly, stood up.

'Kostya,' Johnny said. 'I need you here, mate.'

Tszyu paused. 'I'll go over there.'

With one hand still half wrapped, he walked to a corner with Max and sat cross-legged facing him. Max held his hands and blew on them, transferring his power into Tszyu.

Watching this circus, Johnny was convinced he had made the right decision. You can't stay around a fighter if you're not enjoying it. It's not fair to you or the fighter.

Vince Phillips was everything Johnny feared. He stood up to Tszyu's punches and kept firing back overhand rights, one after another. The big right hands and the hectic pace made Tszyu ragged with fatigue. By the later rounds, Phillips was landing punches almost at will.

He knocked Tszyu down in the tenth, and when he got up he backed him into the only part of the ring Johnny couldn't see clearly. Johnny tried to peek through the ropes. He was sure Tszyu was in trouble. As he tried to find another angle with a better view, the crowd, on its feet and loud, told him something major was happening. Johnny got ready to throw in the towel. He just needed to see what was actually happening. At that moment, referee Benny Esteves Jr stepped in and ended it. Tszyu dropped his head in sickness. The fight was over. The title was gone.

After the fight, they took Tszyu to the hospital. Mitrevski helped him out of the car.

'No, no, no,' Tszyu said, trying to indicate he was all right. Even now, heavy with concussion, he was brave.

Mitrevski hooked Tszyu's arm around his own. 'Stay with me,' he said, and led him inside. Later, back in their hotel room, they sat back and thought, what do we do with our lives?

Only one of them was certain. Max had disappeared. He didn't come back to the hotel, and nobody saw or heard from him again.

When they got back to Sydney Tszyu called a meeting at the Novotel Hotel in Brighton. Others from the Tszyu camp attended as well, and Tszyu went around the table.

'Johnny, what do you think I should do?' Tszyu said.

Johnny had noticed a change in Tszyu since the loss. A quietness. He not only acted differently, he looked different. 'I think you should retire.'

Others offered their opinions. After it was all said, Tszyu thanked them and said he appreciated their views, but he was going to fight on.

'And Johnny, I want you to be with me.'

Johnny had already privately told Mitrevski that he couldn't walk out on Tszyu after a loss. They had to support him in defeat. Mitrevski agreed. But Johnny also knew some changes had to be made.

Later, in private, he sat Tszyu down and for the first time in a long time they got honest with each other.

'What was Max doing there?' Johnny said.

'I thought I could learn something from him.'

'When he called you over when I was wrapping your hands, that really hurt.'

Tszyu apologised. He later told a reporter that he had 'lost communication' with Johnny at some point. Now he recognised that he needed to start listening more to his trainer.

They were going to work together, and do it better this time.

Tszyu's fitness trainer Michael Khmel, a former Russian athletics coach, recommended that they do a stint in Canberra, at the Australian Institute of Sport.

Johnny was unsure, but agreed. Something different might be good. The camp environment at the AIS would be a bit like those Tszyu had known growing up. The two weeks there when they got back to training turned out to be very good for him: athletes training everywhere, all equally committed to success. What Johnny noticed almost from the start was the noise. The buzz in the dining room at breakfast. The sound of ambition.

It was an old noise that made Tszyu feel new again.

Johnny noticed it in the snap of his punch. Every day he seemed to get better.

Eight weeks later, Tszyu fought Ismael Chavez in Townsville, and pummelled him in three rounds. His decision to fight on had been indisputably right.

But the win was bittersweet for Johnny. While they'd been in Canberra, Rowsell had phoned.

'Johnny,' he said, 'I'm gonna go with Bill. I'm sorry.'

Johnny was not surprised. Really, he didn't think Rowsell had a choice.

'Don't you worry about it. You do what's best for you,' he said.

'I'm sorry, Johnny.'

'Don't worry about it, mate, you've got to do what you've got to do.'

Nobody suffered more than Rowsell over the split. As bad as it was, it was about to get worse.

Chapter 25

He was fifteen, and he was fighting by this time. Fighting under Jack Blom and Snowy McFadyen at Newtown Police Boys Club, and weighing about five stone seven pounds. Saturday nights were spent at the old Sydney Stadium at Rushcutters Bay.

Any fighter that was any good around Sydney was there, either fighting for Ern McQuillan or about to be. This night was like every other Saturday night, and Johnny and his mates ran all the way to the stadium to watch the fights.

One of them told Johnny he knew a way in, bypassing the redcoats collecting tickets on the door. Even a bad fight is a good fight when it is for free, and they snuck in and found a spot in the bleachers, up behind the wire fencing, in what they call the cage. Sydney Stadium was a large saucer-shaped stadium with wooden bleachers that ran the circumference of the venue. Each tiered row climbed higher into the stadium so the outer rows were a good four hundred metres or more around. There was plenty of room to stretch out.

Who knows who was fighting this night? Who cared, when the fights were free.

They spread out and sat down on the big empty bleachers, their feet up on the bench in front of them, settling in to watch the fights.

A redcoat snuck right up on them. 'Where's your tickets?'

One of Johnny's mates pulled out a ticket.

'How'd you get in here?' the redcoat asked.

The obvious answer is always the best. 'How do you think we got in here?'

'They're not opening the bleachers tonight,' he said. 'Only from here down. So how'd you get in?'

About this time Johnny noticed a few uniformed coppers making their way up. It was not hard to think what to do next. They all ran.

They ran in all directions and the coppers split and ran after them. A roar went around the stadium.

Four young boys, sidestepping coppers, hurdling bleachers, looking for the door. Every time one of them successfully sidestepped a copper another small roar swung around the stadium. Only they could not find the right door. They did a full lap of the stadium and couldn't find the door they came in. From the inside, and at a gallop, every door looked the same. And they were all locked.

Then one of coppers tripped down a bleacher. He let out a yelp and looked in tremendous pain, and at this the roar from the crowd went up a notch. People actually began to clap.

Then Johnny heard one of his mates yell out. 'Here it is! Here it is!'

All four of them shot through the door, across the road, and kept running until they hit the tennis courts of White City. It was black and none of them were sure if the coppers were still chasing, but they ran into a wall none of them could scale and finally stopped for breath.

There, with fear in their breaths, they figured they weren't free of it yet.

Johnny saw a toilet and told himself he'd hide there until it cooled down. One of his mates hid inside with him, his mate in the cubicle and Johnny behind the door.

Then they heard footsteps.

Johnny stopped breathing.

Hiding behind that door, hearing his own chest beat, he heard his mate being pulled from the cubicle by a copper and, quickly, they were into him.

They're giving him plenty, Johnny thinks.

Hearing more coppers out there, still looking, he remained behind the door trying to see how quiet he could be.

He heard his mate dragged off and the coppers talking. 'There's definitely one more,' one said.

Johnny did not move. He breathed slowly. He was scared as he has ever been. For what felt like an hour he stayed behind the door, his body aching because he was too afraid to move even an inch. But he heard nothing. No coppers talking, no footsteps.

He decided to take a peek around the corner. It was dark and he started leaning around the door, stretching his neck like a turtle coming out of its shell. As his head came around the door he saw that he was clear and …

Stars shattered in his head. Blood flushed from his nose, the bones inside broken.

The copper was waiting the whole time. He dragged him out and pushed him up against the fence and frisked him. Then he put the slipper in.

Later, Johnny was sure he meant to kick him in the arse. But the copper missed and landed slightly higher on his lower back. So much pain shot through Johnny he began to sweat.

They marched him back down to the stadium, his arm up his back, into the stadium and underneath and through to where they had a car waiting out back. As Johnny walked through the stadium somebody who knew him noticed he was one of the boys, and evidently went and found Jack Blom in the dressing room.

The others were already in the car, and when Johnny got in they saw his pain.

'These bastards, what'd they do to you?'

'I'm all right,' Johnny said.

Then one of the older boys said, 'You got any money on you?'

'I've got ten shillings.'

'Mate, put it in your sock, these bastards'll take it off you.'

The ten shillings went straight in the sock.

Back at Darlinghurst station the coppers took them into the interview room.

They started with their names.

As the coppers went down the line Johnny saw his mates were all giving fake names. He was smart enough to follow the lead.

Then another copper walked in. 'Is there anyone here called Johnny Something?'

'No mate,' they all said.

'No Johnny here?'

'No mate.'

They were one in, all in. Mates together. The copper walked out and a detective walked in, playing the full stick. 'Who's the fucking ringleader?'

All this because they snuck in through a door. The coppers kept them there until two, three in the morning. In all his hours there waiting, he thought a lot about friendship. It reinforced all it meant. It was about staying solid, even at the disadvantage to yourself. Nope, no Johnny here.

Just when Johnny was thinking he might be spending the night there the detective opened the door to the room he was being kept in.

'Righto, on your way.'

He walked about ten metres past the detective, who then stopped him. 'Hey! Come here.'

Johnny turned, not knowing whether to go back or turn and run.

'Come here, come back here.'

He walked back.

'Have you got any money?'

He thought of the ten shillings hidden in his sock.

'No mate, no, I've got nothing. I'm gonna run home.'

The detective put his hand in his pocket and pulled out his wallet, pulling from it a ten pound note. 'Get a taxi.'

'No mate, I'm right,' he said, and he turned and began running, all the way home, worried that somebody might find out what had happened.

Next day at the gym Jack Blom cornered him. 'Johnny, what happened?'

Johnny could not lie. He told him it all.

'Mate,' Jack said at the end, 'Harry Miller [the stadium promoter] told me that he rang up to get you out of it and they said there was no Johnny there.'

'Jack,' Johnny says, 'the bloke was asking but the boys said don't tell 'em your name.'

'You silly little ...' Jack said, not finishing his sentence.

It was the way in Erko.

It is easy to understand why, knowing this, that throughout Johnny' earliest days in boxing, first as a fighter and then as a trainer, what kept him in the game was the mateship. Back when the two Jeffs were the stars of the Newtown gym, the times between fights and training would be filled with laughs and pranks. Often after training they'd go down to Erskineville Oval, all of them, for a game of touch football. Steve Mortimer would play, and Joe Bugner, too, big and slow and with no idea but enjoying himself more than he ever thought he would. Johnny would sit and have coffee with a fighter and talk about nothing that was important but enjoy it like few moments he enjoyed anywhere.

Johnny always believed that, to prepare properly for a fight, you needed the right mix of fun and hard work. Without fun, the fighter might be in peak condition physically, but he wouldn't be there mentally.

And that's what he realised was missing, more and more, with Tszyu, even after the move to Canberra and the Chavez fight in Townsville. The connection wasn't there like it had been with the others. Johnny was an employee. For all the joy of the work and the adrenaline of fight night, in the end it was starting to seem like hard slog.

In early 1998, the judge ruled on Mordey's lawsuit against Tszyu. Ordered to pay Mordey $7.3 million plus costs and interest, Tszyu immediately appealed.

By then Warton had Tszyu signed to fight on HBO. He knocked out Calvin Grove, Fenech's destroyer, Rafael Ruelas, Diosbelys Hurtado and Miguel Angel Gonzalez. The improvement in Johnny's relationship with Tszyu after the Vince Phillips loss was only temporary. Tszyu had now broken away from Newtown and signed a lease for his own gym at Rockdale. Johnny had to go there to continue training him. Loud Russian rock music blared as Tszyu skipped and warmed up. When he sparred, the music went off and nobody was allowed to talk. For Johnny, the fun continued to fade.

And here is where the cost is to be measured. After leaving Johnny, Rowsell fought twice under Mordey, then linked up with Fenech, who was now training and promoting his own fighters. While Johnny's fighters were still unwelcome on Mordey's cards, Mordey allowed Fenech to match Rowsell with Lovemore Ndou, a Mordey fighter, for December 1998. Johnny had no doubt Rowsell would win.

He didn't.

The pre-fight press conference almost became a fight in itself. Rowsell and Mordey were not involved, but said they were about to duck under the table when an altercation looked like turning violent. The media rolled their eyes at the staged brawl. But Shannan Taylor gave an indication of how serious he was. 'I kicked off my thongs,' he said. One of the men involved threatened to go and get his gun and come back and shoot everybody. He wouldn't have made it as far as the door, as there were several guns in the room already, and all on the wrong side. The following day Australian Federal Police took away Channel Ten's film of the press conference to identify suspects wanted in other matters. As if this wasn't bad omen enough, Rowsell had also wasted too hard for the weigh-in. He went into the ring hollow-cheeked and pale. Ndou, who made the weight easily, won the fight just as easily.

Shortly after that fight, Rowsell left Fenech to rejoin Bull Parker, Johnny's old fighter. Johnny watched him once again starting from scratch, trying to rebuild a career that had held so much promise. Only now his legs were ageing, his reflexes not quite what they were.

Rowsell and Johnny remained close. They often discussed opponents and what Rowsell should do next. Nobody could read a fight like Johnny, and thus pick an opponent. He also helped Rowsell with his training. He gave him everything except what he needed, and he felt great regret about that.

In April 1999, hail ripped through Sydney and tore holes in the roof of Newtown Police Boys Club. The damage was so bad the council closed the building. When the quote for repairs came in at a million dollars, the council put the building up for sale.

Johnny, initially believing he'd be gymless for only a few months, now had to accept that he was never going back. Newtown was gone. He felt like he'd lost not just a home but an old friend.

Tszyu met secretly with Bill Mordey in mid 1999 and asked him to drop his lawsuit. Mordey knocked him back. Soon after, Tszyu's appeal against the Supreme Court ruling that he must compensate Mordey was dismissed, but the court ordered that half the money Tszyu owed Mordey was to be paid by SKY Channel.

Tszyu made no effort to pay. With interest accruing at roughly two thousand dollars a day, SKY Channel made a business decision to settle, paying the full amount itself in December 1999, then seeking Tszyu's half independently.

'He's crying poor,' a SKY source told the *Daily Telegraph*. 'We know he's in a position to pay.'

Finally, in February 2000, after Tszyu allegedly offered to pay twenty-five cents in every dollar owed, SKY announced legal action against him.

Warton, meanwhile, had discovered that Tszyu had approached Mordey behind his back. Since the split, nobody had done more for Tszyu than Warton. So it was no surprise that he was incensed.

You can hardly blame him. Warton did not promote Tszyu in the traditional manner like Mordey had, or Don King or Bob Arum or any of the world's other big promoters would have. In their case they flipped it around. Tszyu was, in effect, promoting himself, with Warton taking a percentage of the overall take for doing the legwork.

Warton had long been cast in the black hat. Under these lights it looks terribly unfair.

He had not just carried on business. Warton had found ways for Tszyu to multiply his previous earnings. To the public he was the bad guy, the one who had split Tszyu from Mordey. But Warton believed he had saved Tszyu from Mordey. When he found out Tszyu had gone seeking peace deals with him, Warton too, began wondering about loyalty.

MEANTIME, Tszyu had moved to Showtime and continued his run of knockouts with Ahmed Santos in February, 2000. It was all leading to Julio Cesar Chavez, the king of Mexico.

The fight was regarded as a great triumph when it was signed. Chavez was an all-time legend. Once the world's greatest fighter, pound for pound, he had threatened to go a hundred fights without loss, and got to ninety-one before losing to Frankie Randall in a split decision. The Tszyu-Chavez fight looked terrific, and it was nothing of the sort.

It came because Tszyu had always wanted Chavez. But the Mexican was well past his prime now, closing in on thirty-eight with 109 fights behind him, and having lost two of his previous five. He hadn't beaten a top-shelf fighter since stopping Meldrick Taylor in eight rounds five years earlier and hadn't beaten a Top Ten fighter in more than twelve months.

Yet, despite his fading star, Chavez was elevated to the WBC's No. 1 ranking, making the fight a mandatory defence for Tszyu. This was a marvellous piece of luck, since Tszyu and Warton had been after the fight for months. Warton had flown to Mexico, where WBC headquarters is located, to secure the fight, and then to New York to buy the promotional rights from Don King, who still controlled Chavez.

Johnny knew three things about Chavez. He would not be a problem now. The fight would be a big earner. And Chavez could get quite seriously hurt.

An uneasy feeling overtook him once the fight was confirmed, one he hadn't experienced. He told Mitrevski he felt he shouldn't be going into a fight concerned for the welfare of an opponent, yet he was uneasy about Chavez. His toughness and champion's pride, mixed with Tszyu's power, were a strong mix for tragedy.

It is rare for two great fighters to meet each other at the peak of their abilities. In the 1970s there were Muhammad Ali, Joe Frazier and George Foreman, and in the 1980s there were Marvelous Marvin Hagler, Sugar Ray Leonard, Roberto Duran and Thomas Hearns. But more often, fighters on the way down bolster the record of those on the way up or those already at the top.

Most knowledgeable boxing fans knew this was beyond a mismatch.

The big Las Vegas sports bookies refused to offer odds for the fight. That meant traditional venues like Vegas and Atlantic City, driven by hardcore boxing crowds, were out. There were even suggestions the Nevada Athletic Commission was not prepared to sanction the fight.

Warton short-circuited such problems by hosting the fight in Phoenix, Arizona. This was also close enough to the border for Chavez's legion of Mexican fans to come across and fill the Veterans Memorial Coliseum. Even so, after all this the fight went ahead only after Chavez was forced to attend a hearing with the three-member Arizona Boxing Commission. He told them the fight would be his last.

'Let me go with honour and dignity,' he said.

Arizona Senator John McCain, the man behind the Muhammad Ali Boxing Reform Act, wrote to the state's Governor expressing his misgivings, saying the bout was an illegitimate and potentially dangerous mismatch.

As a result of such concerns, Chavez had to pass not only a physical but a series of neurological tests before being passed fit to fight.

The day before the fight, Warton was at the front of his hotel when he saw Chavez returning from roadwork. The way Chavez was running caught his notice. He was labouring. He struggled to the front of the hotel and then collapsed. Warton freaked and rushed to help revive him.

The following night, Johnny said a special prayer for Chavez as he placed the small white cross on the back of Tszyu's hands.

They walked to the ring and the Mexican fans greeted them in the time-honoured manner, pissing in cups and throwing the contents over them. Alongside Johnny and Peter Mitrevski was the third man in their corner, Johnny's mate Chris Condon.

The only surprise in the fight was that it went longer than most expected or would have liked. Tszyu was never in trouble, and after bouncing a series of big shots off Chavez's head during the fifth round he continued the assault in the sixth, putting him down before referee

Robert Ferrara stopped the bout midway through the round.

As they walked out, a Mexican fan king-hit Condon. He turned and tried to retaliate. The bodyguards ushered him away, but he wrestled them the whole trip to the dressing room. Then he wanted to go back and find them. They wouldn't open the door until he cooled.

Tszyu won his victory, and legitimacy in the American market. Chavez announced his retirement after the fight. Five years later, the old lion was still fighting.

Chapter 26

Six months after Chavez, Tszyu fought Sharmba Mitchell, dispatching him in four rounds and adding the WBA title to his WBC belt. Mitchell was a southpaw, and to help Tszyu prepare for the bout sparring partners were flown in from overseas. One of them, Gairy St Clair of Guyana, instantly stood out.

'You're more than a sparring partner,' Johnny said to him. 'Why don't you come back and give it a go here?'

'I'm not even a southpaw,' St Clair said. 'But I'd be interested.'

For a thousand US dollars a week, he was keeping his orthodox style a secret. But even as a southpaw he handled Tszyu in the gym. This, Johnny saw, was a legitimate fighter.

St Clair had moved to the United States to chase his dream but had struggled to find fights. He'd taken the job sparring Tszyu because the thousand dollars a week made him feel like a millionaire.

Johnny organised some businessmen he knew to sponsor St Clair and he moved to Australia, his first fight in his new home occurring in August 2001. He arrived with not much more than the clothes on his back.

Early in 2001, Shannan Taylor left Bill Mordey to be trained and promoted by Fenech. Fenech almost immediately got him a shot at WBC welterweight champion Sugar Shane Mosley. A few weeks before they left, the International Boxing Hall of Fame told Fenech he was to be inducted in the class of 2002.

At that, Fenech knew he had one thing to do. He picked up the phone and called someone he had not spoken to in a long time. He asked Johnny to be with him when they called him to the stage.

Neither knew how it started, but this is how it ended. The standoff between them was broken.

When Fenech flew to Las Vegas for the Taylor–Mosley fight he asked Johnny to assist him in the corner and, although Taylor lost, it made up whatever ground was left for them to cover.

Days after he got back from the Mosley–Taylor fight, someone inside a boxing commission told Johnny that Tszyu was not paying him the full freight. It came to him in a whisper. Since the split with Mordey, Johnny's deal had been the standard trainer's cut, ten per cent of Tszyu's purse. He was told he'd got much less than that for the Sharmba Mitchell fight, and also for the Chavez fight. He fronted Tszyu about it. Tszyu denied it.

Johnny stayed put, but it didn't sit right.

It was now April 2001, and Tszyu was preparing for a fight against Germany's Oktay Urkal with what had become his traditional pre-training camp at the Australian Institute of Sport in Canberra. Before they left, Tszyu called a meeting at his Rockdale gym.

It was the same every time. Johnny would rather have his incisors removed with a hacksaw than go, but he went to maintain team harmony.

'Just before I start,' Tszyu said, standing in front of a whiteboard, 'I want it to be known I am not happy with two of the senior members of the team that have been away and didn't tell me.'

Johnny, who knew the other one was Warton because he'd seen him in Las Vegas during the Taylor–Mosley fight, spoke up. 'Hey, Kostya, are you talking about me?'

'Later, Johnny,' Tszyu said. 'I speak to you later about it.'

'Hang on a minute, I want to know now. Are you talking about me?'

'Johnny, I said wait.'

'No, I'm not going to wait. Am I one of the two?'

Tszyu paused. 'Yes.'

'What's the problem? You were down in Melbourne racing cars.'

Tszyu was in Melbourne for the Australian Grand Prix. 'That's my prerogative.'

'Well it's my prerogative to go to America. You don't own me.'

'But I pay you.'

'Oh, go and get fucked,' Johnny said, standing to walk out.

'Johnny, wait,' Tszyu said.

'No, shove it up your arse,' Johnny said.

'Johnny, come to my place. We'll talk about it.'

'Fuck your place. I'm going.' And with that he walked out. Behind him, somebody in the room started to clap.

'Good on ya, Johnny,' yelled Ron Nash.

When the team left for Canberra, Johnny didn't go.

He was still unconvinced that he was being correctly paid. This little episode only made him more uneasy. Rumours started circulating that he was leaving Tszyu.

After a week, Johnny relented and travelled to Canberra. With no proof that he was being underpaid, what could he do? When he arrived, they resumed working as if no harsh word had been spoken. They simply got on with it.

Initially Johnny thought it was odd. But then he realised the deeper truth—it was all business with Kostya. He paid you, and for that he believed he owned you. Johnny now understood how Tszyu could move on so easily after a blue without any change to their working relationship.

Thankfully Urkal was no great threat. The trick was to get Tszyu through without injury so he could start his next campaign at full gallop.

The fight was in Uncasville, near New London, Connecticut, and Vlad Warton and Ron Nash were already there, making sure everything was in order by the time Johnny, Tszyu, his father Boris and Peter Mitrevski arrived. They would pick the four up at the airport.

Only they didn't.

They stood on the footpath for almost an hour before Nash, navigating next to the driver, pulled up with a thousand apologies. Tszyu was so angry he left his luggage on the footpath and climbed straight onto the team bus, curling up to go to sleep. Nash loaded his luggage.

'How long?' Tszyu barked.

It was about an hour to the hotel. He tucked himself into his jacket and closed his eyes.

All fighters change in the days leading up to a fight. Most get short tempered, unable to stand even small irritations. Few are pleasant to be around. With Tszyu Johnny sensed it was something different. For instance, he would fling open his hotel-room door and explode down the hallway if someone slammed their own door, disturbing him. It wasn't so much pre-fight nerves or psyching-up. It was to do with control. He paid you, he owned you.

'It's like walking on egg shells,' Warton said to him one day in some forgotten corridor at some forgotten fight. By now, Johnny and Warton had brokered a small peace after the blow up years earlier concerning Justin Rowsell.

After a good hour on the road, somebody said he was hungry. The others agreed they could eat a little as well. Tszyu and his dad were asleep. With a McDonald's coming up, they decided to head through the drive-thru.

Never has McDonald's tasted so good.

'Who's eating!?' Tszyu said. The smell of food snapped him awake.

The driver pushed his wrapper down the side of his seat. Johnny pretended he was asleep. Warton pushed his whole burger into his mouth and chewed and chewed.

'Who's buying McDonald's? I'm starving, you know I can't eat this!'

'It's the driver, he was hungry,' Warton said. He turned to the driver. 'You'll have to throw that out.'

'How long until we get there?' Tszyu said.

Suddenly it dawned on them. They were driving in the wrong direction. Nobody had the courage to tell Tszyu.

'I nearly took us to New York,' Nash quietly tells Johnny on the way back.

Tszyu's mood by the time they arrived at the hotel was beyond rage. He strode past reception, ordering Warton to bring his key to his room. Tszyu wasn't talking to Nash at all.

Before each fight, Tszyu insisted that the actual commission scales used for the weigh-in be brought to his room so he could weigh himself each night and be sure he was on schedule. Everyone would nod their head at his professionalism when they heard this. Except Nash. His job was to drive to the commission and get the scales and load them in the car and drive them back and lug them up in the lifts into Tszyu's room.

The night before the fight, he had to take them back. Most times Tszyu would have a final weigh-in before Nash took them away. Now, Tszyu wouldn't let him see his weight on the scales. It seemed only mildly odd at the time, until the next day when Tszyu weighed in heavy. He was forced to skip to strip off the extra weight before another weigh-in two hours later. Tszyu was angry. He told Nash somebody had tampered with the scales. Nash had had enough. 'Johnny,' he said, 'tomorrow I'm going down to the hardware store and I'm gonna buy myself a shovel and hit him over the fucking head with it.'

Urkal took Tszyu the full twelve rounds, but Tszyu took the decision on all three judges' cards. Far more convincing was Zab Judah's performance in the co-main feature. He knocked Allan Vester out in three. This mattered because Zab Judah was the IBF light-welterweight champion, and Warton had pulled off a deal for both him and Tszyu, the WBA and WBC belt holder, to put their titles on the line to become the division's undisputed champion.

A win would reinforce all Tszyu's claims to greatness and earn him the richest deal thus far signed in the light-welterweight division, a five-fight, $15 million deal with Showtime. Australian and other international television rights would be negotiated separately. The money from them would be gravy on top.

Three thousand of Judah's supporters had made the relatively short trip from New York to Uncasville and they booed Tszyu in great doses. The reaction so disturbed Tszyu that after the fight he told Warton to find another venue for the Judah bout.

'Kostya, you know I've already done a contract with the Mohegan Sun casino to do it here,' Warton said.

'I don't want to do it here. I want to go somewhere else.' It was final.

For months afterwards, Warton told everybody he did not want the fight at the Mohegan Sun. On the surface, he looked foolish. After all, he had negotiated the contract and signed it himself. With enough remnants of the Mordey fallout still floating about, those looking for a reason to knock Warton found this an excellent one. No one knew it was Tszyu's decision, but once again Warton copped the public kicking.

Warton wrote Tszyu a three-page letter. He explained that the fight belonged on the east coast. The west coast opened up whole different possibilities. He also told him the Mohegan Sun would almost certainly sue. It was a major casino, and now he was interfering with their business.

Still Tszyu refused.

Finally, in desperation because he could not find a way out of the deal, Warton read a copy of the letter to Showtime boss Jay Larkin.

'I didn't realise you were the guy that was taking all the bullets [for Tszyu],' Larkin said. 'Now I know.'

Sympathising with Warton, Larkin helped shift the fight to the MGM Grand in Las Vegas.

Yet, as seemed to happen, in the months leading up to the fight, we saw why Tszyu was so adored by the Australian public.

There existed a wonderful simplicity in his language that helped sell him to a public wanting heroes. He spoke with absolute confidence, and the simplicity of his language removed all pretension.

When they arrived in Las Vegas, Judah went all ghetto-speak on Tszyu, taunting him and ridiculing him with childish jibes. Tszyu spoke in plain language. 'I've been in this business for some time and been in the big fights many times,' he said. 'I'm cool, relaxed and ready to go.'

Such simplicity unnerved Judah. When Tszyu held his stare, shortly after the weigh-in, the American was suddenly looking at a fighter he had never seen before. So much a part of Tszyu's edge was his mystique.

Tszyu even stayed cool when the weigh-in nearly erupted.

As he stepped on the scales, Johnny stepped aside to let Judah's men watch him weigh in. They all then moved aside for Judah to weigh in.

Johnny began hustling forward to see what Judah weighed and check that no one was slipping a foot under the scales or standing close enough to allow Judah to lean on him and 'lose' a few ounces.

'Excuse me, mate,' Johnny said, nudging past Judah's bodyguard.

'Get your hands off me,' the bodyguard said, shoving Johnny back. Another one stepped up next to him

'I'm entitled to step in and have a look,' Johnny said.

'Back off,' another bodyguard said.

At that, Johnny's mate Chris Condon launched forward.

'Don't touch him, you low fucking dogs,' he said.

Judah's bodyguards, tough guys with their shoulders pinned back, shrank when Condon came through the crowd with nothing to back him but intent.

That night, Tszyu's bodyguard Glen Jennings, famously absent in those earlier hours, spoke up at dinner.

'I thought Chris was totally out of order there today, Kostya,' he said.

'What?' said Johnny, interrupting.

'He could have started a war, the way he carried on.'

Johnny almost spat the words out. 'Well I'm glad he did because one of them was getting ready to throw me to the back of the auditorium,' Johnny said. Johnny wondered where Jennings was during it.

Tszyu listened.

'And realistically,' Johnny said, 'that was another mental edge for us. When Judah saw his bodyguards melt he shrank a bit himself.'

Tszyu seemed content with that.

The next night, Tszyu delivered.

Judah's hand speed gave him the opening round on all three judges' scorecards. He consistently beat Tszyu to the punch. It looked like a dark night. But Tszyu is not just one of the biggest punchers in the division. He is one of the shrewdest. Johnny believes he is very likely the smartest fighter ever. As the second round began, Tszyu subtly changed the distance between him and Judah. Where in the first round he had stood at the end of Judah's punches, the perfect distance for Judah's superior hand speed to be most effective, in the second Tszyu closed the gap. It was just a few inches, but suddenly Judah's timing was out. Tszyu crowded him, no longer at the end of his punches, instead bringing Judah onto his own.

He was on his way to winning the round when he jabbed at Judah and the American, a southpaw, slipped to the right, on the outside of the jab.

It was a mistake that altered Judah's career. As he brought his head back to regain his centre of balance, Tszyu was already bringing the straight right hand down the line behind the jab. Judah actually moved his chin into the punch, which multiplied its effect.

Judah fell and tried to regain his feet too quickly. He rose stiff-legged with his right toes turned in, his gloves upraised, in queer fashion, and then he stumbled across the ring and fell again. Referee Jay Nady immediately waved him out at the second fall.

Judah recovered shortly after. Realising what was lost, he attacked Nady. He put his glove to his throat and seemingly tried to strangle him. A brawl erupted in the ring as Judah's posse finally came good. Judah was later fined $US75,000 and suspended for six months, but he'd lost far more than that. The three belts—WBA, WBC and IBF—now belonged to Tszyu.

He called the result 'Destiny'.

Judah's bright star was tarnished. He would continue to fight and even win the welterweight title but, now that it was confirmed his chin was suspect, he always came with a question mark. He was considered just off the very best.

A MONTH after the Judah fight, after finally agreeing to pay SKY Channel his full share of the money owed to Mordey, Tszyu missed the first payment deadline. The amount had whittled down to $2.5 million, and the first instalment was for $1 million. When Tszyu missed the payment, SKY demanded $500,000 immediately and asked for the remaining $500,000 to be added to the $700,000 due the next fight. Showtime would now garnishee Tszyu's purse. From his next fight, the first in his new five-fight, $15 million deal with the network, it would deduct $1.2 million to pay SKY.

Chapter 27

It came delivered on a coaster.

The front of the coaster advertised a Chinese restaurant and the back represented a change in life for Johnny. There, scribbled in blue ink, were the names of Tszyu's opponents and the sums Tszyu had got for fighting them. This information was supposed to be private, but Johnny's source was impeccable. It was easy for him to work out ten per cent of those figures. In every case, the result was more than he'd been paid.

The coaster was delivered in August 2002, more than sixteen months since Johnny had first fronted Tszyu about mispayments. He looked over the figures and with each new figure the hurt cut deep.

It was not just the deception. Tszyu had known Johnny was struggling financially, yet he still underpaid him.

Back in the Mordey days, Johnny's accountant had stolen more than $700,000 of Johnny's savings. Or that was what he was convicted of stealing. In fact, he had stolen closer to $900,000. All Johnny had. The accountant did three years and change in the nick, which pleased Her Majesty but did nothing to get Johnny's money back.

It was gone.

Johnny, now in his fifties, was back to square one. He had a small terrace house in Erskineville, as wide as a single-car garage. After his father died in 1996, his mother Marge had moved into the spare bedroom. It was small and the best he could do. No longer working, either, he had begun fighting back financially on the strength of Tszyu's emergence as one of the world's best fighters.

Now, tallying up the figures, Johnny saw that the shortfall carried enough zeroes to change the whole way he was living. It was more than a million dollars.

His mind went back to 1995 and the day Tszyu had turned up on his doorstep and said he needed him. The decision he'd made that afternoon had cost him his friendship with Mordey and badly strained his relationship with Fenech, and it had very likely cost Justin Rowsell a world title.

All that for doing what Johnny had felt was the right thing to do.

He sat there, trying to take it all in.

Before fronting Tszyu Johnny called Mitrevski to tell him what he had learned. Mitrevski was hardly surprised. Since signing his own deal he hadn't received anywhere near what he should have either.

Then he called Tszyu.

Once again, Tszyu denied it. But now Johnny knew the truth. He had the coaster, and he trusted its source. Tszyu dug in. Johnny refused to be thrown off. They hung up.

Johnny brought it up again. And again. For weeks they went back and forth.

Then Johnny got a call from his friend, the radio broadcaster Alan Jones. Tszyu had asked Jones to help him convince Johnny that he was not lying. 'Johnny, I've been through Kostya's contract,' Jones said. 'I'm afraid you've got it wrong.'

'Did he show you the other contract?' Johnny said.

Johnny held his ground. Eventually Tszyu called a meeting.

'Are you going to be honest with me?' Johnny said.

'I promise I will tell you everything.'

'One lie and I go,' Johnny said.

'Everything,' said Tszyu. 'Who are you going to bring to the meeting?'

Johnny hadn't thought about taking anybody.

'I'm going to take my accountant,' Tszyu said.

Johnny called James Dack, Steve's brother. Dack was one of Sydney's biggest real estate agents and had been helping him sort out his finances.

Johnny was certain that unless the money issue was sorted out he could no longer work Tszyu's corner.

'I couldn't,' he said, 'knowing he's done that to me.'

The story broke in the press the next morning. Interviewed on radio, Tszyu said it wasn't a serious enough issue to cause a split with Johnny. Then he called Johnny himself. They met at a coffee shop in Stanley Street, Darlinghurst, and as they sat down a Channel Seven camera truck rolled past, in search. Seven had been ringing around trying to find where the meeting was being held. All they'd got was the suburb.

Johnny sat down with his paperwork. One lie, he told Tszyu, and I'm gone.

He plucked a bout off his list, one fought in America.

'How much did you get for this fight?' he said.

Tszyu told him. It checked with the number on the coaster.

'Now, for this fight, did they pay you in American dollars?'

Tszyu screwed his forehead in thought. 'No, they pay me in Australian.'

'Kostya, we'd be the only people that never got paid in American dollars when they fight over there.'

'Australian dollars.'

'So you're telling me that you fought in America and they paid you in Australian dollars?'

'Yes.'

This was important. At the time of many of these fights the Australian dollar was drifting around fifty cents American. Johnny was being paid in Australian dollars. Based on that one fight, he was banking around half of what he should have earned.

'Mate, I asked you not to lie to me and you started off with a lie,' Johnny said.

'I'm not lying.'

'Kostya, they don't pay us in Australian dollars. So what are we going to do?'

Tszyu went through his paperwork again. He sat back in his chair, thinking.

'Yes,' he conceded, 'I think it was American.'

'Listen, mate, that's one lie. One more and I'm going. OK, how much did we get?'

Tszyu told him his figure.

'Thank you. Now, what about the other cheque?'

'What other cheque?'

'Are you telling me this is the only cheque?'

'Yes.'

'Mate,' Johnny said, rising out of his chair, 'you're a low fucking dog. I've had it.'

Tszyu jumped up and grabbed Johnny by the arm. 'Johnny, you're like a father to me.'

'Fuck off,' Johnny said, flinging his arm away.

People sitting around them in the courtyard soon cleared out.

Dack stood to try and calm him. 'Johnny–'

'You fuck off, too.' Then Johnny turned towards Dack—and winked at him.

He walked out.

Tszyu didn't know that Johnny knew. What Johnny had discovered. More than one cheque was being written.

Of every million dollars in a purse, Tszyu was having part, say $400,000, paid to him directly and the rest paid into his company, Top Ring Events Pty Ltd. Johnny was paid only out of the first portion. The amounts varied for each fight, but the greater share always went into the company bank account, away from Johnny's view. For every million dollars Tszyu was paid, based on the previous example, Johnny was earning about $40,000 instead of $100,000.

Peter Mitrevski, as Johnny's second in the corner, was supposed to be paid $5,200 a fight. He had been underpaid for the last three fights and not paid at all for several fights before that.

Dack spoke to Tszyu about it.

'I fix this problem with Johnny, but I don't like Peter,' Tszyu told him. 'I don't want Peter in my corner.'

Dack spoke to Johnny about it. This could bring the whole deal undone.

'Peter stays, mate,' Johnny said.

Another meeting was organised at Dack's office suite in Edgecliff.

Tszyu arrived this time with his wife Natasha. Johnny has a lot of time for Natasha.

'Johnny, is everything going to be all right?' she asked.

'Don't worry about it, darl, it'll be fine.'

Dack walked Johnny and Tszyu into an office and left them alone. He had already gone through the figures with Johnny, telling him how much he was short. 'In cold, hard terms,' he said, 'you want a million.'

Tszyu offered him $800,000. He explained he was doing it tough with all these other payments he had to meet, notably the SKY Channel bill for the Mordey settlement. This was the most he could afford.

Johnny didn't believe him, but everything he had learned since the day he was born told him to take the money. You don't knock back money for promises.

A deal was worked out. Tszyu would write a contract paying part of the $800,000 now with the rest to be made up from the purse from his next two fights, on top of the full ten per cent fee.

As for Mitrevski, Tszyu claimed he'd never agreed to pay him at all. Eventually, with the involvement of lawyers, a deal was struck and a compensation payment was made. Mitrevski was required to sign a confidentiality agreement to accept the deal.

Then Tszyu said he would not pay him in the future.

Johnny insisted that Mitrevski had to be in his corner. Tszyu held firm. So Johnny told Mitrevski that from now on he personally would pay him $10,000 a fight.

Tszyu blamed it all on a misunderstanding.

'I learn in Australia that everything has to be written on paper.'

It was a nice throw-off.

Don Majeski, who continued working with Warton after the Mordey split, had a deal with Tszyu that paid him five per cent of Tszyu's gross for each fight. 'I don't think they perceive the business as an industry over there,' he told the *Sunday Telegraph*. 'But when people are making millions of dollars there is no excuse. In America, managers take thirty-three per cent of the fighter's purse. [Tszyu] felt everything was for nothing and he was getting away with paying people five and six per cent or whatever it was and he thought it was OK. And unfortunately a lot of us went along with it.' Majeski hadn't been paid in several fights.

'I guess Kostya didn't want to pay me either. I don't know what it is. I've been paid up until the fight with Chavez and Sharmba Mitchell, so I can't say I haven't made money. But I never got an explanation. Vlad said Kostya didn't want to pay me. I'd like to know his response.'

Johnny weighed what to do. On the one hand, he wanted to walk away. Now he had to stay two more fights, at least, to get the money he was owed. And he was fifty-eight, and he needed that money. Oddly—because he had no choice but to stay—he now found it easier to continue working with Tszyu.

Initially he sensed that Tszyu was a little embarrassed, even remorseful, at having been caught out. But things soon returned to normal, Johnny taking him through the pads as if it had never happened.

Tszyu's next fight was against the American Jesse James Leija. It was held in January 2003, in Melbourne, at the then Telstra Superdome, a football stadium with a retractable roof. It was his first fight in Australia in nearly five years, and while many Australians appreciated the opportunity to watch Tszyu live, the promotion was a disaster. Warton, voted *Ring Magazine*'s Manager of the Year the previous year, was for some reason forced to split that role with Channel Seven's TalentWorks subsidiary. It didn't make sense, but none of what happened in Melbourne made much sense. The size of the stadium and the supposed astuteness of the promotional team had people's eyes spinning over the money they were going to make and in their haste they made mistakes. Television deals were made that crossed over other television deals. Blackout periods were ignored and blackout areas omitted. The TV contract called for a five-hour telecast when they had three hours of content. Extra fights had to be found, new negotiations had to take place. Finally, Tsyzu was forced to underwrite the fight for 30,000 tickets from his share of the television rights.

The undisputed light-welterweight champion of the world stopped Leija in six rounds in front of a crowd estimated at just 28,000.

Chapter 28

At about ten o'clock one night in 2003, Michael Dann's phone rang. Phone calls at this time of night are generally either good news or bad news. Dann was an optimist.

'Michael.' It was Bill Mordey. 'I'm at the casino. Why not come down?'

Dann was in his pyjamas. 'You're kidding, aren't you? Who are you with?'

'I'm going to tell you something,' Mordey said, 'and I don't want you to tell another person bar Margaret.' Margaret was Dann's wife. They had been married for thirty-seven years. She could keep a secret better than he could.

'I'm here with Kostya,' Mordey said.

'What?'

'No one is to know about this. We might get back together.'

'Really.'

'I'm buggered if I know whether I'm doing the right thing.'

'I think you are.'

'Well, at times you've got to bite your pride ...'

Mordey spoke about forgetting old wounds, almost as if he was thinking aloud. He was already working on a plan. If they got back together, he said, Tszyu was going to fight this bloke and that bloke and that bloke.

'We're going to work out what Kostya's already paid out in this legal suit and we're going to reimburse him that, and then the sky's the limit.'

'I agree.'

'So I want you off your arse and we're going to get this going.'

'Bill, I'll be looking forward to it.'

'We'll catch up tomorrow.' Before Dann could hang up, Mordey said, 'There's only one fly in the ointment. Kostya's worried about his old man. He's going to ring me in two days and give me a decision. At this stage it's ninety per cent going ahead.'

'Bill, I think it's great. Speak to you tomorrow.'

After the problems that had throttled the Leija fight, Tszyu was now clearly looking elsewhere. He'd called Mordey out of the blue. It was the first time they'd spoken in years.

They had dinner in a little restaurant at the casino. Tszyu paid.

Three days later, having kept his secret, Dann got the call from Mordey.

'I should have fucking known,' Mordey fumed. 'I should have fucking known better. He's pulled out.'

'Oh, well,' said Dann.

'I'm crooked on myself for even meeting.' No one revealed the secret.

Tszyu stuck with Warton and the new management team—and the Tszyu Express moved on. Mordey never got an explanation but believed Tszyu's father had stopped it. After Leija, Johnny wanted Tszyu to have one more fight, a big-money fight against Arturo Gatti, and retire. As with Harding and Mitrevski, Johnny saw things in Tszyu that he didn't see himself. He wanted Tszyu to go out as a champion, quite possibly the greatest light-welterweight ever.

While Tszyu was the undisputed champion, Gatti was the greatest draw in the division. It was a simple concession to this one indisputable fact: while boxing is a sport, the money comes from entertainment.

When Tszyu had fought Ghana's Ben Tackie in Las Vegas eight months before Leija, the fight was a snore. Who knew who Ben Tackie was? The guy was unrecognised on his own street. Pay-per-view sales on Showtime reflected as much. Warton, who'd guaranteed Tszyu's purse, took a bath. At the same time Gatti was slugging it out with Micky Ward on HBO, punching from the first bell to the last. *Ring* magazine named it Fight of the Year.

Fight fans, above everything, want to see a *fight*. Too many fights these days feature one-sided mismatches designed to pad the record of the guy with the big reputation and keep him safe for his next pay-per-view, while picking the pockets of the audience. Sure, Tszyu wore three title belts, but fans recognised where the better fight was. On HBO.

So it seemed inevitable. Gatti was the next opponent.

After the Leija fight, Tszyu said he would think about his future, even contemplate retirement, and would talk to family. He made no mention of Gatti.

It was almost twenty-two months before he fought again, in a rematch with Sharmba Mitchell in Phoenix. By then, there was no more talk of retirement. Mitchell had not stopped complaining that his knee injury cost him the first fight. Anybody who knew anything knew he could have taken a bat into the ring and still not got near Tszyu, but if he wanted a rematch, Tszyu was happy to give him his lumps.

The reason for the delay between fights was that Tszyu suffered a shoulder injury. Johnny concentrated on his other fighters in the gym, working the local circuit. On a Friday night near the end of April 2004, he went to Newcastle to watch the Australia–New Zealand rugby league

Test. He didn't know at the time but, also in Newcastle, Bill Mordey had checked himself into the Mater Hospital for chemotherapy treatment.

The next morning Johnny opened the paper and read that Mordey had died. He was sixty-seven and had suffered an adverse reaction to the chemotherapy. Fenech and Harding and Tszyu and Johnny all paid tribute in the press. Privately, though, Johnny said he wasn't going to the funeral.

They hadn't spoken in nine years. He didn't think it would be right. Why would Mordey want him there?

Then Brian Mills called.

'Craig and Gwenda [Mordey's partner] would really like you to go,' he said.

Johnny said, 'OK.'

Tszyu and Fenech arrived together. Dozens of other boxers also found a pew. Crooks and desperates and horse trainers, a few bookies, some of the biggest names ever involved in rugby league, even people just off the street, filled St Mary's Cathedral in Sydney to say goodbye. Johnny took a seat near the back.

When Tszyu's shoulder healed, they flew to Phoenix for the Mitchell rematch. On the way, Johnny learned of Tszyu's meeting with Mordey. By now, though he found it difficult to admit, he was hardened to Tszyu's lack of loyalty.

He wondered if Tszyu, when he was considering returning to Mordey, had given any thought to the rift he had caused between them. He wondered if he cared. How could he have even imagined that Johnny could go back and work with Mordey after all that had happened? And did Tszyu think for a second about Justin Rowsell, who never got the world title he deserved, all because of Tszyu's ambition? Nobody paid the price for Tszyu's success more than Rowsell.

Tszyu put Sharmba Mitchell down four times in three rounds before the referee stopped the fight. By now, though, the Gatti fight was looking unlikely. HBO said it was not interested in matching its guy against Showtime's Tszyu. HBO wasn't interested in a match-up with rising lightweight Floyd Mayweather either.

It was a small blow for Tszyu. By now he was looking for the big-money fights, the kind that define a career, the box-office blockbusters. His problem was that few in the States were interested. The fights against the likes of Mitchell, Leija and Tackie had deadened his appeal in America. The bloke shaping as the most likely contender for Tszyu was Britain's Ricky 'Hitman' Hatton. As Mordey had done years earlier with Tszyu, Hatton's promoter Frank Warren manoeuvred Hatton to the No. 1 ranking to make the fight mandatory.

If there was anything growing up around Erko and Newtown taught him, it was friendship. Here he is, struggling to deal with Tszyu who, on the surface, has so many fine qualities to him you wonder how it can be any problem at all. It is easy to like somebody's strengths—to nominate somebody as a particularly good bloke because they are a wonderful boxer, or a good footballer, or talented at whatever it is they do. We all have good qualities.

Johnny understood the trick was to accept someone's weaknesses. Can you put up with their limitations, the areas they fall short? That is what defines friendship, he believes, because that is what defines the man. So, as the year closed out, he got in a car with his partner Ingreed and drove many hours north to Grafton. After sixteen years, Russell Cox was in Grafton jail and up for parole. Many people protested that a notorious and violent criminal was being allowed out early. Their voices never change. From the multitude, though, two voices were heard above all others.

NSW Corrective Services superintendent Steve Tandy told the Parole Board he 'could not offer a bad comment' on Cox.

'Personally, I think he has had enough,' Tandy said.

Tandy was a young warder at Long Bay in 1975 when he looked up to see Russell Cox running at him with a pistol aimed at his head. It was part of the failed jailbreak that saw Cox moved to Katingal, the escape-proof prison in the Long Bay complex, from where, after four months, he escaped.

Tandy believed all prisoners could be rehabilitated, and Cox was the example. 'They have got to have some light at the end of the tunnel,' he said.

The other voice, of great clarity, was NSW Supreme Court Justice Jeremy Badgery-Parker, who had changed Cox's jail term from life to twenty-nine years under truth-in-sentencing laws. He recommended Cox's release. He said he believed Cox's 'maturation' from incorrigible to model prisoner had begun while he was on the run from 1977 until 1988.

During which time he just happened to have bumped into Johnny a few times.

'It seems that he was able, to a very large extent, to conduct his life in what would be regarded as a normal way,' the judge said.

Cox had appreciated Johnny's visits more than Johnny ever knew. During those brief contacts he felt … normal. 'He was a really big influence in my life,' Cox said. 'John gave me a sense of family, in some respect, in that way. I'm still not close to my own family, but I understand how important it is, that sense of having a close family. I try to do that with friends now.

'And that's something that I really seen in John, you know. Making the effort of bringing people in you didn't know, because he wanted you to be in touch with people, to have this outside influence. A lot of people I knew couldn't come and visit me anyway. It would have caused them too much trouble in their own lives. But he'd always be turning up with somebody that you didn't know and introducing them to you. And treating you like family, which was a really nice thing.'

Johnny had always told Cox that the day he got out, he'd be there at the gate to meet him.

He drove to Grafton and waited at a friend's house.

Reporters and cameramen were also there, at the gate. Cox walked out under a broad-brimmed hat with a manila envelope shielding his face so you couldn't tell who was behind it, and got straight into a waiting car.

Johnny was thrilled to see him.

Later that evening, he and Ingreed, and Cox and his partner, Helen, took a walk along Brushgrove, the island in the middle of the Clarence River. It was a warm evening in a lovely summer and they walked for more than an hour, Cox trying to take in all that was new around him. He was free for the first time in sixteen years, and was truly free for the first time in a lot longer than that.

'What are you going to do with yourself now, Russell?' Johnny asked. They talked long into the night. The next morning Johnny said goodbye. He and Ingreed headed back to Sydney. Cox, needing to fulfil his parole obligations in Brisbane, got into his car and headed the other way.

Chapter 29

Ricky Hatton was tough and honest and undefeated. You cannot find three better qualities in a prizefighter. Johnny acknowledged that, and worried about it.

To win this fight, Tszyu's wonderful talent alone would not be enough.

They needed to fight smart, and everything needed to be perfect.

Johnny watched tape of Hatton and saw a lot to be concerned about. Almost all his opponents tried to outsmart him, outbox him, before eventually getting rolled by his strength and aggression. Johnny wanted Kostya to outsmart him, but another way. He wanted him to outpunch him. You weren't going to finesse a win against Hatton. You had to thump one out of him. Beat him at his own game.

When they started work in the gym, Johnny walked in close on Tszyu during pad work, preparing him to fight short. He had him work on nice, short uppercuts and tight little hooks.

Tszyu resisted.

His fight strategies were most often decided in quiet conversations in the corner of the gym with his father, and here they decided Tszyu should fight Hatton at a distance. Tszyu was confident he could bring Hatton on to his punches. Johnny didn't like it. Whether Tszyu liked it or not, he said, Hatton was going to be pushing up on his chest.

No, said Tszyu. He wanted to fight Hatton like he had fought Vernon Forrest, fourteen years earlier, in the final of the world amateur championships. 'I can push Hatton back, punch with him toe to toe, or jab and move like when I beat Forrest,' he told reporters. 'Maybe I will give him big surprise and try all three.'

The problem was, it wasn't fourteen years ago.

The one argument Johnny could not bring up was the most basic and inarguable: Tszyu was not the fighter he was. He no longer had the reflexes he once did, and to plan to fight like he had fought Forrest was to bank on them being there. If Johnny's assessment was right, Hatton would be able to pick Tszyu off and come in behind his jab to fight his fight. On Tszyu's chest.

More than thirty years of training told Johnny he was right. But they also told him he could not say it. For in boxing, the fighter needs to retain a supreme vision of himself. Doubt is weakness, and in the stress and violence of the contest even small weaknesses can become excuses.

Johnny was sure that if Tszyu trained to fight Hatton close, he would soon find the angles to work the body and bring the power to break Hatton down. But he needed to train for that. His body needed to be conditioned for it. While he was not a typical twelve-round fighter, and while most of his knockouts came early in his fights, Johnny was confident Tszyu could get Hatton late. If he fought him the right way.

Tszyu preferred his way.

In the end, though, Johnny did all he could do, which was have faith. He knew that if there was any fighter in the world capable of changing style mid-fight and still being successful it was Tszyu.

Only the best fighters can recognise subtle shifts and adjustments during a fight and react to them. Tszyu recognised them quicker than anybody, and always made the right adjustment. When Jan Bergman had cut him at Newcastle years earlier eighteen months after he won the title, Johnny had sat him down and held the cut together. In that minute, Tszyu sensed the cut was bad and that he could be in danger of losing the fight on cuts if he did not do something fast. Bergman failed to finish the next round.

In the bout against Zab Judah, Tszyu's subtle change of distance between the first and second rounds threw Judah's timing out and brought him on to his own right hand, the one that stopped the fight.

So Johnny trusted. Initially, the prospects looked good.

Michael Katsidis, a young Australian lightweight, a brawler who fights better the tougher it gets, was brought in as a sparring partner, along with Americans Kendall Holt, a future light welterweight world champion, and Emanuel Augustus, once the IBF's No. 2 ranked light-welterweight.

When training began, Tszyu determined his daily work. Every time he fought he kept a diary of his training program. One of his ploys for combating the toll of ageing was to go to the diary for his last fight and see what he'd done in training on whatever day of preparation it was. For the coming fight, he would do more. Age cannot catch you so long as you exceed your best, or so Tszyu's thinking went.

So when he told *The Australian*, 'I'm training the same way I did years ago, even harder, and I don't have any guessing games with my shape,' he was telling the straight truth.

Early on, his sparring partners paid for it.

Holt was dropped with a body shot in sparring. The American took such a beating he left camp ten days early. He needed to save himself for his own next fight. As for Augustus, Tszyu dominated him so much Johnny wanted to sack him.

'I'm worried about this bloke's safety,' he told Peter Mitrevski.

Johnny was happy with the way it was going. Watching Tszyu spar, he believed that for all the courage Hatton would bring, Tszyu had too much firepower. He looked sharp and strong.

The fight was to be held at Manchester's M.E.N. Arena. To suit pay-per-view schedules it would be fought at 2 a.m. on Sunday, prime time Saturday night in the United States, and Sunday afternoon in Australia.

Johnny was the first to notice the change in Tszyu's sparring when they got to England.

He was not dominating the contest like he had in Australia. Rather than going up a notch, as it always had ahead of a fight, the quality of his sparring diminished. If anybody had walked in off the street, they might have believed Katsidis was the star of the gym. Now even Augustus was giving more than he took.

It worried Johnny tremendously. Tszyu was not a lazy trainer. Indeed, he fought like he trained, and here he was, the most focused athlete Johnny had known, looking lethargic. His hair, his eyes, his whole body showed he was fatigued.

After a couple of days with no improvement, Johnny decided they had only one direction left. 'We might have it very easy today,' he said. As with Fenech in Las Vegas, before Azumah Nelson, he knew he had to freshen Tszyu, drop the load and let his body recover. By now Tszyu had trained for twelve and a half weeks. He still had a week and a half to go. This was not unusual for Tszyu, though most boxers trained between eight and twelve weeks for a fight. But at thirty-five, Johnny worried his body was over-tired from the work.

Tszyu said no.

He knew what he had to do. His diary told him so. A slave to his diary, he pushed through. Frustrated, Johnny couldn't change his mind. He knew Tszyu could not see the drop in his performance in the gym. If ever there was a time a fighter needed to listen to his trainer, it was now. Tszyu had not factored in one basic fundamental of training. As the athlete ages, the body needs more time to recover from heavy workloads. His body wasn't getting that time.

Watching on, Johnny could see it. If anybody else could, they weren't saying.

Now came the most important moment in their relationship. They had failed once before, admitting it only after Vince Phillips knocked Tszyu out. Now they were back at that point. Was there enough in their fighter-trainer bond for Tszyu to acknowledge it?

No.

He needed to trust Johnny, and in the end he didn't trust him enough.

He continued training hard, trying to work his way out of his problem, confident that he knew himself better than anybody else. In some ways his stubbornness was understandable. He had achieved such success, why should it be different now?

So when Tszyu failed to finish his roadwork days before the fight, he told no one. Only Warton knew.

Each day, security staff supplied by promoter Frank Warren accompanied Tszyu on his run through the countryside. Early on, one particularly fit young guard returned from an early roadwork session and marvelled at how well Tszyu ran. 'He's a runner and a half, this lad, I can't keep up with him,' he told Warton, who was hearing none of this for the first time.

Days before the fight, the guard sought him out.

'We've got a problem,' he said.

'What's that?'

'Kostya's liver hurt and we stopped running halfway through.'

While Hatton was going to be tough, few believed he could win. But he had advantages. Tszyu was almost nine years older than Hatton, and in the previous two-and-a-half years he had fought just three rounds. It was a long lay-off, with no warm-up, against a genuine threat. Also, Tszyu had to drop some twenty kilograms during camp, which takes a tremendous toll. He eventually weighed in heavy, and was forced to return to his room and skip and shadow-box to get the last few grams off.

Whether it worried Tszyu, Johnny did not know. But he had said early in training that he had no concerns about his condition yet failed to make weight. Surely that must have told him something had gone wrong somewhere.

Johnny was disappointed that Tszyu had failed to make weight again. Around every gym he'd ever worked, it was considered a mental victory for a fighter when his opponent failed to make weight. It showed something in his training was not quite right, and for a finely tuned prizefighter, that alone could be a big concession to an opponent. Johnny felt Tszyu's weight failure gave Hatton a mental lift.

There was also the fear of what could happen to your own fighter. Too often, when the fight was on the line, the problem festered and became the excuse that justified quitting. It provided an out.

After the weigh-in they had dinner, and lunch together the next day. It was an unusually long fight day, given the 2 a.m. start, but while the odd yawn escaped as the night got later, adrenaline pumped them along.

They left the hotel at a quarter past ten.

Johnny felt good when they got in the ring. The adrenaline of another world title ran through his body. Tszyu looked sharp during the warm-up. And the big Manchester crowd was bringing something extra.

During the ring introductions, Hatton watched Tszyu the whole time. It was a window into his intent. The time had come.

From the first bell, Hatton backed Tszyu up, going straight into his roughhouse strategy. When Tszyu fired, Hatton slipped his punches and, rather than fire straight back as Tszyu had anticipated and trained for, he bullied forward. Then, he went to the body.

In Tszyu's favour, Hatton was wild, missing his punches.

Though Hatton won the first, it was not a lot to be concerned about. Tszyu could sometimes give away early rounds to look at his opponent's style so he could figure out how to combat it. In the second, Tszyu took back the centre of the ring behind his combinations.

Towards the end of the second, Hatton pushed Tszyu onto the ropes and landed three clean uppercuts, each snapping Tszyu's head up. But Tszyu was brave, ending the round by rolling off the ropes and turning on Hatton, taking the angle to fire lefts and rights. 'Now give it to him, Kostya,' called Mitrevski from the corner.

By the third, Tszyu was becoming more ragged as he kept Hatton's pace. If he could not turn this around, he ran the danger of fighting the Vince Phillips fight all over again.

Then the genius of Tszyu began to show itself. Between rounds, he recognised he was losing the exchanges. So at the start of the fourth he met Hatton centre ring with a small adjustment. Before engaging, he stepped back slightly to create room. If he was unable to punch Hatton off him, or find the distance to keep him at the end of his punches, he would create the room another way. Taking a half step backwards, he started throwing long, straight right hands that began bouncing off Hatton's forehead.

When the fourth ended Johnny kept it calm in the corner. He called for ice as Tszyu sat down, then got to work wiping him down, cleaning him up for the next round.

'Put your hands down, mate,' Johnny said. Tszyu rested his gloves on his thighs.

By the fifth Hatton had almost abandoned the jab as a weapon. He simply waited for Tszyu to lead, slipped it, then roared in behind with left rips and hooks and overhand rights.

But Hatton was taking more than he was giving. Tszyu was taking the round.

Then the fight changed.

Collapsing into a clinch, Hatton threw a barrage of short right hooks and then, as Tszyu backed away, a long left hook caught him and he stumbled against the ropes. The Manchester crowd, 22,000 strong and cheering every punch Hatton landed, lifted their man. Just as Johnny hoped Hatton would begin to tire, fatigue left his body.

While Johnny had anticipated a fast start from Hatton, nobody thought he would still be keeping it up by this point. Through the middle rounds, the two continued warring.

Towards the end of the seventh Tszyu landed a blow, a left rip that hit Hatton on the belt line causing Hatton to take a knee. It was ruled a low blow by referee Dave Parris. So no knockdown.

At the end of the seventh, Hatton's trainer, Billy Graham, put him back on the game plan: 'I want you to get him back on the ropes where he's not as dangerous.'

Hatton tried his best as, outside the ring, the English crowd found song. 'There's only ooonnne ... Ricky Hatton.'

As the eighth ended, Tszyu swayed against the ropes and gasped with an open mouth. He was beginning to wear the strain. The fight appeared to be turning again.

'Make him miss, Kos,' Johnny said. 'Make him miss and then jump on him, mate.'

'More water,' said Tszyu.

They wiped him down and smeared Vaseline on his face. They pushed away the swelling from around his eyes with an End-Swell.

'Don't be on the ropes,' Johnny said. 'Kostya, it's important to jab him hard. Jab him hard and bring him onto it. He's going to rush out, mate.'

Tszyu had not abandoned the jab, but its effectiveness was gone. He was now using it merely as a blinder while bringing the straight right hand behind it. Johnny tried hard to keep Tszyu to their own plan. They needed to save this fight.

Hatton was still strong. He was wild and loose and perfect, and despite taking the cleaner punches he continued to walk forward and force Tszyu backwards. Only now he was doing it through presence. Even when he wasn't punching, Tszyu was retreating. Hatton had won the battle for authority.

That might sound strange, given that Tszyu was the bigger puncher and landing the cleaner shots. But only half the battle is to land the bigger shot. The other half is to take it, and Hatton was wearing Tszyu's punches far more comfortably than Tszyu was absorbing his.

After Tszyu was warned for another low blow Hatton seemed to figure, Well, if that's the way it's going to be … He moved in and threw a punch that was low and deliberate and hit square on Tszyu's protective cup, and he crumpled to the canvas.

Tszyu, courageous and game, declined to take the full five-minute rest allowed for the deliberate foul. But it took whatever was left.

Hatton, showing the stamina of a three day march, somehow picked it up again in the tenth. For the first time in his career, Tszyu fought on the retreat.

They mauled each other, throwing rabbit punches, sliding elbows off each other. Tszyu was being beaten, but if anybody ever wondered about his bravery, and there was certainly never a reason to doubt it, it was here to see. Every time he began to fade, he tried to rally.

He fought beyond himself.

He fought bravely.

He fought until he was finished.

The British commentators ringside finally realised that Hatton was about to do what they had only hoped. On Showtime, the American broadcasters read it perfectly.

'Constant pressure by Ricky Hatton,' said Steve Albert, 'and even if it's not always effective, it's dictating the pace and tempo of this fight.'

'It was billed as the fight of Ricky Hatton's life, but it's turning out to be the fight of Kostya Tszyu's life,' said Al Bernstein.

'He has not faced this in a long, long time.'

'He is being pushed to the brink.'

When the bell ended the eleventh, Tszyu sat down and Johnny leaned through the ropes, resting his hand over Kostya's heart.

'Are you OK?'

He failed to answer, looking blankly out in front. Johnny cupped his cheek and turned his head to get his attention. 'Are you OK?'

Again there was no answer.

Johnny turned and looked for Parris. The referee walked towards their corner and Johnny shook his head. Parris turned and waved his big arms above his head, waving Tszyu out. Hatton leapt from his stool and collapsed. Every battle raises the emotions to just below the skin, and now that it was over the Briton fell into his trainer's embrace, crying.

Tszyu, a picture of dignity, rose from his stool and walked across to congratulate the new champion. He did not complain. He did not make excuses. He simply congratulated Hatton and wished him well.

Back in the corner, Johnny had no doubt that if he had picked Tszyu up and pushed him to the centre of the ring for the final round he would have gone without question. It wasn't lack of courage that held him back. He was spent and, when asked the question, Johnny did not get the answer he needed.

If there was any small consolation, it was that Tszyu trailed on all three scorecards, 104–105, 103–106 and 102–107. He would have needed a knockout in the last to win.

After interviewing Hatton, the ring announcer found Tszyu. 'I am a proud man,' Tszyu said. 'I am a very, very proud man. I'm not saying this is the end of my career, maybe yes, maybe not. But I am saying that today I lost to the better fighter. There is no shame for me to say this. I am a strategic fighter and I am planning lots of things for this fight, but today Ricky was better than me everywhere.'

The walk back to the dressing room after a loss is always heavy, but it was made lighter by the warmth of the English crowd. Responding to Tszyu's sportsmanship in defeat, and the heart he had brought to the ring, they lifted him.

The dressing room was quiet and lonely, despite all the people there. They always are. Salvaging what they could, people quietly congratulated Tszyu for the way he fought, and for the way he'd accepted defeat.

Later, he was taken to hospital for precautionary tests. He was urinating blood from the kidney punches and the low blow in round nine.

After a short sleep, Tszyu found Johnny and, ignoring his own injuries, asked, 'How are you feeling, mate?'

Johnny looked at his bruises, at the swollen eyes. 'Mate, I'm proud. I've been proud of you in victory so many times, and I'm equally proud of you in defeat today.'

Already criticism had begun in some sections of Tszyu quitting on his stool. It was cheap and ignorant and most definitely wrong. The Tszyu camp soon set that right. It had been Johnny's decision to stop the fight, not Kostya's.

So the critics turned on Johnny.

Two days later, radio newscasts began reporting a 'rumour' that Tszyu had sacked Johnny because he'd stopped the fight early. Within a few hours it emerged that the story had come from Russian sports paper *Sovietsky Sport*, which allegedly quoted Tszyu's manager since 2003, Matt Watt. Perhaps in a bid to sell the story, the paper quoted Vlad Warton as confirming that it was Johnny who'd stopped the fight.

'Kostya wanted to continue, but Lewis felt that he was losing the fight,' Warton reportedly said. 'It wasn't Kostya's decision to end the fight. He would never have stopped his own fight.'

Reuters, the wire service, picked up this 'breaking news' and sent it around the world. It was on the radio in Australia within minutes. The story ran until Tszyu's publicist reached Matt Watt during the Tszyu team's stopover in Bangkok and told him what was happening. She then officially denied the story. Tszyu and Johnny at least had a heads-up. They prepared for a grilling when they landed in Australia.

At Sydney airport they all stood together, and Tszyu backed Johnny's right to stop the fight. The reports of a dispute were bullshit, he said.

'I just look at it this way,' said Johnny. 'For eleven rounds Kostya had done his best. I felt at the end of the eleventh he had really given his all. I think Hatton had the younger legs, and with 22,000-odd Mancunians cheering him on I didn't want to put Kostya in a position where I would have regretted it.'

Then he found a perspective that few had considered.

'The greatest thing for me today was when I walked out here and [Tszyu's wife] Natasha came over and hugged me and thanked me. That means more to me than anything. I am proud of what I have done, because I know that Kostya is as good as gold.'

Days later, Tszyu quietly checked himself into hospital. He was having headaches and there was blood in his urine. Johnny learned about it from a doctor. 'Johnny, I just want you to know that if you had any doubt as to whether you stopped the fight at the right time, you did,' the doctor said. 'If he had fought another round he could be dead. Dead.'

Johnny was filthy that nobody had told him Tszyu was in hospital. He called Watt to ask why. Watt was apologetic. Tszyu wanted it kept private, he said.

When the story of his injuries broke, Tszyu's public-relations company sent out a press release denying the seriousness of the injuries, and quoting Tszyu's doctor. It's bad business for a fighter still looking for fights to be known to be damaged. The commissions might get concerned.

What was never revealed was that Tszyu's great problem was dangerously high blood pressure. Doctors were unable to bring it down without admitting him.

Tszyu and his people denied it then, and they will probably deny it now. All that has changed in the meantime is that Tszyu has gone from a beaten fighter still hopeful he might fight again to a retired fighter. His past injuries only underline his bravery.

Yet always, if any doubt remains as to the seriousness of his injuries, you go back to the words of the doctor.

Dead.

While Johnny has never spoken publicly about that phone call from the doctor, he finds comfort in it. He did the right thing.

Forty years and four world champions after Jimmy Carruthers first noticed Johnny's unusual concern for his fighter, nothing had changed.

Chapter 30

He was finished. The energy to get up once more for the Hatton fight, the likelihood that it was Tszyu's last fight despite his refusal to announce his retirement, had worn him down.

He was sixty-one. The Newtown gym was long since closed, and he still wandered from gym to gym. He trained at the PCYC at Woolloomooloo or the HK Ward gym at Sydney University, or South Sydney PCYC or Marrickville PCYC, staying six months, twelve months, before moving on to the next one. None of them was Newtown.

Then Paul Briggs asked him to take over his training. Briggs's trainer was doing an involuntary stint, and he too had wandered from one gym to another, looking for the right fit. Johnny was reluctant at first. Briggs was good, world rated and had just lost a fight for the title, but Johnny wondered whether he had the enthusiasm for another campaign.

For a long time he said no. Briggs persisted, though, and lit something inside him. The enthusiasm came back.

In 2006, Johnny was awarded the Medal of the Order of Australia for services to boxing and rugby league and he agreed to take over Briggs.

Earlier that year Briggs had lost a majority decision against Poland's Tomasz Adamek for the WBC light-heavyweight title, Jeff Harding's old belt. Now, with Johnny in his corner, he was confident he could reverse it. They set about training for the rematch.

MEANWHILE, Gairy St Clair was back in his old country, Guyana. He had just buried his mother when promoter Angelo Hyder phoned from Australia.

'I've got you a shot for the IBF belt in South Africa,' Hyder said. 'It's not much money, but it's for the title.'

'Forget about the money, all I want is the title,' said St Clair.

'Well, you'll have to come back to Australia straight away.'

St Clair flew home from his mother's funeral and walked into Johnny's gym. It was short notice, and it was going to be tough. The champion was Cassius Baloyi, a hard-punching, hard-fighting South African.

St Clair, who had somehow been reduced to a boxing journeyman, recognised the fight for what it was. After years working as a sparring partner for better-recognised fighters, failing to get the world title fight because he didn't have a promoter backing him, or fighting on undercards because more hyped but less skilled fighters had sold out the arena, this was his chance. He was regarded as a fill-in fight for Baloyi, a night off while the South African stalked more fancied opponents for bigger purses.

But for Gairy St Clair, this was his shot.

He didn't want to blow it. 'The only one who can train me for this world title is Johnny Lewis,' he told Hyder.

They had just four weeks.

For Johnny, St Clair was in the same class as the other great movers, Justin Rowsell, Johnny Famechon, Phil McElwaine. A beautiful, clever boxer. And it wasn't going to be enough.

'Gairy, we're gonna have to fight this another way, mate,' he said.

'We're not gonna win this by boxing him. We can't hit him with six or seven punches and then make him miss with ten. We're gonna have to fight him.'

St Clair knew it went totally against his style. But he looked at Johnny and said OK.

'Whatever you want you get,' St Clair said. 'That's the discipline of a real champion.'

From their first day in the gym, they trained to fight. To stand and trade. Much as it should have been with Tszyu–Hatton, it was crucial they prepare for the way they needed to fight. St Clair surrendered all the clever tricks and subtle skills that had made him world class and instead trained his body to be a puncher, ready to fight twelve hard rounds.

But this fight was going to test St Clair in many ways. En route to South Africa, their plane broke down. It wasn't ready to fly for more than a day. For St Clair that meant two days of training lost, just a week out from the most important fight of his life.

They got to Gauteng, South Africa, and picked up training without a hiccup. It all looked good.

Then St Clair's girlfriend called from Australia. She had miscarried.

It is not unusual for a single emotional blow, like a mother's death, to focus a fighter. All that short-term emotion galvanises the spirit and often comes out in performances above anything seen before. Buster Douglas's mother, for instance, died weeks before he caused one of boxing's biggest upsets by knocking out Mike Tyson in 1990.

But two?

Worried now, Johnny kept an eye on St Clair while Hyder, who read emotion like a Gypsy fortune-teller, worked hard to lift the energy in camp. He took St Clair's mind away from his troubles, found ways to bring laughter into camp. Johnny enjoyed himself like he hadn't since back in the 1980s.

It was not only good for Gairy.

Come fight night, St Clair seemed ready. He went to the ring relaxed and calm and single-minded.

Nothing had changed Johnny's mind. They were not going to win the title, in Baloyi's homeland, by boxing clever. You might win the fight, but you won't win the decision. So from the opening bell St Clair, as Johnny had trained him to do, stood himself in front of the hard-punching Baloyi and went punch for punch.

Given that Baloyi was a banger more than a boxer, it took tremendous courage to make that stand. And then to fight the way he was …

For round after round, St Clair traded. He started strongly, and each time he came back to the corner Johnny asked how he was.

Still going good.

'He's knocking him off his front foot,' Hyder said, not so much in concern as disbelief. As he and Johnny watched Baloyi rock St Clair with his big shots, they saw St Clair pick up his gloves and wade back in.

He was fighting the way they'd trained to fight and, Johnny believed he was winning. Just so long as the altitude didn't hit him all of a sudden, leaving him gasping for oxygen . . .

When St Clair walked back to the corner after the bell to end the eleventh, Johnny knew he was a round away from winning the title. All he had to do was see out the round, avoid getting stopped, and after twelve years as a professional fighter he would be a world champion.

The bell rang and St Clair walked to the centre of the ring, as he had eleven other times, and again he stood and he traded.

The decision was unanimous.

The three scorecards read 116–112, 115–113, 115–114.

Johnny felt brief pain. They couldn't do it to him, could they?

'The winner, and the new IBF super-featherweight champion of the world …'

St Clair had won it.

He had simply refused to be beaten. Even when he had a barrowful of very sound excuses to lose the fight, he would not cop one. Johnny ranks that bout alongside Jeff Harding's first win over Dennis Andries as the greatest show of guts he has ever seen.

THREE months later, Briggs got his rematch with Adamek.

He dropped him in the first round, putting Adamek in all sorts of hurt. When he got up, Briggs dominated the round, landing cleanly and severely. But for some reason Briggs stayed within himself. At the bell Johnny told him to step it up, go on with it, and let's get home early. Briggs, hearing his own voice instead of Johnny's, stayed fighting at a twelve-round pace, and eventually that's what it went. Adamek pulled back into the fight and again took a majority decision. Briggs fought only once more before retiring.

Johnny returned home frustrated. He was coming to the end of his career now, he knew that. There were more days behind him than in front. This fight had been there to be won and they hadn't taken it.

Without really being conscious of it, Johnny began winding back his training after the Briggs' defeat. The fighters in the gym were thinning out. At home, Brent and Leisa had grown and started their own families, but he now had two more young sons, Jackson and Johnny Jr. He wanted to give them his time.

Yet he could never break fully away from the gym. Some fighter always had one more fight coming up. They still do.

He worked briefly with Billy Dib, and took him to the International Boxing Organisation (IBO) featherweight title in 2008, his sixth world champion.

Justin Rowsell never got his world title. He returned to Casino, on the NSW far north coast, and now trains fighters in between driving a truck. Johnny speaks to him often and still can't come to terms with him never winning a world title. Of all the people who deserved it . . .

In 2009 Jeff Harding's old sparring partner, Steve Dack, suffering depression, took a gun and shot himself. Johnny gave Steve's eulogy. His ashes were to be buried under a tree in Sydney's Centennial Park, and his friends took turns carrying the ashes so they had their time to say goodbye. Near the end of the walk, Steve's sister offered the ashes to Johnny. He looked at the small white box. 'I can't,' he said.

Julian Stewart, whom Steve used to call Sunshine, climbed out of his wheelchair and walked the final furlong, long and laborious, in tribute to his friend.

For months afterward, Steve would suddenly pop into Johnny's head and, just as suddenly, he would break down. He still talks to Steve's brother James almost every day.

At a function at Balmain Leagues Club in 2009, Tommy Raudonikis told a crowd: 'One of the blokes I really want to thank in my life is Johnny Lewis.' Johnny happened to be in the crowd.

'Gee, it meant a lot to me,' Johnny said about it. 'He didn't know I was there.'

They all come into his life, and they all stay. Perhaps because he gives so much of himself to them.

Jeff Harding spent more than a decade as an alcoholic after losing his title to Jamaica's Mike McCallum in 1994. Many friends tried many ways to help him beat his addiction, without success. Johnny said everyone he'd ever spoken to who knew anything about alcoholism had told him it took tremendous courage to beat it. 'If that's so, then we're OK,' he said. 'Nobody has more courage than Jeff Harding.'

In 2009 Harding, clean and sober for some months, was told he was to be inducted into the World Boxing Council's Hall of Fame. It would be his first gentle step back into public life. Harding gave a long moment's pause at the news ... 'So they still remember the Hitman, hey?'

He continues taking baby steps to a full life again. He stays close to those that have value in his life.

The last time Harding was seen in public, he was working the corner with Johnny.

Alongside them, always, is Peter Mitrevski. More than thirty years of his life have been spent next to Johnny in gyms around the world and in fighters' corners, with Mitrevski yelling out Johnny's instructions. Mitrevski still works every corner with Johnny, who now trains his son, Peter Jr.

Despite never having announced his retirement, Tszyu has not fought since losing to Hatton. He is doing all right, though. After finally settling with SKY Channel, he sued the law firm Eakin, McCaffery, Cox for negligence for advising him that he could break the Mordey contract. The judge found in his favour and ordered the firm to pay him $4 million in damages.

Tszyu made around $25 million in purses in one of the richest careers in his division, and his name features in any argument over who was history's best light-welterweight. He now spends much of his time chasing business opportunities in Russia, where he has even hosted his own reality-television series.

Johnny sees Tszyu only rarely, almost always at a fight. Their lives are no longer intertwined.

With Jeff Fenech, things are different.

For a long time after Fenech's retirement, as we know, the two did not speak. The rift started with a misunderstanding and continued through stubborn pride. It hurt Johnny, and Fenech too.

All these years later, Johnny won't forget the gift Fenech gave him. Nobody, he is sure, will ever do what Fenech did with what he had to do it with. Two fragile hands, the constant struggle to make weight, and yet he achieved greatness.

Fenech says he loves Johnny as easily as he says he loves his family. In the important moments in their lives, they are always there for each other. When Fenech announced a comeback in 2008, it seemed natural to get Johnny in his corner. At first, a comeback for Fenech sounded absurd. He was forty-four and hadn't fought in twelve years.

Connections of Samart Payakaroon had proposed a rematch to give Payakaroon the chance to recover what he'd lost all those years earlier. He still had a large following in Thailand, so plenty of fans would be willing to pay to see the fight. Fenech got interested and started training, only to have Payakaroon withdraw.

Then Azumah Nelson agreed to one more fight.

While Johnny had always been against comebacks, this one was different. 'If I thought there was a chance of him getting seriously hurt, I wouldn't be part of it. But Jeff's forty-four, Azumah's forty-nine. They'll be OK.'

Fenech won the decision and retired, again and forever, finally content. Their friendship remains.

THERE IS a coffee shop along Erskineville Road called Shenkin. It used to be an old butcher shop. Sawdust on the floor. They made their own sausages.

Johnny sits there this day with Graeme Langlands, the former St George rugby league great, because he sits there nearly every morning with Langlands.

The waiter comes along and asks for their order.

'How long have I been coming here?' Langlands says. 'And you've still gotta ask?' He has a hot chocolate and if it ain't hot, it's going back. He is joking, of course. Or at least they think he is. What they don't know can't hurt them.

Soon, they bring the hot chocolate and, with it, Johnny's flat white, weak and hot.

Johnny has a coffee with Langlands each morning before he heads to the gym. As he sits at the table near the window an elderly man walks past.

'Hey, Johnny,' the man says through the window.

'Hello mate,' Johnny says.

They talk briefly. It could be anyone this day, because at some point they all walk past. And they all stop and say hello, these last few survivors from streets that no longer exist, and in all these conversations with all these people the same qualities shine, like a great light, and it takes only a small intellect to understand that here is his secret. The six world champions, the trust of a thousand others, come from these streets.

This morning at Shenkin he talks about the recent funeral of a friend and how, as he sat and listened to the eulogy of this man's life, he thought about his own life.

'I'm at an age now where I'm going to more funerals, missing more friends that I've known all my life,' he said. 'Sitting there at this particular bloke's funeral, I just thought, it's strange ... every now and again you think, hey, what have we gone, six-eighths of the journey, seven-eighths of the journey or what? You tend to think, I wish that everybody could have had the life that I had.

'I think it all comes back to, I honestly do believe, the first twenty years—the first decade of my life, and then the next one after that really firmed up what I was to be like. Living where I lived, knowing the people that I got to know and, being young and in an area where all the older blokes mixed with the younger blokes. Every day was a learning curve about life.

'It wasn't about going to university or anything like that; it was just the nitty-gritty of what life is about. Good stories, sad stories. As I sat there in the church I imagined what it would have been like had I been born and bred in Hurstville or Brookvale or whatever. The one thing I am really grateful for is Erskineville. It's been in my life for so long, and the people that I met, the schools that I went to, everything was so perfect for me.'

I asked him about the small white crosses. The small pieces of tape he puts on the back of his fighters' hands. Why does he do it, and where did it come from? It seemed as good a time as any, as he had never struck me as particularly religious.

He could not remember at first.

He thought about it for a good while and then he said it began, he believed, with a Mexican fighter brought out to fight on an Ern McQuillan card sometime in the 1960s. The Mexican arrived without his trainer and Johnny was brought in to work his corner. He had been training only a few years by then and, before he began taping the hand, the Mexican fighter asked if he could put a small white cross on the back of his fist to keep him safe.

While not the religious type, Johnny does believe.

So he taped the cross to the back of the Mexican's fist and, switching to the other hand, taped an identical cross to keep the other fighter safe, too.

He has done it for every fighter he has had since then, and it is always the same. In the beginning they ask why. He has no answer other than to say that it just makes him feel better before sending them out to the ring.

But there it is again, in something as simple as taping hands.

It is the trust it fosters. With Johnny, everything always starts with good intentions. So they give themselves to him.

And from there comes the other great secret to Johnny Lewis.

It is there the day in 1981 when Jeff Fenech walks into the gym and Johnny gets Mark Cribb to start ripping him up the guts and Fenech, stirred to battle, squares up and comes back. It is in Jeff Harding rising from his stool at the end of the eleventh, behind on points and needing a knockout to win.

It is in Tommy Raudonikis turning and vomiting into a bucket of sand as he pushes himself like no man Johnny has seen push himself before.

In Reggie Marbuck and Ces Rolls, and young Loopy Hammond, outnumbered twelve to four and saying, 'Who's your best?'

It is in the people he grew up around, and it is what he came to look for in the fighters he trained. The ones that had it found greatness.

They were staunch and, when the moment came, they gave.

Like Johnny Lewis gave.

ACKNOWLEDGEMENTS

Much of this book is written from the recollections of Johnny Lewis and I have tried, as best as possible, to match Johnny's memories with what records exist. If there are discrepancies, I apologise.

I would like to thank those that willingly gave their time to talk about Johnny and his influence in their lives—Jeff Fenech, Justin Rowsell, Peter Mitrevski, Vlad Warton, Ron Nash, Tommy Raudonikis, Steve Mortimer, Michael Dann, Craig Mordey, Russell Cox, Steve Crawley, Bobby Lanigan, James Dack, Julian Stewart, Reggie Marbuck, Graeme Langlands.

I would like to thank my editor Stuart Neal for his guidance and, most of all, reassurance.

Most of all I want to thank Johnny. There are few special men in this life. We have one here we should cherish.

—Paul Kent

First of all I'd like to thank anyone I've ever been in the corner with. You are the reason for it all.

I'd also like to thank my partner Ingreed, my son Brent, and Russell Cox for their help.

I'd also like to thank Paul Kent. I probably multiplied his time and effort by 80 per cent by not being there all the times he wanted, yet we spent plenty of time together writing this, and a lifelong friendship was forged.

—Johnny Lewis